GW00691977

Towards a
BETTER
FUTURE

A Review of the
Irish School System

John Coolahan | Sheelagh Drudy

Pádraig Hogan | Áine Hyland

Séamus McGuinness

Published by the **Irish Primary Principals' Network** and the
National Association of Principals and Deputy Principals

Published in Ireland by IPPN (the Irish Primary Principals Network) and
NAPD (the National Association of Principals and Deputy Principals)

IPPN, Ballinglanna, Glounthaune, Co. Cork
T (+353) 21 4824070; F (+353) 1890 212224; info@ippn.ie

NAPD, 11 Wentworth, Eblana Villas, Grand Canal Street Lower, Dublin 2
T (+353) 1 6627025; F (+353) 1 6627058; info@napd.ie

Copyright © 2017
(IPPN / NAPD / John Coolahan, Sheelagh Drudy, Pádraig Hogan, Áine Hyland, Séamus McGuinness)

This publication may be reproduced, distributed, or transmitted for non-commercial purposes in any form or by any means,
including photocopying, recording, or other electronic or mechanical methods, without the prior written permission of the
publisher, provided the authors and copyright holders are duly acknowledged in any reproduction, distribution, or transmission.
Any reproduction, distribution, or transmission of this publication without duly acknowledging the authors and copyright
holders is not authorised and will be considered a breach of copyright.

This publication may not be reproduced, distributed, or transmitted for commercial purposes in any form or by any means,
including photocopying, recording, or other electronic or mechanical methods, without the prior written permission of the
copyright holder.

Design by Brosna Press, Ferbane, Offaly
Printed by Cityprint Ltd, Cork

ISBN 978-0-9555050-5-8

Notes on Contributors

Dr. John Coolahan is Emeritus Professor of Education at the National University of Ireland Maynooth. He has lectured extensively in Ireland and abroad, is author of three books, has published over 120 articles in Irish and international journals, and has edited several educational publications. Professor Coolahan has had extensive involvement in a public service capacity as an adviser on educational policy in Ireland. At international level, he has been a consultant on education to the EU Commission, the Council of Europe, the World Bank and the OECD. He has recently chaired the National Forum on School Patronage and Pluralism, and is Chairman of the Implementation Group for the Arts in Education Charter.

Dr. Sheelagh Drudy is Emeritus Professor of Education and former Head of the School of Education at UCD. She has been a teacher educator for many years at NUIM and UCD and was previously a second level teacher. She has published books and articles on the sociology of education. She has been involved in educational policy development, having served on a variety of national and international bodies. She is a former Research Fellow and Visiting Fellow at Lucy Cavendish College, Cambridge. She was a member of the first Teaching Council and currently serves as a member of the Council of the National Council for Special Education.

Dr. Pádraig Hogan is Senior Lecturer in Education at the National University of Ireland, Maynooth. He has a keen research interest in the quality of educational experience and in what makes learning environments conducive to fruitful learning. Since 2003, he has led the research and development programme 'Teaching and Learning for the 21st Century'. This programme currently involves the university with eleven Education Centres, Dublin & Dún Laoghaire ETB and over 70 second-level schools. To date, he has published over 100 research items, including books, journal articles, book chapters and commissioned pieces. His most recent book is *The New Significance of Learning: Imagination's Heartwork*.

Dr Áine Hyland is Emeritus Professor of Education and former Vice-President of University College Cork, Ireland. She has been active in education circles in Ireland and internationally for over 50 years. She started her career as a civil servant in the Department of Education, and was a secondary teacher in the 1970s. Since 1980, she has been involved in teacher education – in Carysfort College, University College Dublin and subsequently as Professor of Education in University College Cork. She has been a member of various education boards and has published books and articles on the history of Irish education, educational policy, educational disadvantage and curriculum and examinations.

Dr. Séamus McGuinness is a former Senior Lecturer in the School of Education, Trinity College, Dublin. He served as a member of the Secretariat of the National Education Convention and as chair of a number of Department of Education committees, including The Technical Group on the Establishment of the Teaching Council, The Expert Group on the Allocation of Teachers to Post-Primary Schools, The Education Sector Performance Verification Group (ESPVG). He is currently chair of the New Schools Establishment Group. He has also worked as a consultant for a number of national and international organisations in the areas of system and programme evaluations and has co-authored a range of related reports.

The **Irish Primary Principals' Network (IPPN)** is the professional body for over 6,000 leaders of Irish primary schools and works with the Department of Education & Skills (DES), the National Parents Council, management bodies, other education partners, unions, and children's charities towards the advancement of primary education. IPPN's vision is 'Empowered Leaders - Inspired Learners'. In achieving this vision, our mission is to support and advocate for exemplary school leadership – Tacaíocht, Misneach & Spreagadh.

Leading and Learning

www.ippn.ie

The **National Association of Principals and Deputy Principals (NAPD)** was established in 1998 to provide a united voice nationally for Principals and Deputy Principal on issues of common concern. As a professional association, NAPD seeks to promote the interests and welfare of second-level school leaders.

www.napd.ie

In 2015, IPPN collaborated with the DES and the NAPD to establish the **Centre for School Leadership (CSL)**, which is responsible for the coordination and quality assurance of CPD programmes for current and aspiring school leaders.

www.cslireland.ie

Foreword

The idea for *Towards a Better Future* was inspired by a review of the Finnish education system presented by Professor Pasi Sahlberg at a conference for school leaders. It prompted the question of whether it would be worthwhile to undertake similar research on the Irish education system. To our knowledge, there is no publication that gives a comprehensive overview and analysis covering contemporary early childhood, primary and second-level education in Ireland.

The Irish Primary Principals' Network (IPPN) and the National Association of Principals and Deputy Principals (NAPD) were established on the cusp of the new century, in recognition of the key role school leadership plays in modern education, and of the desirability of a collegial voice on school leadership. IPPN and NAPD collectively represent 8,000 school leaders and provide support, advice, training and advocacy on school leadership issues. Through conferences, research studies, publications and participation in public debate, they contribute to enriching the discourse and practice of qualitative educational endeavour. In the recent past in Ireland, a significant range of reforms for all aspects of the school system has been initiated. This has coincided with a period of economic recession. The impact of the recession on the education system has seriously impeded the successful implementation of the reform programme, which the system needs. IPPN and NAPD are well aware of the difficulties faced by school leaders, particularly in seeking to address the many demands made on them to promote desired reforms in these unfavourable circumstances.

It is in this context that IPPN and NAPD considered that the time was ripe for a thorough study to be undertaken of the contemporary education system, from pre-school to the end of post-primary school. The following terms of reference were designed for the study:
- to undertake a research-informed analysis of the Irish education system at the present time in order to identify what are the main strengths, the main shortcomings, and the main opportunities for development
- to include within the scope of the analysis early childhood education, primary education and post-primary education
- in relation to strengths, to highlight what is educationally distinctive, referring as appropriate to concrete instances and to relevant research, in Ireland and internationally

- in relation to shortcomings, to illuminate the factors that give rise to these, again referring as appropriate to experience and research, both Irish and international
- in relation to opportunities for development, to identify what factors currently impede the utilisation of such opportunities and to comment on what kinds of approaches might prove promising in tackling impediments.

IPPN and NAPD invited five distinguished educationalists to undertake this work – Professor John Coolahan, Professor Sheelagh Drudy, Dr. Pádraig Hogan, Professor Áine Hyland, and Dr. Séamus McGuinness. It is a true reflection of their profound commitment to education, and of their generosity of spirit, that they have conducted this considerable body of work entirely voluntarily. We are both humbled by and deeply grateful for this. On behalf of all Irish school leaders, we thank each and every one of them for their work and for their service to education, both in Ireland and further afield. It has been a joy to work with people of such high calibre.

In the course of its research, the group has consulted with various personnel, but has conducted its work independently of IPPN and NAPD. What was sought was an objective, evidence-based appraisal of the recent past and current issues in Irish schooling, with a view to the review leading to a better future. We considered 2016 to be an appropriate time to conduct such a study, with a key focus on promoting good educational practice for Ireland's young generations.

IPPN and NAPD take pleasure in publishing this work at this time. We believe that a careful reading of the text will be of value to all stakeholders and to those interested in the good of Irish education. The review provides a conspectus for policy-makers, practitioners and participants of the comprehensive range of issues and concerns relevant to the achievement of the reform programme. Neither IPPN nor NAPD has influenced the work in any way. We see the publication as a contribution, in line with our tradition, of cultivating enlightened awareness of educational issues, with a view towards a better future.

We would like to say a special word of thanks to Geraldine D'Arcy (IPPN) and Derek West (NAPD) for their work in copy-editing and proof-reading the text.

Clive Byrne (Director, NAPD) & **Seán Cottrell** (CEO, IPPN)
March 2017

Introduction

A significant and enduring feature of Irish educational history is the deep-rooted desire and respect for education evidenced by Irish parents. Even in times of great political and economic hardship, parents sought schooling for their children. As the school system evolved, parents took advantage of every opportunity made available to them to improve the access of their children to schooling. An associated striking feature of Irish educational tradition has been the respect and status thathas been accorded to the role of the teacher, and the high quality of applicants attracted to the profession. These traditional features form a valued strength of the contemporary schooling system.

The primary, secondary and vocational school systems have their roots in the era when Ireland formed part of the British Empire. Their origination and structure were shaped by the political, religious, economic and social forces of the period. Following political independence, three eras of particular policy change occurred – 1922-1934, the 1960s, and the 1990s, which have further shaped the school system of today. However, legacy issues from all stages of development continue to have an influence on aspects of current schooling policy.

The following table sets out some summary facts of the contemporary education system for the year 2015-16.

Totals	Schools	Teachers	Students
Primary & Special Schools	3,262	34,576	553,380
Second-level Schools	735	26,804	345,550

Rapidly-growing Student Population
- Primary: 553,380 in 2015 expected to grow to 574,000 in 2018
- Secondary: 345,550 in 2015, to grow to 411,000 by 2025
- Immigrant students comprise 10.6% of primary students and 12% of post-primary students

The proportion of early school leavers in Ireland, at 6.9%, is smaller than the EU average, which is 11%. In relation to performance, the 2014 National Assessment Survey at primary level has shown significant increases in achievement in English, Reading and Mathematics when compared with the previous survey in 2009. The performance of Irish students as measured by the most recent international assessments available is indicated in the following summary points:

PISA 2015 (15-year-olds)
- Reading: significantly above OECD average
- 3rd out of 35 OECD countries, seventh out of all participating countries
- Mathematics: significantly above OECD average (though not among high-performing countries)
- 13th out of OECD countries, 18th out of all participating countries
- Science: significantly above the OECD average and significantly better than 2006 when Science was first tested
- 13th among the OECD countries, 19th out of all participating countries.

PIRLS 2011 (Reading at primary level, 4th grade)
- Irish students scored significantly above international average
- Ranked 10th out of 45 participating countries
- Students in only five countries scored significantly better.

TIMSS, 2015 - Primary
- Mathematics: 9th out of 49 participating countries
- Science: 19th out of 47 participating countries.

TIMSS, 2015 - Post-Primary
- Mathematics: 9th out of 39 participating countries
- Science: 10th out of 39 participating countries.

When one notes the pattern of completion of education of Irish students and students internationally, one detects a major change for the younger age groups, reflective of the advances made in Ireland in recent decades on educational provision. In 2015, 92.7% of Irish 20-24 year olds had attained Leaving Certificateor its equivalent, the third highest proportion of the 28 EU member states. Indeed, Irish 25-34 year olds are above both the EU and OECD averages in completing secondary education.

People who have completed upper secondary education

2014	Ireland	EU 21	OECD
People aged 55-64 years	59%	68%	66%
People aged 25-34 years	86%	84%	82%

The percentage of the same Irish age group who have completed higher education is significantly higher than their peers in the EU and the OECD, as is recorded in the following figures.

People who have completed higher education

2012	Ireland	EU 21	OECD
People aged 55-64 years	25%	22%	24%
People aged 25-34	49%	37%	39%

(Sources: DES Annual Statistical Reports; DES Annual Statistical Reports International)

The economic recession of 2008 to 2015 had a serious injurious impact on what has been arguably a fourth significant period of educational policy change and development. Financial cutbacks and retrenchment of services have impeded the successful implementation of a range of new policies, without throwing them altogether off course. Despite the difficulties, the change agenda is still operative and the concern for further reform is being sustained because of its centrality to the social and economic well-being of the nation.

Within this context, the Irish Primary Principals'Network (IPPN) and the National Association of Principals and Deputy Principals (NAPD) invited a small group of educational researchers to carry out an appraisal of the state of the schooling system as Ireland comes out of the recession. The group was asked to undertake a research-informed analysis of the Irish school system in order to identify what are its main strengths, the main shortcomings and the main opportunities for development. The aim was to take various relevant aspects of the system, to contextualise the current situation by reference to recent developments, to analyse current trends, issues and problems in a succinct way, and to propose lines of action which might maximise opportunities for achievement for each sector, into the future. The sub-themes selected for appraisal were: Teaching and Learning; Early Childhood Education; Curriculum; Assessment – Primary and Junior Cycle; Transition from Second Level to Higher Education; Educational Leadership and Governance; Equality, Inclusion and Rights; The Inspectorate; Finance and Resourcing of Education; Initial Teacher Education and Induction; and Professional Development in Teaching.

A summary of the main aspects of the reform era of the recent and current period indicates aspirations for improvements throughout the school system. There has been an extended new focus on early childhood education in terms of provision, curriculum and quality. The primary curriculum and its pedagogy are undergoing a reform process, with an initial emphasis on literacy and numeracy. Sustained efforts are being made to reform the Junior Cycle curriculum. Modes of assessment at primary and Junior Cycle are high on the reform agenda. Attention is being focused on improving the transition process between second-level schools and higher education institutions. Renewed policy attention is being focussed on special education and the education of pupils with various disabilities. There is policy concern for the education of the increasing numbers of immigrant children and asylum seekers. Efforts are being made to reform the inherited school patronage system, in the context of a more multi-cultural society. The vocational school system is being restructured under new statutory arrangements.

Reform efforts are afoot to change inherited patterns of school life and culture. Collaboration and greater co-operation between school staffs is being encouraged. Schools are now required to engage in whole-school planning and in school self-evaluation. New forms of school leadership, with an emphasis on educational leadership, are being fostered. The work of school leaders has been greatly extended in many ways. The establishment of IPPN and NAPD is reflective of this new emphasis. The traditional role of the Inspectorate has been greatly changed and now involves a variety of forms of inspection, with

> " **Modes of assessment at primary and Junior Cycle are high on the reform agenda. Attention is being focused on improving the transition process between second-level schools and higher education institutions.** "

an emphasis on co-professional relationships with teachers and more public reportage for accountability and evaluation purposes. Teacher education has been undergoing what is, arguably, its most significant reform period ever. Under the aegis of the Teaching Council (established 2006) Initial Teacher Education (ITE) programmes have been extended in duration and been significantly reconceptualised. It is now officially accepted that teacher education is a lifelong process. Accordingly, a programme of teacher induction is being progressed for all teachers. Provision for continuing professional development (CPD) for teachers throughout their careers is being devised.

The education reform policy in contemporary Ireland outlined above, amounts, in accumulation, to a major new direction for the inherited school system. The elements involved have been gestating for some time and have evolved through consultative processes between key stakeholders. One of the striking features of the reform programme, in contrast to most of the international pattern, is its consultative basis, rather than a more traditional 'top-down' approach. The key elements of the policy are regarded as being well based on research and in line with good international practice.

However, research also emphasises that the successful achievement of major educational reform is a complex process, involving many requirements. Crucial among these are resources, goodwill and time. When a lot of change is occurring, or proposed to occur simultaneously, it can put strains on the system. During the economic recession, financial resources and personnel resources have been seriously reduced. Changes such as reductions in salaries and allowances, the removal of middle management posts, reductions in support staff, dis-improvements in pupil-teacher ratios, embargos on appointments in various staff categories of the system and reduced capitation fees have had deleterious effects on the system and on staff morale. While this is a reality, it is greatly to the credit of personnel in the system that so much of the qualitative aspects of the education system have been maintained. Nevertheless, the various cutbacks have had a downward impact on the system. Personnel feel over-stretched, tensions exist in the system, goodwill and positive engagement and sense of ownership of the reforms is less in evidence than would be desirable for such a reform programme. The reform agenda has encountered a context that is unfavourable to its progression. Yet, the reform agenda is too important for the future of Irish society to be jeopardised. A realistic appraisal of the situation needs to be taken so that the sought-for progress can be made. Central to this is the realisation at government level and by society at large that, among other inputs, greater resourcing of the reform agenda is crucial. There are helpful signs that some of the damage caused by the recessionary cutbacks is being addressed, but a much greater and sustained commitment is required.

The authors of the following overview and appraisal of the school system have sought to highlight the key issues in each of the sectors examined. Against a background of recent change, they have identified the major policy issues that face us. They have affirmed many strengths of the system and identified how best these strengths can be built upon, and what new emphases are required. While the sub-themes are dealt with individually, there is an overall connectedness in the holistic reform involved for the system. Points made are supported by relevant national and international research. It has been thought that a succinct style of treatment, rather going into a detailed approach, best serves the purpose of this overview. Chapters vary in length relating to the sub-themes being dealt with.

As a small island nation, with a strong and distinctive educational tradition, we have a duty to use our best collective wisdom to design the school system in such a way that it can serve the needs of a changing society within the globalised world of the 21st century. Continual reform is an in-built need of modern education systems, at some periods particularly crucial. Ireland is at such a period now, and the way forward is being charted in impressive ways. It is the task of this generation to ensure that the challenge is met and that the current and evolving reform agenda is successfully achieved and implemented. The agenda for change is such that it needs sustained support from a number of relevant government departments, as well as the Department of Education and Skills.

Contents

CHAPTER ONE ● ● ● ● ● ● ● ● ● ● ● ● ● ● ● ● ●
Teaching
and Learning

INTRODUCTION

Teaching and learning constitute the heart of educational action and there are many ways in which key issues in this very broad topic could be investigated. For instance, one might survey prevalent trends in different countries, as Organization for Economic Cooperation and Development (OECD) reports regularly do, and seek to draw insights for what is commonly called 'best practice.' Alternatively, one might concentrate on analysing the outcomes of teaching and learning as measured by examinations, tests and other instruments that yield substantial numerical data. On the other hand, one could undertake research chiefly from a psychological perspective, or a sociological one, thus putting a critical spotlight on personal, social and family factors that might remain in the background in other forms of enquiry. The approach taken in this chapter is one that puts the joint work of the educational practitioner and his/her students at the centre of the picture. That is to say, it seeks to disclose the experience of teaching and learning from the inside. At first sight, this may look a bit subjective, especially when compared to the objectivity associated with the empirical procedures of the social sciences. In fact, however, this approach is even *more* empirical: it seeks to pay attention to features of the experience of teaching and learning that are *central and inescapable* ones. Yet many of these features are routinely passed over, not only in educational policies that equate evaluation with measurement, but even in the professional discourse and actions of teachers themselves. Uncovering the experience of teaching and learning from the inside brings to the foreground questions about purpose and values, but not in a way that calls to mind familiar things like mission statements or school philosophies. Rather, the real focus of any searching exploration of teaching and learning needs be on the values and purposes that are actually embodied in the practices carried on every day in our schools. Invariably these practices involve implicit assumptions, some of which might be questionable if they were made explicit. Therefore, an incisive understanding is called for, of what actually happens in the experience of teaching and learning itself, if educational policies and practices are to be adequately informed and evaluated.

THE BACKGROUND

The abolition of the Primary Certificate in 1967 and the introduction of a new primary curriculum in 1971 opened the way for a different quality of educational experience in Ireland's primary schools; different both from the official 'cultural nationalist' emphasis that had prevailed in the era since independence and the 'traditional didactic' emphasis of the era before independence. The 1971 curriculum was largely devised by the Inspectorate of the Department of Education. Not all primary teachers embraced at once its central idea that children were to become more active participants in their own learning. By the time the revised primary curriculum of 1999 was in preparation, however, Ireland's primary teachers had in the main become practitioners of more experiential forms of teaching and learning. The ultimate authors of the 1999 curriculum could be said to be primary teachers themselves, through their heavy representation on the syllabus committees of the National Council for Curriculum and Assessment (NCCA) that produced the draft curricula for approval by the Minister for Education. As the appendices for the curriculum handbooks show, moreover, almost all of the committees were chaired by primary teachers (Department of Education, 1999). The advisory and support services for the 1999 curriculum were also very largely staffed by primary teachers. This historic shift of emphasis at primary level from exam-led teaching to a focus on the quality of the students' educational experiences is not, however, a fully-accomplished project. Perhaps it can never be. As will be reviewed later, work remains to be done on enhancing teachers' professional capacities in a number of respects to promote such higher quality educational experience among students.

It can fairly be said that the major shift that has taken place in the cultures of teaching and learning at primary level has not been mirrored at post-primary level. That is not to say that there have not been serious efforts to bring about such a shift (see Chapters 3, 4 and 5 of this review). In launching the Junior Certificate programme in September 1988, the then Minister for Education, Mary O'Rourke, voiced her anticipation that the kinds of educational experiences which were now a central feature of primary education would follow through into second-level. There are many

> " It can fairly be said that the major shift that has taken place in the cultures of teaching and learning at primary level has not been mirrored at post-primary level. "

reasons why this did not happen and these are reviewed in Chapters 3 and 4. Chief among these reasons has been a reluctance among post-primary teachers over more than three decades to accept changes in curriculum and assessment that would give them a role in assessing the work of their own students for certification purposes.

An important consequence of the points sketched in outline above is the discontinuity between the kinds of teaching and learning that are pursued at primary level and those pursued at second level. Recent studies of national samples of second-level schools carried out by the Economic and Social Research Institute (ESRI) in association with the NCCA highlight some serious concerns here (Smyth et al., 2004; Smyth et al., 2006). These prominently include: the negative effects of the discontinuity between primary and post-primary; a decline in students' positive attitude towards school during Second Year and into Third Year; a disengagement from learning by students that is associated with heavy reliance on practices like 'teaching from the book' and lack of constructive feedback to students.

Teaching and learning at the Senior Cycle remain heavily influenced by perceptions of what the Leaving Certificate assessments are deemed to reward, with resulting negative effects on the purposes for which teaching and learning are themselves pursued. This point was underlined in the 2014 research report *Predictability in the Irish Leaving Certificate*, commissioned by the State Examinations Commission at the request of the Transition Reform Group, which was established by the Minister for Education (Baird et al. 2014). Although this research (carried out by researchers from Queen's University Belfast and Oxford University) was concerned mainly with issues of predictability in the Leaving Certificate exam, it also produced findings on teaching and learning more widely at Leaving Certificate level. These findings confirm some long-standing criticisms of prevalent practices in the Senior Cycle, including: an over-emphasis in some subjects on knowledge recall to the detriment of higher-order skills; a narrowing of the curriculum scope in the subjects that were analysed (English, Economics, French, Design & Communication Graphics); the prominence of 'mock exams'; and a thriving grinds industry (45% received some private tuition in 2013). The following overall comment by the researchers on the dominant practices of teaching is revealing:

> Teachers did agree that they taught towards the format, structure and style of examination questions and shared their understanding of the messages given within mark schemes of what responses are required and what is of value. They indicated that how they end up teaching can seem like spoon-feeding students but they are conscious that 'students want points, parents want points.' Many teachers showed us their own analysis of the types of questions that come up year on year and they felt they were fulfilling their duty as teachers by sharing these analyses with students
> (Baird et al. 2014, p.84).

PURPOSES IN TEACHING AND LEARNING: CONTROVERSY AND COHERENCE

In Ireland as elsewhere, when teachers are asked about their purposes, about what has brought them into teaching, they rarely if ever reply in such utilitarian terms as those cited above from the *Predictability* report. More characteristically, they report that they want to make a difference for the better in the lives of their students; that they wish to help students to reach their potential as human beings; that their work as educators will help to strengthen community, cultural and civic life (Lawlor, 2014, Ch.5). A critic or sceptic might claim that such motivations assume too sanguine a view of teachers' scope for agency; that such optimism fails to recognise the social and historical constraints in which teaching is embedded; that the institutionalised interests, which invariably secure a decisive say in the control of schooling, are being disregarded. Moreover, clearly there is abundant evidence on which such criticism can draw, both in historical and in empirical research studies. Rather than defeat the purposes of improvement, however, such evidence needs to be explored with discernment, incisiveness and a keen sense of the practicable. Only thus can the attractions and dangers of a fool's paradise be kept at bay.

Before proceeding further, the issue of tensions between teachers' scope for agency on the one hand and the weight of inherited traditions and institutionalised powers on the other needs some preliminary investigation or clarification. On such clarification depends much of the coherence of teaching itself as a social good and a defensible practice.

The idea that the guiding purposes of formal education are to be decided chiefly by those who have secured a position of institutional power became deeply lodged in Western civilisation. Educational historians have traced the beginnings of the long ascendency of this idea to the early 9th century (Boyd & King 1999; Bowen, 2003). Early versions of the idea were championed by the institutional churches; more recent ones have become manifest in an international educational discourse about the needs of economy and society. For all its apparent naturalness, however, this idea is a distortion and an impediment. It defines formal education as an essentially paternalistic undertaking. In its preoccupation with controlling the right contents for curricula, it cloaks some of the most important consequences of teaching, even from teachers themselves. It deprives teaching of the coherence and integrity that should properly belong to anything called a practice, and to the practitioners of that practice. In short, it tends to make formal education a vehicle for one or other dominant 'ism'. For instance, the guiding purposes of education can be seen to be placed in very powerful hands – and cast very differently – if we take the following illustrative examples from the history of Western education: European countries in Medieval Christendom; European countries after the Reformation; England in the mid-19th century; Ireland in the later 19th century; Eastern European countries after the Second World War; Ireland in the early period of independence; England after the Education Reform Act of 1988. In each of these examples, one can identify a dominant family of values characteristically associated with bodies or groups that have secured some enforceable powers in society. Moreover, one can readily find in such examples, disputes, shifting alliances and recurring jostling among the influential bodies. What is difficult to find here, however, is much scope for original thought and action by teachers as practitioners; indeed the very idea of teacher as practitioner seems a stranger in such contexts.

Such conceptions of education can broadly be described as 'paternalistic', although 'authoritarian' might sometimes be more appropriate. In addition, they can find plausible warrant in classical Western philosophy, particularly in selective or uncritical readings of Plato and Aristotle. From such readings arise the apparently natural idea that one's 'philosophy of education' must spring primarily from one's 'philosophy of life.' It is only a small step from here to the familiar mantra that 'education is an essentially contested arena': a phrase whose self-defeating character would be readily evident if used in relation to practices such as nursing or medicine. In saying this much, however, we must clearly acknowledge that practitioners in any field are neither fully autonomous beings nor clones of each other. Any practice that is in good order not only identifies a set of common purposes, it also allows for debate and ordered conflict on how the practice might be improved (Dunne, 2005, pp. 152-158; Hogan, 2010, Chapters 3 & 4; Williams, 2007, Ch. 1). A practice that is in good order also allows ample scope for the personal qualities brought into play by individual practitioners. These include depth of commitment, imagination in action, resilience and discerning judgement, and the capacity to extend and renew the practice itself. It must be recognised of course that a democratically elected government, as legitimate guarantor of the public interest, has responsibilities in regulating practices, in ensuring their fruitful contribution to the public good itself, and in ensuring that practices are duly answerable for the public resources committed to them.

> " The idea that the guiding purposes of formal education are to be decided chiefly by those who have secured a position of institutional power became deeply lodged in Western civilisation. "

Anything that is to be recognised as a practice in its own right must have some publicly acknowledged purposes, purposes that are worthy of the commitments and actions of its practitioners, notwithstanding their different outlooks in matters of politics, religion, lifestyle and so on. It is largely counter-productive then to approach the question of educational purposes in the historically dominant ways reviewed above (viz. associating educational purposes with 'isms' or personal 'philosophies of life'). This is especially the case where formal education as a practice in a pluralist democracy is concerned. A more fertile approach is to start with the practice itself and its practitioners. One can now begin to identify from within this context some key purposes that are educationally promising as practical forms of action; purposes, moreover, that seek to be socially defensible in a universal sense. Among such purposes that can initially be identified are the following three:

- uncovering constructive potentials that are native to each individual
- cultivating such potentials through renewed imaginative engagements with inheritances of learning and seeking to broaden the range in each case
- promoting practices of learning that acknowledge and respect differences, and that dispose learners to seek to benefit others as well as themselves.

To put the matter like this is to say that a learning environment that is truly educational is marked less by adherence to a particular party, church or group, or indeed to any version of the question 'what knowledge is of most worth?' A truly educational learning environment is oriented primarily to the needs of the students. It seeks to open up a range of study possibilities that answer promisingly to these needs, while promoting co-operative learning practices and ensuring that competitive impulses remain healthy. It is marked firstly by a commitment to building and sustaining a vibrant community of enquiry that is as inclusive as is earnestly practicable. In such a learning environment teachers characteristically seek to uncover students' real potentials, and to acknowledge the manifest plurality of the human condition. This entails further that teachers, as far as possible, need to become imaginative authors of their own work and discerning, co-operative critics of their own practice. The kind of orientation for a practitioner ethic that comes to light here distinguishes teachers from a workforce whose actions are mainly dictated by conformity with unquestioned routine or with imposed directives. Equally, this ethical orientation distinguishes practitioners' actions from workplace cultures that are marked largely by negativity or resistance where proposals for renewing and enhancing the practice are concerned. In such learning environments, moreover, students are encouraged and helped to become more fluent, more capable, more active and more responsible participants in their own learning. The quality of educational experience in such environments contributes crucially to enhancing the students' human capacities and to discovering continually new aspects of their own identity.

SHIFTING PERSPECTIVE:
AN INTERPLAY AS DISTINCT FROM A TRANSMISSION

It is worth taking stock briefly of the path taken to this point, while also anticipating a few turns that lie ahead. Adequately understood, teaching and learning in formal education have a higher purpose and responsibility than meeting a society's demands for economic and social skills. It is not that the latter are unimportant. However, anything called a social or economic skill is itself properly nurtured in a healthy learning environment; i.e. focused on the disclosure and cultivation of capabilities that are linked to a personal sense of identity and enablement. To speak of capabilities in this educational sense is to recognise them as authentic expressions of learners' native potentials. While justified restraint is an essential feature of such learning environments, coercion in any form is detrimental.

The key purposes of teaching and learning are also misconceived if they are regarded as part of the evangelical mission of a church or the political imperatives of the state; or indeed as an exercise in the transmission of cultural heritage to younger generations. Despite the prevalence of such conceptions in the history of educational practice – even to our own day – they do an injustice to those they would purport to help. It is not that churches, political parties and various cultural groups do not have legitimate aspirations to extend their influence and to win more members. Whether transmission is the appropriate way to encounter the teachings or values of such bodies is not our concern here. Where education is concerned, however, the prevalent notion of transmission presents a difficulty, indeed an injustice. The injustice resides in regarding the student or pupil as a submissive, or more commonly an acquiescent participant in educational endeavours. The fact that such a diminution might nowadays be more subtle than overt in the cultures of schooling tends to becloud the point that something invidious might be routinely practised, hand-in-hand with the commendable work of teachers (Carr, 2006; Hogan, 2003; Oakeshott, 1981).

Even the more benign conceptions of transmission are prone to overlook an insight of critical importance. They overlook the significance of the *joint* nature of teaching and learning. Teaching and learning is invariably a joint event, experienced from different standpoints –sometimes radically different – by teachers and students. This remains the case even when the fact is unacknowledged by either teacher or students. As a joint event, the notion of an active interplay provides a more fertile basis for understanding what actually takes place than any notion of transmission ever could. No less than in any game that is played in public, the stakes can be high for both teachers and students in the to-and-fro of this interplay. Fear of

> " The key purposes of teaching and learning are also misconceived if they are regarded as part of the evangelical mission of a church or the political imperatives of the state; or indeed as an exercise in the transmission of cultural heritage to younger generations. "

embarrassment, of ridicule, or of any other form of belittlement can be very real for students, and for the teacher, even where such fears might be largely misplaced. Discipline codes have characteristically sought to remove such sources of danger. Nevertheless, they have generally been articulated from one side much more than the other: as formal regulations and requirements, enforceable by the school authorities.

When conceived as an active interplay, the primary emphasis in teaching and learning falls more on relationships and responsibilities than on regulations and requirements. More particularly, from the teaching side of the interplay, the key challenges for the teacher now appear as those of opening up new imaginative landscapes for the students in the particular subject(s) being studied. The interplays of teaching and learning become properly fertile when students become gradually more at home in these landscapes and incrementally more proficient in negotiating their own paths through them – individually and co-operatively. Of first importance here for teaching is the painstaking work of building environments of learning that are vibrant and venturesome, respectful and safe. Such environments are more communities of enquiry than places of transmission. They enable inheritances of learning – scientific, historical, mathematical, religious etc. – to be brought to life and encountered in ways that are engaged, sustained, and age-appropriate. They also enable such inheritances to be questioned, debated, and explored further.

The rules necessary for supporting and sustaining such environments need to be identified, discussed and agreed by the different parties to the interplay. Teachers of course have a particular leadership role in this, and can draw profitably on insights from their professional knowledge and previous experiences. Nevertheless, whenever an experienced teacher embarks on this work with a new cohort of students, the teacher travels a familiar path in new ways, ready to learn older things anew and to learn many other things for the first time.

> " When conceived as an active interplay, the primary emphasis in teaching and learning falls more on relationships and responsibilities than on regulations and requirements. "

Where this experience is commonplace among teachers the practice of teaching itself is likely to be in a healthy state. In Ireland's schools, it is more common at primary level than at post-primary, though by no means unknown in the latter.

External controls – whether from government directives, official school policies or another source – have sometimes reduced to negligible proportions the scope for the exercise of such leadership on the part of teachers. To the extent that this happens, and educational reforms in more than one jurisdiction in recent decades have made it happen regularly, teaching as a practice may become not merely constricted, but even disfigured on a wide scale. Ironically, teachers themselves can be authors of such a sorry state of affairs, as for instance where educational reforms conducive to the rationale explored above have been promoted by government policy, but rejected by teachers.

ENHANCING THE ENVIRONMENTS OF TEACHING AND LEARNING

Practices of teaching that seek to promote a high quality of educational experience need to be alert to the unintended as well as the intended consequences of teachers' actions. Let us recall here the extract from the *Predictability* report quoted earlier. This reveals that many teachers at the Senior Cycle of second level are discomfited by the consequences of some of their own regular practices (e.g. spoon-feeding and teaching-to-the-exam). It should not be assumed, however, that the prevalent approaches to teaching at primary level are free from shortcomings of this kind. Inspectors' reports on primary schools in recent years have urged the necessity for greater attention to evaluation of the actual consequences of teaching, particularly in the assessment of English lessons (DES, 2013, p.45). Recent efforts to address this issue at primary level are considered in Chapter 4.

In connection with this alertness to unintended consequences, it is worth citing a key insight from Dewey, which is pertinent to practices of teaching at all levels:

> Perhaps the greatest of all pedagogical fallacies is the notion that a person learns only the particular thing he is studying at the time. Collateral learning in the form of enduring attitudes, of likes and dislikes, may be and often is much more important than the spelling lesson or the lesson in geography or history that is learned. For these attitudes are fundamentally what count in the future. The most important attitude that can be formed is that of desire to go on learning.
> (1938/1996, p.48)

Unless the kind of attentiveness Dewey highlights here becomes a central part of the discipline of teaching, many of the best opportunities for enhancing teaching itself are likely to be bypassed. To recognise this gives to self-evaluation an importance in teaching that it has very largely lacked historically. Such a recognition, moreover, properly gives a secondary, or supportive role to evaluation by others, whether by colleagues or by inspectors. Equally important, it provides an agenda for self-evaluation that has not been too familiar, especially where professional development has been mainly understood as the upskilling of a teaching force.

We will return to the issue of evaluation in the next section, but prominent on the proper agenda of professional development would be the uncovering of hidden as well as overt influences in teaching and learning. Such professional development would accordingly promote a capacity to build learning environments with features like the following: that are non-coercive in character; that are inviting to newcomers; that help to uncover one's previously undiscovered potentials *and* limitations; that characteristically subject to scrutiny both received wisdom and unacknowledged assumptions; that embrace developments in ICT, but with a discerning eye for their pedagogical promise; that seek new ways to advance higher levels of proficiency so that enquiry can more fruitfully proceed; that promote *through concrete learning experiences themselves* a deeper understanding and tolerance of human differences; that encourage the unfolding of a vibrant sense of personal identity, while supporting a similar unfolding among fellow-learners; that cultivate an ethos of community where diversity is also affirmed.

This list of features of an enhanced educational practice is of course far from exhaustive. However, it highlights the myriad influences that come and go with endless play – to paraphrase Wordsworth – in educational experience daily. Influences that are strongly at play in either in the background or the foreground can, moreover, work harmfully as well as constructively. Discerning the more important ones in any particular instance calls attention to the kinds of perceptiveness and adroitness on the teacher's part that help to make educational experience truly fruitful. It is also important to mention here that where daily practice becomes preoccupied with just one or a few prominent features – e.g. with the measurement of achievements in tests and exams – the other factors at play do not thereby fall dormant. For instance, attitudes that are divisive or invidious could be learned very powerfully, and inconspicuously, while all overt efforts are devoted to the promotion of demonstrable cognitive advances. It is all too rarely acknowledged that the long-term ethical significance of education lies more in the quality of these daily experiences than in the contents of a particular body of ethical teachings on the school curriculum. It is in the tenor of these experiences, moreover, that that the real significance of the classical Greek notion of *ethos* can be found in education. To become aware of this is also to realise how mistaken it is to associate the term *ethos* mainly with the powers, privileges or prerogatives of any of the patron bodies in education. Against such commonplace errors, Dewey's insight cited above has a compelling force.

THE EVALUATION OF LEARNING

The evaluation of learning in Irish schools is customarily associated with two distinct but complementary functions: (a) the carrying out of assessments and examinations, (b) the work of the schools Inspectorate. Depending on how adequately examinations or assessments are conceived, or how broadly or narrowly the work of inspectors is understood, evaluation can be an informative, an ambiguous, or even a misleading affair. In this connection, Chapters 4 and 5 provide an illuminating account of different forms of assessment and a review of developments and current issues of concern in the assessment systems at primary and post-primary level. Chapter 8 on the Inspectorate highlights some historically characteristic approaches to inspection and traces some welcome developments in the nature and scope of inspection practice, especially in recent years.

However, let us assume for a moment that the formal systems of assessment and of inspection are all in good order. Even then, the combined fruits of assessment and inspection would still provide a far from complete picture of the benefits which evaluation, as a crucial dimension of educational practice, can yield. As touched on earlier, the important thing to stress is that the primary benefits of evaluation arise when evaluation itself is constructively and insightfully embodied in the everyday work of educational practitioners themselves. 'Practitioners' in this wider sense include not only teachers and school leaders, but also inspectors, researchers, professionals in the support services, managerial bodies and associations, statutory agencies in education, and so on. This is not, it should be stressed, a matter of widening the range of approaches in order to have more effective as distinct from less effective forms of evaluation. The very notion of 'effectiveness', for all its prominence in the research and policy literature on education, fails to capture the heart of what is involved in the evaluation of learning and teaching. If the various kinds of practitioners involved in education understand evaluation primarily in terms of effectiveness, then the best insights that evaluation itself has to offer may be largely bypassed. No more can one capture the core of the matter in this restricted way than can a drama critic review a play based on the playwright's text alone.

To suggest that evaluation needs to be embodied constructively and insightfully in the actions of practitioners means that the practitioners have to become their own most capable and perceptive critics. Evaluation thus understood is hospitable to what the DES promotes as school self-evaluation, and is conceived as a co-operative or team endeavour, not as an exercise in compliance, or individual display. It is what is properly referred to by the phrase 'reflective practitioner', and it lies at the heart of teacher education – both in its initial and professional development modes. The latter now includes the

> " ...the primary benefits of evaluation arise when evaluation itself is constructively and insightfully embodied in the everyday work of educational practitioners themselves. "

induction phase that is currently expanding as *Droichead* (See Chapters 8 and 9). Where the education of teachers involves them habitually in analysing and reviewing the collateral as well as the more explicit dimensions of learning in their classrooms, evaluation becomes quite naturally an integral part of the work of teaching itself. Familiarity with criteria of excellence in appraising the consequences of different kinds of pedagogical actions can be systematically cultivated here, hand-in-hand with a capacity to provide regular, informed feedback to students.

The benefits of such forms of teacher education go far beyond the domain of skills, and become manifest in the teacher's ethical orientation and sense of professional identity. Accordingly, a range of worthy human qualities also comes actively into play in the learning experiences of teachers themselves, whether as newcomers or practitioners that are more experienced. Examples of these qualities, all of which involve a refined exercise of judgement, include sensitivity to interpersonal dynamics – in both classroom and staffroom; a keen ethical awareness where differences in outlook are concerned; openness to constructive criticism; commitment to working co-operatively; and not least, a disposition toward taking leadership initiatives with colleagues and students. One could call such qualities the creative habits of heart and mind that are appropriate to the conduct and evaluation of teaching as a distinct form of human action.

Embodying such qualities centrally in daily practice not only gives teachers the capacity and moral energy to debate educational issues in a surefooted way with school leaders, inspectors, students and parents. Equally important is the point that evaluation itself here becomes richer – i.e. more incisive, more inclusive, more thorough. To give a concrete example: where achievements ('outcomes') in learning are being evaluated by teachers, such achievements are now seen as multi-dimensional, as distinct from one-dimensional. Teachers' accounts of students' progress are now seen to include not only informed judgements about their advances in cognitive matters, but also about changes in their *practices of* learning and their *attitudes towards* learning. An accomplished evaluative capacity on the teacher's part can monitor and appraise significant developments on each of these three dimensions. The kind of illuminating professional communication this makes possible – with students, colleagues, parents, inspectors and others – discloses the fuller purposes of evaluation as a central feature of educational practice. It also reveals the bland character of a discourse on evaluation where notions of effectiveness predominate.

THE CHANGING NATURE OF TEACHING AS A PRACTICE

Just over two decades ago, the then Department of Education and Science issued a circular called 'Time in School'. That 1995 circular, withdrawn some months after its introduction, made no acknowledgement of the variety of professional activities teachers carry out daily. A basic assumption underlying the circular was that teachers' time in school should be spent entirely in teaching their classes. If such a conception of teaching were a faulty one in 1995, it would be quite misplaced in 2016.

OECD figures for annual contact time in the middle school (i.e. Junior Cycle) range from almost 1,000 hours in the US, to around 730 in Ireland, to around 600 in Finland. (Data for 2013, published in OECD 2015, p.452. See also Fig.5 in Chapter 11). The low total for the Finnish figures attracts attention, particularly in view of the esteem in which Finland's schools are held internationally. The high-quality learning environments of Finnish schools are yielded by a 'less is more' rationale where the school timetable is concerned (Sahlberg 2011, Ch.2). This allocates teachers' time with keener discernment than in most other countries: proportional reductions in teaching time, proportional increases in time for collaborative planning, reviewing and evaluating activities. Research in Ireland and elsewhere shows that it is practitioners' capacity in these latter activities that enables schools to take ownership of their own professional work and to grow as professional learning communities.

(Hargreaves & Fink 2006, p.255ff; Hogan et al. 2008, pp. 22-23, 83; Sahlberg 2011, Ch.3). Where policy and practice are concerned, if scheduled time isn't made available for such activities, it's difficult to see how things like school self-evaluation, mentoring of newcomers to the profession, or indeed systematic feedback to students, can become hallmarks of the professional cultures of teaching. In this connection it is significant that a recent DES circular envisages the 'provision of professional time for teachers', within the scheduled weekly hours, for professional and collaborative activities (DES 2016a, pp.16-17).

There are big issues here, which must be carefully identified and faced. The initiative on the provision of professional time for teachers is a welcome new departure by the DES. However, the changing nature of teaching as a practice means that the time-in-school question needs to be looked at anew, by *all* of the education parties, as does the ratio between teaching time and non-teaching time. Progress in this endeavour would need to be made through a series of changes that are clearly seen to be significant and meaningful. For instance, an important early step might see the unloved idea of 'Croke Park hours' profitably replaced by a negotiated settlement on the use of teachers' time; a settlement that does justice to the necessities of 21st century educational practice. Such a departure would need take due account of EU norms for the average working week and to study in some depth the ingredients that have brought about sustainable improvements in jurisdictions that are broadly comparable to Ireland. In short, this points to the necessity for a newly-designed working agreement, or contract, for teachers in Ireland's schools rather than for self-contained agreements on individual issues. Some form of a New Deal is appropriate here. The original New Deal concept is associated with President Franklin D. Roosevelt's initiatives that closed the curtain on the Great Depression in the US in the 1930s and focused collective energies on achieving a brighter future. A New Deal begins with a public acknowledgement on all sides of the hurts and hardships caused by a prolonged economic downturn. Against this background, it continually keeps an eye on the larger picture, including relevant international policies, when devising strategies for remedy.

In this connection, the most recent EU data available on teachers' contracts and working conditions has many illuminating things to say, including the following comparative note:

> In the great majority of European countries, teachers' working time is largely determined by their teaching hours. However, in most cases, additional activities are also included. The number of hours they must be available at school for other activities, such as meetings or management duties, may also be specified, as occurs in 18 countries. Overall working time is a concept used in the majority of countries covered, and corresponds to the total number of working hours a week, as set down in collective bargaining agreements or other contractual arrangements.
> (European Commission, 2013, p.73)

When studying international comparisons from an Irish perspective, developments in countries of roughly comparable population and resources are particularly worth looking at: e.g. Scotland, Denmark, Finland (Basis: GDP per capita of $40,000 or over, at purchasing power parity). The agreement reached in Scotland based on the McCrone Report of 2001 provides an interesting case study here (Scottish Government, 2001). This recommended a new approach to how teachers' professional time might be spent and led to an agreed and lasting settlement. There are significant cultural differences between Ireland and such countries of course, and these need to be carefully taken into account in any comparative studies. In the case of countries such as the above three, however, the differences are much less pronounced than they are with jurisdictions in the Far East. This point needs to be highlighted when comparisons are made with 'leading' Far Eastern jurisdictions that are often cited in so-called 'best practice' comparisons: e.g. Singapore, Korea, and Shanghai.

> " When studying international comparisons from an Irish perspective, developments in countries of roughly comparable population and resources are particularly worth looking at: e.g. Scotland, Denmark, Finland "

This chapter has sought to identify and review some of the key issues – sometimes overlooked ones – that lie at the heart of teaching and learning and that exert a decisive influence on how education is thought about and practised. As Ireland emerges from the unhappy experience of recession it is timely to focus on these issues with an eye to a more inspiring educational provision that can be sustained through successive changes of government. Recognising our very considerable strengths, it is not an unrealistic goal to aim to ensure that our educational practice is second to none. Pursuing this goal calls for some crucial shifts of policy and perspective, however, as is suggested in this chapter and illustrated in a recurring way in the chapters that follow.

CHAPTER TWO • • • • • • • • • • • • • • • • • •

Early Childhood Education

A BACKWARD LOOK

Prior to the late 1990s, early childhood care and education (ECCE) did not receive significant attention in educational discourse and policy in Ireland. Very little research on early childhood education had taken place. There was an underestimation of both the significance and complexity of early education issues.

Strategic statements in the mid-1990s, by international organisations such as the OECD in 1996, UNESCO in 1996, and the EU Council of Ministers of Education in 1997, signalled that early childhood education should be a serious policy concern. Ireland, as a member of these bodies, also signalled a new approach at this time, as is set out below.

In the Programme for Government of 1997, early childhood education was selected as an area for policy action, with a commitment to provide a specific budget for it. Subsequent years witnessed much more focussed inquiry, multi-lateral dialogue and formal reports on early childhood education. In March 1998, a major public consultative forum of all major stakeholders took place – the National Forum for Early Childhood Education. This produced a major opportunity for reflection and deliberation on all aspects of early childhood care and education. This was captured in the Forum's *Report,* which was published in the summer of 1998. In the following year, the government published the first-ever White Paper on early childhood education – *Ready to Learn* (Government of Ireland, 1999). In 2002, the Centre for Early Childhood Development and Education (CECDE) was set up and published a range of valuable documents on the theme, until it was closed down in 2008, as the economic recession set in. In 2003, the National Council for Curriculum and Assessment (NCCA) published *Towards a Framework for Early Learning* (NCCA, 2003a), which it described as 'a milestone for the NCCA.' As a response to a request from the Department of Education and Science (DES), the OECD conducted 'an intensive review' of early childhood policies and services in 2002. Its report, *Thematic Review of Early Childhood Education and Care Policy in Ireland* was published in July 2004. The National Economic and Social Forum (NESF) also took this issue under its remit, conducted a consultative investigation on ECCE and issued its report, *Early Childhood Care and Education in* September 2005. In 2006, the Early Years Education Policy Unit was set up, co-located, at the time, between the DES and the Office of the Ombudsman for Children.

Contemporaneous with this cluster of initiatives focussing primarily on early childhood education, there was a sequence of important developments on children and childcare. These included the establishment of the National Childcare Strategy, 1991, the National Children's Strategy, 2000, The Children's Act, 2009, the Children's Ombudsman, 2003, and the Minister for Children, 2005.

This unprecedented concentration of reports, policy documents and institutional initiatives collectively formed a framework of reference for the sector. A rationale for action, which set out principles, policies and guidelines for action, was established. Among a range of elements addressed was the need for co-ordination of effort; research; standards, quality and training; resourcing; database; curricular guidelines; priority needs of minority groups; and conditions of work for ECCE personnel.

However, the implementation of policy proposals and the concrete realisation of plans for ECCE on the ground were slow to happen. The OECD Review commented:

> It is clear that 'a national policy for the early education and care of young children in Ireland is still in its infant stages'. The review called for 'The urgent formulation of a National Plan for Early Childhood Services Development,' and for 'A significant increase in ministry budgets for early childhood services, so as to quickly reach the average rate of public expenditure for OECD centres
> (OECD, 2004a, pp. 6-10).

In its report of 2005, the NESF commented:

> It is clear that a rich base of ideas, understandings, recommendations, research findings and records of good international practice is available to Irish policy makers. The research and consultative basis is very deep ...the most striking feature which has emerged is that of a great vacuum in policy implementation, even on issues that have been agreed by government ... What is needed is a comprehensive, co-ordinated and streamlined policy implementation process.
> (NESF, 2005, pp. x – xii).

A DEVELOPING ECCE CONTEXT

While this call for a streamlined implementation process has still to be met, it is heartening to note the implementation in recent years of a range of policies, which hold out much promise for early childhood education.

Curriculum

In the area of curriculum, the CECDE produced *Síolta* in 2006, which broke new ground in this field. In 2009, the NCCA published *Aistear,* drawing on a wide consultation process and best international practice in curricular design for ECCE. This curricular work has been refined further and incorporated in the NCCA's *Aistear / Síolta Practice Guide*, published in 2015. This is a resource of major value to practitioners in early childhood care and education, but is challenging for staff with qualification levels of less than NFQ Level 7. The subtitle is indicative of the 'toolkit' aim of the publication *Curriculum Foundation and Pillars: Overviews, Activities, Self-evaluation Tools and Action Planning Templates.* It is envisaged as being used by a wide range of practitioners working in early childhood settings. The introduction states:

> The Practice Guide includes a range of resources to help practitioners to critically reflect on their curriculum and identify what works well. Additionally, the resources can help practitioners to identify priorities for development and to plan actions for positive change. In this way, the Practice Guide can be used for on-going review, development and improvement by individual practitioners, practitioners working together and by practitioners supported by a mentor.
> (NCCA, 2015a, p. 2).

The DES is also in the process of organising improvements on the primary school curriculum of 1999. It is concentrating on the early years at first and on language teaching in Irish and English and in Mathematics teaching as a priority area. There is close liaison between the DES and the NCCA with a view to incorporating best early childhood curricular practice in the new design. Hitherto, there has been a dysfunction between the integrated approach of *Aistear* and the more subject-focussed infant school curriculum. The new Primary Language Curriculum will be available in two versions, for Irish-medium schools and for English-medium schools. The final drafts of the volumes are very attractive, well-illustrated and colourful, and contain much guidance and articulation of learning outcomes for teachers. They include data on learning outcomes, progression criteria, support materials and examples developed by teachers and children. However, the continuing existence of very large numbers of pupils in many reception classes in infant schools is a serious impediment to good practice.

Extended Provision of State Aid for ECCE

Traditionally, in Ireland children have been permitted to attend the infant sector of the national school system from the age of four. Following recommendations from various agencies, the government introduced the free pre-school year in 2010. This is the first universal state-funded provision of ECCE in Ireland for children in the year prior to attending primary school. It provides for free provision for three hours per day, over a 38-week year. Its popularity was immediately evident when in excess of 68,000 children, 95% of those eligible, chose to attend the 4,200 services participating in the scheme. The providing services are required to adopt the *Aistear / Síolta* curricular approaches. In 2015, the decision was taken to extend the scheme from September 2016. From this date, children from age three to five-and-a-half may avail of an average of 61 weeks of ECCE provision in pre-schools prior to enrolment in primary schools. This has resulted in a further increase of 60,000, leading to a total of 128,000 children benefiting from the scheme.

> " Following recommendations from various agencies, the government introduced the free pre-school year in 2010. This is the first universal state-funded provision of ECCE in Ireland for children in the year prior to attending primary school. "

In 2014, the *Better Start* initiative was established by the Department of Children and Youth Affairs (DCYA), in conjunction with the DES, to bring an integrated national approach to developing quality in ECCE for children from birth to six years. This service involves a cadre of skilled and experienced early years' specialists working directly in a mentoring capacity with ECCE services. These staff are using the *Aistear / Síolta Practice Guide* as a core approach in their work. Favourable staff provision is also maintained in DEIS schools, Early Start, and schools in the Giving Children an Even Break schemes.

In the *Programme for Partnership*, spring 2016, the government promised a broad range of measures comprising '…a targeted investment approach based on international best practice for young children.' This is reflective of a welcome prioritisation of this concern, now that the recession has eased. Over each of the last two years, there has been an increase of 35% in the national budget for ECCE. The budget for 2017 allocated an extra €121.5m. to this sector, bringing the overall allocation to €466m. The 2017 budget for the related sector TUSLA, the Child and Family Agency, involved an increase of €37m., bringing its full budget to €713m. Such improvements go some way to easing pressure on the early childhood sector, but need to be sustained to answer the needs involved.

Concern has been expressed that traditionally children with disabilities have tended to be neglected in the provision of early childhood education. A major new initiative in September 2016 was the Access and Inclusion Model (AIM), which seeks to allow children with disabilities to engage fully in ECCE. A new higher education programme, LINC, was set up in 2016 to train up to 900 preschool staff (graduates) each year to work as Inclusion Co-ordinators in the ECCE setting. The Better Start scheme is also supportive of the AIM initiative and, in 2016, recruited 50 new early years' specialists in this context. A *Diversity, Equality and Inclusion Charter and Guidelines* has been published to assist in promoting good practice. Focused attention has been given to the needs of children such as those with Autistic Spectrum Disorders. This progressive move has implications for professional training and appropriate resources to ensure satisfactory implementation of policy.

Teacher Education for Early Childhood Education

The contemporary era has seen significant reforms in teacher education under a co-operative partnership between the DES and the Teaching Council. The concept of teacher education as a lifelong process involving initial, induction and continuing professional elements is now established. The initial teacher education courses have all been extended in duration and reconceptualised regarding content modules, research experience, school practice and elective specialisation. The initial teacher education programmes for primary teachers have extended their provision for early childhood education and have incorporated elective specialisms in the area. There has also been a very large increase in the provision of bachelor degree courses in early childhood studies. A Workforce Development Plan is in existence, which aims to assist and standardise training for staff in early child education and care centres. The minimum grade required is grade 5 of the National Framework of Qualifications standards, but strong efforts need to be made to help staff attain higher grades. The statement in the *Action Plan for Education* (DES, 2016j) – 'We recognise that the provision of high quality professional development opportunities for early years practitioners is needed' (p.31) – is welcomed. The commitments for the support of early years' education in Objective 3.1 are important. Within these the commitment in 2016 for 900 pre-school staff to be enrolled on a National Level 6 Programme for Inclusion Co-ordinator (p.34) will be a significant support. However, there is a need for a much higher proportion of staff to be at grades 7 and 8. It is also the case that personnel in many ECCE settings, of which there are about 4,500, largely female, experience unsatisfactory working conditions and inadequate payment for their services. To assist the continuing professional development of teachers the NCCA, in conjunction with the regional education centres, have been providing courses with a key focus on *Aistear* methodology. A beneficial scheme of tutors, in association with Sligo Education Centre, has been nurtured in sustaining this work. Some of the Master in Education courses have incorporated specialist strands on ECCE, increasing the pool of expertise within schools.

Inspection

While over recent years, the school Inspectorate has been developing greater expertise in ECCE, a major new development occurred in 2015 with the establishment of a specialist core of ECCE inspectors within the DES. Those recruited to this Early Years Inspectorate have very high levels of expertise and experience in this area. The initial cohort of ten such inspectors had been increased by another six in 2016. A key focus of their work is to promote continuous improvement in ECCE settings by affirming good practice and making recommendations for improvement. They work in association with the Tusla pre-school inspectors, focussing on the quality of the educational service provided, while the Tusla personnel have responsibility for the health, safety and quality of infrastructural provision. The first reports of the DES early-years inspectors were published in June 2016. About five hundred inspections were carried out and published by the end of 2016. Helpful also in promoting good practice was the issuing of *Revised Regulations for Pre-Schools* in 2016. The Inspectorate has prepared a *Quality Regulatory Framework* for issue in 2017 to provide guidance on the expectations set out in the *Revised Regulations*.

Research

The research base for ECCE has been greatly increased over recent years, largely due to more specialist staff and new courses in the higher education institutions. Staff are also maintaining reciprocal co-operative links with international colleagues in the field. The outcome of seminars, conferences and published papers on ECCE is greatly enriching understanding, policy and pedagogical approaches.

LOOKING AHEAD

While progress has been recorded over recent years in the provision and quality of ECCE, it is an area that requires sustained policy attention and support. The traditional under-financing of the sector needs to be addressed. Efforts need to be made to raise the percentage of GDP allocated to the sector from the current 0.1% towards the OECD average allocation of 0.8% (OECD, 2016, p. 310). The improved training of personnel in many pre-school centres is a matter of urgent importance, as is improved remuneration and working conditions. There is a large number of agencies in the ECCE sector and there is a need for much greater co-ordination and co-operation so that provision for children from birth to six years of age is a more cohesive, and unified experience. The hope is that the Strategic Alignment Group between officials of the DCYA, the DES, Pobal and Tusla, as well as the Early Years Forum, set up in 2016, will be successful in ensuring greater cohesion and harmonisation of the diverse agencies in the ECCE field. Work is afoot to improve the harmonisation of effort between pre-schools and the infant sector of primary schools, and this needs to be further developed. Furthermore, the current efforts to reform the infant school section of the state primary school curriculum need to be promoted further, with greater attention to the large size of infant classes in many primary schools. The engagement of an agency such as IPPN can be productive in easing transitions. There is a need to synchronise the subject-based primary curriculum with the *Aistear / Síolta* approach of ECCE. The *National Early Years Strategy*, which is being currently developed and is expected to be published in 2017, provides a good opportunity for locating on-going reform initiatives on ECCE within a broad national plan.

CHAPTER THREE ● ● ● ● ● ● ● ● ● ● ● ● ● ● ● ●
Curriculum

INTRODUCTION

This chapter traces the development of the primary and second-level curriculum in Ireland from 1922 to the present day. It outlines the many efforts made over the past forty years to reform Junior Cycle curriculum, including the new Junior Cycle Framework that was agreed between the teacher union leaders and the Minister for Education and Skills in May 2015. It explores the strengths and weaknesses of the learning outcomes approach to curriculum design adopted by the NCCA since 2009, cautioning against an undue or slavish adherence to specifying curriculum solely in terms of topics and learning outcomes, especially at Leaving Certificate level.

PART ONE: HISTORICAL BACKGROUND

In 1922, the new Irish Free State inherited an educational system that was un-coordinated and fractured, with three different Boards responsible for the three separate sectors of education - primary (national) education, secondary education and technical education. One of the first actions of the new state was to bring together the three sectors under one Minister and one Department of Education (Minister and Secretaries' Act, 1924). While there was undoubted political commitment to the setting up of a single department, in practice it was to be many decades before there was any real co-ordination between the different sectors of Irish education. This lack of co-ordination was reflected in the lack of continuity in curriculum planning between primary and post-primary education.

National School Curriculum, 1831 – 1971

The national school curriculum prior to 1922 had undergone various revisions since the setting up of the national school system in 1831. The curriculum was initially highly prescriptive, based on textbooks (referred to as 'readers' by the Board of National Education), and the progress of pupils was strictly monitored by the Inspectorate. From 1870 to 1899, a 'payment by results' system was in place and teachers were paid on the basis of the results of their pupils in annual examinations. The curriculum was revised in 1900 when payment by results was abolished. From 1900 to 1921, the Revised Programme gave greater flexibility to schools and encouraged discovery and activity-based learning (Walsh, 2016).

Following Independence in 1922, the primary school curriculum was significantly reformed to emphasise the Irish language, Irish culture and Irish history. The child-centred and discovery-based approach, which had underpinned the curriculum from 1900 to 1921, was abandoned, and in 1922, the first National Programme was framed on nationalist lines (National Programme Conference, 1922). The range of subjects was reduced (to Irish, English, Mathematics, History, Geography, Singing, Needlework and Drill) and the content and focus became Irish and Gaelic in orientation. The Irish language was to be taught to all children for at least one hour a day and the work of the Infant classroom was to be entirely in Irish. Because of difficulties encountered in the implementation of the 1922 National Programme, the curriculum was revised in 1926 (National Programme Conference, 1926). The revisions were relatively minor and the philosophy and much of the content of the 1922 programme were endorsed. The programme was revised again in 1934 (Department of Education, 1934) and in 1948, when the Revised Programme for Infants was introduced (Department of Education, 1948), but the emphasis on Irish language, culture and history remained. It was not until 1971 that a major review and revision of the primary curriculum took place.

Secondary School Curriculum, 1878 – 1970s

From 1878 until 1924, the Intermediate Board's examination system dominated teaching and learning in Irish secondary schools. Under a system of payment by results, there was a strong incentive for secondary schools to adopt the Board's examination syllabi. Throughout this period, there were three levels of examination – Junior Grade, Middle Grade and Senior Grade, with a wide range of subjects, and the syllabi for these subjects at the three grade levels were prescriptive and content-based (Coolahan, 1981). For some years, a fourth grade, Preparatory Grade, was also available but this grade was discontinued in the early years of the twentieth century.

> " Following Independence in 1922, the primary school curriculum was significantly reformed to emphasise the Irish language, Irish culture and Irish history. "

Payment by results at post-primary level was abolished in 1924 and new Intermediate and Leaving Certificate programmes and examinations were introduced. These programmes initially rejected prescribed texts, and open courses were introduced in language and literature subjects. Examinations were less predictable, and rote learning of set texts was no longer rewarded. However, following pressure from teachers, open courses were dropped and set texts were re-introduced in 1942. From 1924 until the 1980s, the Intermediate and Leaving Certificate programmes continued to consist largely of a disparate set of syllabi for a range of subjects – as had been the case under the old Intermediate Board. The Intermediate and Leaving Certificate examinations continued to dominate teaching and learning in second-level schools and 'the examination was the tail that wagged the curriculum dog' throughout the 20th century. (Hargreaves, 1989)

In spite of significant curriculum changes at primary and secondary levels after 1922, there was little or no co-ordination between the new National Programmes at primary level (First and Second National Programme Conferences 1922 and 1926) and the Intermediate and Leaving Certificate programmes. Until the 1980s, review and revision of primary and secondary curricula were largely a matter for the Inspectorate, which submitted their proposals to the Minister for Education for approval (Coolahan with O'Donovan, 2009).

Technical and Vocational Education, 1899 – 1970s

The curriculum in technical schools had never been centralised, and even after the Vocational Education Act was passed in 1930, there was no national curriculum for vocational schools. It was not until the Day Group Certificate examination was introduced in the late 1940s that the semblance of a national curriculum and a national examination was introduced for vocational schools, and even after that date, individual schools had considerable autonomy in relation to curriculum and assessment (Hyland, 1999).

The Reports of the Council of Education, 1954 and 1962

The Council of Education was set up by Minister Richard Mulcahy in April 1950. It sat for over a decade between 1950 and 1962. It published two major reports – one on the primary school curriculum (1954) and one on the curriculum of the secondary school (1962). Both reports were informed by Catholic philosophy and Catholic social teaching and emphasised the religious purpose of education. The report on the primary curriculum stated that 'the school exists to assist and supplement the work of parents in the rearing of their children;' that '(the parents') first duty is to train their children in the fear and love of God' and that 'that duty becomes the first purpose of the primary school'. While in some respects the report was conservative, it raised a number of issues relating to the curriculum of the primary school and recommended that the curriculum be broadened and that greater flexibility be given to schools in the implementation of the curriculum (Department of Education, 1954).

The report on the secondary-school curriculum, published in 1962, 'approved generally of the existing regulations which provide the framework for the Junior and Senior Cycle curricula'. The report stated that the 'ultimate purpose of secondary schools in Ireland is to prepare their pupils to be God-fearing and responsible citizens' and that 'liberal or general education (i.e. an all-round formation of the faculties) is the immediate object of the secondary school'. The Council considered that 'a well-balanced course of general education is one having humanist and other subjects as its basic core, the balance being in favour of the humanist group'. In general, the tone of the report of the Council of Education was uncritical and self-satisfied and suggested that there was no great need to reform the curriculum at either junior or Senior Cycle. At a time when free second-level education had become the norm in other European countries, the report dismissed the suggestion that such a reform be implemented in Ireland, describing free secondary education for all as 'utopian'.

> " At a time when free second-level education had become the norm in other European countries, the report dismissed the suggestion that such a reform be implemented in Ireland, describing free secondary education for all as 'utopian'. "

Remarkably, the Council refuted any suggestions that there was a lack of co-ordination between the curriculum of the primary and secondary schools stating that 'we cannot admit that (this allegation) has any substance ...' (Department of Education, 1962).

Investment in Education Report, 1965

Within a very short period, however, the findings of the report of the Council of Education were challenged by the Investment in Education report (Department of Education, 1965). The report raised questions about the functionality of the education received by some pupils at primary level, and highlighted the limited nature of the curriculum of Irish secondary schools which it referred to as a 'classical grammar-school type'. It showed the relatively low number of students (especially girls) taking science subjects and the low number of boys taking modern languages. In the context of a country that was hoping to develop its international industrial and business focus, the findings of the Investment in Education report indicated that curriculum reform would have to be a priority.

The numbers of pupils in second-level education increased significantly following the introduction of free second-level education in 1967 – within less than ten years second-level enrolment in Ireland had increased from 148,000 in 1966/7 to 239,000 in 1974 (Coolahan, 1981, p.195). While some individual syllabi were reformed in the 1970s, some vocational schools began to offer the Intermediate, and Leaving Certificate programmes after the introduction of free education, it was not until the 1980s, that a fundamental review of second-level curriculum was undertaken.

The New Primary School Curriculum, 1971

The new primary school curriculum of 1971 was drafted by a committee of inspectors in the late 1960s and revised syllabi for individual subjects were piloted in various schools throughout the country before the full curriculum was finalised and approved by the Minister. The 1971 curriculum was radically different from its predecessor, in terms of its philosophy, content and methodology. It provided a wide range of subjects and emphasised guided discovery learning methods. There was a greater focus on the Arts; Social, Environmental and Scientific Education, and Physical Education than had been the case in previous curricula. Flexibility was given to schools and teachers in the choice and balance of subjects and teaching approaches, and school-based curriculum planning was introduced (Department of Education, 1971). The aims of the 1971 curriculum were summarised as follows:

- To enable the child to lead a full life as a child
- To equip the child to avail of further education, to go on to live a full and useful life as an adult in society.

The curriculum was based on a philosophy of education that incorporated the following five principles:

- The full and harmonious development of the child
- The importance of making due allowance for individual difference
- The importance of activity and discovery methods
- The integrated nature of the curriculum
- The importance of environment-based learning.

The integrated nature of the curriculum was spelled out in Chapter II of the Teachers' Handbook – The Structure of the Curriculum. The integration of the curriculum was seen 'in the religious and civic spirit which animates its parts' and the Handbook stated that 'the separation of religious and secular instruction into differentiated subject compartments serves only to throw the whole educational function out of focus'. This emphasis on the integration of religious and secular instruction was to become controversial in subsequent years, but simply gave substance to Rule 68 of the Rules for National Schools (1965) which stated 'Of all parts of a school curriculum Religious Instruction is by far the most important …. Religious instruction is …. a fundamental part of the school course, and a religious spirit should inform and vivify the whole work of the school' (Department of Education, 1965).

It is notable, however, that no effort was made in drafting the 1971 curriculum to ensure continuity between the primary and secondary school. If anything, the gap between the learning experience of pupils at primary and secondary level was widened by the introduction of the new primary curriculum, which emphasised a child-centred approach as opposed to a rigid exam-based curriculum at second level. During the consultation period prior to the introduction of the new curriculum in 1971, this anomaly was pointed out in a submission from the Teachers' Study Group, but to no effect (Coolahan, 2016).

The Report on the Intermediate Certificate Examination, 1973-5

In 1970, a committee was set up by the Minister for Education to advise on the reform of the Intermediate Certificate Examination (ICE). The committee published an interim report three years later and a final report in 1975. The ICE report recommended that the centralised examination of pupils at the end of Junior Cycle should be discontinued and that a system of school-based assessment should be introduced. It envisaged a comprehensive system of moderation of school-based assessment by a 'moderation and educational assessment service (MEAS)', organised through groupings or consortia of schools. In addition, it recommended that support should be made available to teachers to ensure that they had the necessary skills to engage in a range of modes of assessment such as essay-type questions, objective tests, oral and practical tests and project and coursework assessment (Department of Education, 1975).

No action was taken by the then Minister for Education, Richard Burke, on the ICE report and the examination-led Intermediate and Leaving Certificate programmes continued to dominate teaching and learning until the end of the 20th century.

Curriculum and Examinations Board, 1984-1986

A decade later, the issue of curriculum reform, especially at second level, became a major national educational policy issue. In January 1984, the (interim) Curriculum and Examinations Board (CEB) was established by the newly-appointed Minister for Education, Gemma Hussey. Her intention was to set up the board as soon as possible on a statutory basis. The CEB, which was chaired by Ed Walsh, President of the then NIHE Limerick, was asked to make recommendations on a new unified system of assessment for Junior Cycle at second level as well as to undertake a review of the Leaving Certificate (CEB 1984).

As the primary school curriculum was relatively new, was popular with parents, primary teachers and the Inspectorate, and insofar as evidence was available, seemed to be reasonably effective in achieving its aims, curriculum review and reform at primary level was not a priority. However, the CEB was concerned at the lack of continuity between the primary and second-level curriculum. One of its first actions was to set up a Joint Committee to review the curriculum for the compulsory school period (Infants to the end of Junior Cycle) with a specific brief to propose a framework for second-level Junior Cycle curriculum (building on the primary school curriculum). The Joint Committee consisted of more than forty members, including teachers representing the primary, secondary and vocational sectors, representatives of management bodies, as well as parents and business representatives.

The first CEB consultative document, *Issues and Structures in Education*, published in July 1984, was outspoken and radical. The board proposed a fundamental reform of Junior Cycle curriculum, and a reformed system of assessment 'which should permit the involvement of teachers as part of their professional work. It should be sufficiently flexible to allow for the development of alternative programmes … (and) the scope and range of skills and qualities assessed should be broadened considerably'. The report added: 'If one is to provide an assessment of a comprehensive range of content and skills, if one is to achieve congruence between course objectives and examination procedures, and if the increased autonomy of schools and teachers is to be promoted, then it seems inevitable that at least part of the examination procedure will be school-based'. It pointed out that change from external to internal assessment, especially at the end of the compulsory school period, had taken place in many countries, including Australia, Canada, Denmark, France, Sweden and New Zealand and it was time for Ireland to follow suit (CEB, 1984).

Following a period of public consultation, and taking account of the views submitted, a framework for curriculum and assessment – *In Our Schools* – was issued by the CEB in March 1986. The influence of some of the principles underpinning the 1971 primary school curriculum was evident in the proposed Junior Cycle framework. In contextualising its recommendations for reform, the CEB recognised the need for Ireland to re-assess its educational goals in the context of the late twentieth century. School programmes 'should be framed within a cultural context which emphasises creativity, enterprise and innovation more than conformity and passive learning'. Students must be encouraged 'to think in terms of identifying problems and considering solutions rather than always seeking absolute right or wrong answers to problems'. In order to achieve this, reform of the assessment system was vital. According to the board, the role of assessment in promoting student learning should take precedence over its role for the purpose of certification, and information about the progress of pupils should be 'an integral and recurring part of teaching and learning'. The report recommended that external examinations at the end of Junior Cycle be phased out and replaced by school-based assessment.

> "
> School programmes 'should be framed within a cultural context which emphasises creativity, enterprise and innovation more than conformity and passive learning'. Students must be encouraged 'to think in terms of identifying problems and considering solutions rather than always seeking absolute right or wrong answers to problems'.
> "

The Teachers' Union of Ireland (TUI) supported those recommendations – their members were willing to assess their own pupils for certification – they had done this since the 1940s for the Group Certificate and Technical Subjects exams (known as TS exams). The Association of Secondary Teachers (ASTI) had reservations – but more particularly in relation to high-stakes examinations like the Leaving Certificate.

The reforms proposed by the Curriculum and Examinations Board were not, however, implemented. In early 1986, in a government Cabinet re-shuffle, Gemma Hussey was removed as Minister for Education. Her successor, Patrick Cooney, was cautious. Advised by officials in the Department of Education, he distanced himself from the recommendations of the CEB. He referred the report back to the board, suggesting that 'alternatives' to some of the recommendations be considered (Coolahan, 2014). Shortly afterwards, the coalition government fell and Fianna Fáil came back into power. The CEB was disbanded and was replaced by a new board – the National Council for Curriculum and Assessment (NCCA). Unlike the proposed statutory CEB, the NCCA would not have responsibility for examinations – its role would be an advisory, not an executive one.

National Council for Curriculum and Assessment

Within a short period of taking office, the new Minister for Education, Mary O'Rourke, announced that the Intermediate and Group Certificate examinations would be abolished and that a new unified certificate, the Junior Certificate, would replace them. It was envisaged that the new Junior Certificate would encompass the best aspects of curriculum and assessment of both the Group and the Intermediate Certificates and would include, as the Group Certificate had done, some elements of school-based assessment. However, this did not happen and the Junior Certificate, which was introduced in 1989, was modelled much more closely on the Intermediate Certificate than on the Group Certificate. School-based and continuous assessment, which had been a key feature of the Group Certificate, was largely discontinued except for a small number of subjects.

A review of the Junior Certificate, undertaken ten years later by the NCCA, was critical of the influence of terminal examinations on pupil learning (NCCA, 1999). It stated:

> It was intended that the Junior Certificate would be awarded on the basis of a wide range of modes and techniques of assessment. …. In contrast to what was originally envisaged, the assessment of the Junior Cycle programme is dominated by terminal written examinations.

The review stated that 'there is an ongoing mismatch between the aims and principles of the Junior Certificate programme and the modes and techniques currently in use for the formal assessment of that programme'. It emphasised that the need for change was urgent and called on all the education partners 'to engage fully as a matter of urgency and agree a way forward'.

Primary Curriculum Review Body, 1990

In the meantime, Minister for Education, Mary O'Rourke, set up a Review Body on the Primary Curriculum, which reported in 1990 (Department of Education 1990). The review body broadly endorsed the underlying philosophy and principles of the 1971 curriculum but concluded that the curriculum required revision and re-formulation 'in its aims, scope and content, in the manner in which it was implemented and in the way in which pupil progress was assessed'. It made a number of specific recommendations in relation to the use of Information Technology and it also recommended that a new Science programme be introduced. The report included specific recommendations about the implementation and resourcing of its recommendations and recommended an improvement in the overall funding of primary education.

Primary Curriculum, 1999

Following the publication of the report of the Primary Curriculum Review Body, a further decade elapsed before a revised primary curriculum was published. As indicated in Chapter 1 of this publication, the 1999 curriculum was designed largely by primary teachers who played a major role on the relevant committees of the NCCA (O'Toole cited in Looney, 2014). The 1999 curriculum retained many of the features of the 1971 curriculum and was designed 'to nurture the child in all dimensions of his or her life – spiritual, moral, cognitive, emotional, imaginative, aesthetic, social and physical' (Department of Education, 1999). The general aims of the curriculum were almost unchanged from those of the 1971 curriculum, and were re-stated as follows:

- To enable the child to live a full life as a child and to realise his or her potential as a unique individual
- To enable the child to develop as a social being through living and co-operating with others and so contribute to the good of society
- To prepare the child for a continuum of learning.

The underpinning principles redefined the two basic principles of the 1971 curriculum as follows:

- Celebrating the uniqueness of the child
- Ensuring the development of the child's full potential.

The three pedagogical principles of the 1971 curriculum - activity and discovery methods, an integrated curriculum and environment-based learning - were subsumed into a wider range of learning principles. Guided discovery learning and active learning, promoting the active involvement of children in an imaginative and stimulating learning process, were emphasised. The overall vision was to enable children to meet, with self-confidence and assurance, the demands of life, both now and in the future. The curriculum aimed to help children to become lifelong learners and to develop the motivation and the skills that would enable them to do so. There was a strong focus on literacy and numeracy while at the same time the Arts, Science and Technology played an important role.

The curriculum was presented in six strands of learning, some of which were further sub-divided into subjects:

- Language: Gaeilge and English
- Mathematics
- Social, Environmental and Scientific Education (SESE): History, Geography and Science
- Arts Education: Visual Arts, Music and Drama
- Physical Education
- Social, Personal and Health Education (SPHE).

In addition, a seventh strand - Religious or Ethical Education – was provided for, but this strand would be the responsibility of the different school patron bodies, not of the Department of Education and Skills.

The 1999 curriculum documentation is impressive. When it was launched, it was made available in printed form, beautifully produced in a boxed set of more than 20 volumes. There were two volumes for each strand / sub-strand of the curriculum – one volume containing the aims, detailed learning outcomes and planning guidelines and the second (Teacher Guidelines) containing up to 200 pages of resource suggestions, guidelines and sample lesson plans with exemplars and illustrations. The curriculum was also made available in electronic form, accessible online. Printed copies of the 1999 curriculum are no longer available but the curriculum is available online and on a USB stick.

The curriculum contains a balance of knowledge, concepts and skills, and in all subjects, assessment is regarded as an integral part of teaching and learning. One of its essential features is a recognition of the principle that there are different kinds of learning and that individual children learn in different ways. The curriculum articulates, therefore, not only the content to be learned and the outcomes to be achieved, but also a wide range of approaches to learning. Strong emphasis is placed on developing the ability to question, to analyse, to investigate, to think critically, to solve problems, and to interact effectively with others.

In the light of recent debates about religious instruction and religious education, it is interesting to note that the 1999 curriculum referred to the seventh strand as 'Religious or Ethical Education'- as opposed to 'Religious Instruction' - which had been used in all previous national curriculum documents, and in the *Rules for National Schools*. The 1999 Handbook also differed from previous curriculum documents in stating that responsibility for Religious or Ethical Education curriculum would be the responsibility of the school patron bodies, not the responsibility of the Churches, which had been the formal position before 1999.

Notably, there is no mention in the 1999 curriculum of the integration of religious and secular education. Whereas in the 1971 curriculum it was stated that 'the separation of religious and secular instruction into differentiated subject compartments serves only to throw the whole educational function out of focus', in the 1999 curriculum, the following statement appears (Department of Education, 1999):

> For the young child, the distinctions between subjects are not relevant: what is more important is that he or she experiences a coherent learning process that accommodates a variety of elements. It is important, therefore, to make connections between learning in different subjects. As they mature, integration gives children's learning a broader and richer perspective, emphasises the interconnectedness of knowledge and ideas and reinforces the learning process.

The curriculum document also states that:

> The strands are not discrete areas of learning, as they overlap and interact to form a holistic learning experience for the child. They will also assist teachers in identifying possibilities for integrated learning within subjects and curriculum areas, and throughout the curriculum as a whole. At the end of each curriculum statement, the purposes of assessment are delineated, and several approaches and recommended tools are explained.

The Teacher as Curriculum Developer and Planner

While the 1999 curriculum provided a clear and structured national framework, it built on the recommendations relating to school-based planning in the 1971 curriculum. The 1999 curriculum strengthened the flexibility for schools and teachers 'to plan a programme appropriate to the individual school's circumstances and to the needs, aptitudes and interests of the children'. In planning its programmes, schools were expected to adapt and interpret the curriculum to meet their own unique requirements. The planning process is described as 'involving a continuous cycle of development' and is stated to have 'the potential to enhance pupil outcomes through focusing on teaching and learning, monitoring progress, and enabling schools to build their capacity to manage change'. As indicated above, extensive guidelines and support materials were provided both in print and online for schools and teachers to enable them to engage in curriculum planning and development.

While the 1999 curriculum documentation was impressive and was generally welcomed by the education partners, in practice the effectiveness of its implementation varied, as had been the case with the 1971 curriculum (NCCA, 2005). This finding should not have been unexpected in the case of a curriculum that allows flexibility for teachers and schools in planning, development and implementation.

Junior and Senior Cycle Curriculum, 2000-2009

During the first years of the new millennium, debate continued about the reform of junior and Senior Cycle curriculum and assessment. Research undertaken by the ESRI provided new insights into the effect of the Junior Certificate on student participation and achievement. It noted that many students became disengaged at an early stage of Junior Cycle. It found a curriculum that was seen as inflexible and overcrowded, with relatively little flexibility for teacher or students. It highlighted the dominating effect of the Junior Certificate examination on teaching and learning, and indicated the narrow range of assessment activity (Smyth et al, 2004, 2006, 2007 and 2011).

However, efforts by the NCCA to reform the Junior Certificate met with resistance from the teaching profession. Proposals for reform of Leaving Certificate assessment presented by the NCCA to Minister for Education Mary Hanafin in 2005 were met with scepticism by the Minister, who described them as a 'Rolls Royce' model of change (Murray, 2007).

In 2007, the NCCA announced that the syllabus for two new Leaving Certificate exam subjects – Physical Education and Politics and Society – would be sent to schools within a year, as would proposals for revised assessment of the three Leaving Certificate science subjects, Physics, Chemistry and Biology. However, there was to be considerable delay in moving forward in all of these areas. The ASTI made it clear that their members would not support 'ill-judged, superficial or inadequately resourced reform'. They would support change 'that is valid in itself, is in the interests of their pupils, and which does not undermine the strengths of the education system' (Murray, 2007).

> " Research undertaken by the ESRI provided new insights into the effect of the Junior Certificate on student participation and achievement. It noted that many students became disengaged at an early stage of Junior Cycle. "

Questions were also raised about the model of curriculum reform and implementation that was beginning to be adopted by the NCCA. Teachers (especially secondary teachers) had in the past been familiar with a technicist approach to curriculum where the teacher's role was to implement a clearly-defined curriculum, prescribed centrally. The rationale underpinning the NCCA's new model of curriculum planning was informed by the practice perspective on curriculum 'with its associated emphasis on teacher agency in any change and development process' (Looney, 2014 and Hammond et al, 2011). While in itself, this model is to be welcomed (see Chapter 1), for many second-level teachers, who were comfortable with exam-led and textbook-based approaches, the new approach would be quite a challenge.

PART TWO: A NEW APPROACH TO CURRICULUM DESIGN

Leading and Supporting Change in Schools, 2009

In 2009, the NCCA published a discussion paper on *Leading and Supporting Change in Schools* that, *inter alia*, identified the key role of teachers in the implementation of change and explored how lasting change in teaching, learning, school culture and implementation could be achieved. The document emphasised that 'realising deep educational change can only happen through teachers and school management and their interactions and relationships with the learner.' It recognised the need to give schools greater autonomy in setting the agenda for change at the local level and the need to involve teachers and schools in both planning for change as well as involving them in the process of change (NCCA, 2009).

As a result of debate and discussion, and in line with developments in curriculum planning internationally, the NCCA made significant changes in its approach to curriculum and syllabus planning and design in 2009. The NCCA's revised approach emphasised a 'learning outcomes' approach to curriculum design, the role of teachers as curriculum developers and the use of an online portal.

Learning Outcomes Approach

Under the 'learning-outcomes' approach, new curricula and syllabi would be specified in terms of topics and learning outcomes – it would be a matter for individual teachers to interpret these topics and learning outcomes and to plan their teaching accordingly.

A learning-outcomes approach to curriculum and programme planning has been widely adopted internationally in recent years. It is used by many OECD countries for designing early years, primary and second-level curricula and has been adopted in the US, Australia, New Zealand, and Singapore, as well as in the 50 countries of the European Higher Education Area (under the Bologna agreement) as a tool for designing higher education programmes (Hyland et al 2007). In the early 2000s, the Australian Curriculum, Assessment and Reporting Authority (ACARA) produced a national curriculum framework for primary and second-level schools that has many parallels to the NCCA's approach. In 2012/13, the council of federal, state, and territory education ministers in Australia endorsed a revised Senior Cycle curriculum 'as the agreed and common base for the development of state and territory senior secondary courses'. A learning outcomes approach was also adopted in 2010/11 in the curriculum frameworks developed by Education Scotland – Scotland's national curriculum authority (Hyland, 2014). However, there is an important distinction between those countries and Ireland. In the case of Australia and Scotland, there is an intermediate structure between the national curriculum body and the schools, which mediates and interprets the national curriculum and provides detailed guidelines and support for individual schools. As indicated above, each Australian state and territory has its own education ministry and Scotland has 32 individual local education authorities. In Ireland, there is no such intermediate framework, apart from the Education and Training Boards for vocational schools and community colleges.

Moreover, while a learning-outcomes approach is learner-focused and provides clear information on what a learner is expected to know and to be able to do following the completion of a programme, defining a curriculum solely in terms of learning outcomes has its limitations. Learning outcomes are statements of essential learning, and as essential learning, they are written at minimum acceptable or threshold (pass/fail) standard. The learning described in learning outcomes is the learning that must be attained in order that the learner can be deemed to have passed a minimum threshold (Moon, 2000). For implementation purposes, it can be argued that a curriculum requires greater specification in order to enable teachers to ensure that the level and depth at which the subject is being taught is appropriate to the stage of progression of their students. A curriculum or syllabus that focuses only on (minimum) learning outcomes is at risk of under-estimating and under-challenging higher achievers and failing those with learning difficulties.

Teachers as Curriculum Developers

In explaining the emphasis on teacher involvement in the NCCA's revised model of curriculum planning, Anne Looney, CEO of the NCCA, described teachers as 'agents of curriculum development' and stated that 'their practice is valued, not as a site of curriculum 'implementation' but as a context for innovation' (Looney, 2014). Her colleague, John Hammond, made a similar point in 2011 when he said '… In the context of developments in curriculum and assessment, these things are best achieved by growing the capacity of schools as centres of innovation and change, by supporting and developing the professionalism of teachers, thereby improving the most important interaction in education which is between the teacher and the learner in the classroom' (Hammond et al, 2011).

It goes without saying that teachers play a hugely significant role in planning, developing and implementing curricula. There is nothing new about this realisation. Experience of school-based and teacher-based curriculum development is not new in Ireland – especially at primary level, where schools and teachers have been encouraged since 1971 to use a school-based approach to curriculum planning. Curriculum and lesson planning has been a significant component of initial teacher education programmes for primary teachers since the 1970s. However, for many second-level teachers and principals, a school-based approach to curriculum planning and development is a relatively novel development and one of which many have little (if any) expertise or experience. For many generations of second-level teachers, the Junior and Leaving Certificate syllabi were their 'bible', and they have traditionally relied unduly heavily on the prescribed syllabus and on textbook-based teaching.

That is not to say that second-level teachers in Ireland have no experience of curriculum development and innovation. There have been many school-based curriculum initiatives in the second-level sector over the years. In the 1970s and 1980s, the City of Dublin VEC Curriculum Development Unit supported school-based curriculum development, e.g. the Integrated Science Curriculum Innovation Project (ISCIP) and City of Dublin Humanities Project; the Shannon Curriculum Development Unit also supported school-based curricula; and many school-based curriculum interventions were supported by EU funding. The popularity of school-based curriculum development was evidenced by the existence of an active and dynamic Irish Association for Curriculum Development (IACD) from the mid-1970s to the late 1980s (Trant 2008). In more recent years, teachers involved in the Junior Certificate Schools programme, Transition Year and the Leaving Certificate Applied designed, developed, delivered and assessed bespoke programmes (Hyland 1998). And some university-led initiatives such as TL21 (Teaching and Learning for the 21st Century), a project led by the Education Department of NUI Maynooth (Hogan et al, 2008); the Multiple Intelligences, Curriculum and Assessment project (Hyland 2000) and the Bridging the Gap project in University College Cork (Hyland 2005) also supported school and classroom-based curriculum planning.

> " The popularity of school-based curriculum development was evidenced by the existence of an active and dynamic Irish Association for Curriculum Development (IACD) from the mid-1970s to the late 1980s "

However, these initiatives applied to a limited number of schools and were usually supported and backed-up by resources and professional expertise and training from their sponsoring organisations or institutions. The experience of these initiatives indicates both the strengths and the pitfalls that can arise in the case of school-based curriculum initiatives – in particular, the risk that teachers might not set sufficiently high learning targets, especially for pupils from educationally disadvantaged backgrounds. In situations where a spiral approach to curriculum planning was adopted, there was always a risk that, without monitoring and oversight, the level at which topics were taught might not adequately differentiate the depth of treatment appropriate for different grades/years.

The approach adopted from 2009 onwards by the NCCA relies on a highly professional and well-educated teaching force to interpret and 'customise' the curriculum in a way that best suits their school and pupils, as well as time and resources for planning and for in-service support. While the recently extended teacher education programmes in Ireland will ensure that newly-qualified teachers in future will have the required expertise, it is to be expected that some existing teachers may feel challenged by the new approach, that they may not have the skills or confidence to engage effectively with curriculum development, and/or are likely to require ongoing support and training to enable them to design and implement their own programmes.

Online Portal

In addition to delegating responsibility to teachers for developing and customising the curriculum, the new approach and rationale places a heavy reliance on the NCCA's online portal (www.curriculumonline.ie). The portal provides opportunities for teachers to share ideas, sample lesson plans, resources, and suggestions and the clipboard function of the portal allows teachers to customise the curriculum for classroom use.

While an online portal has undoubted potential as a source of exciting and innovative resources for teachers and learners, undue reliance on an online portal can be problematic. There are likely to be some teachers who are less than comfortable with accessing the web, and it should be borne in mind that significant problems of online access still exist, especially in rural areas of Ireland. A survey carried out in May 2016 by Amárach found that a third of people living outside the five largest cities of Ireland say that slow and unreliable internet speeds currently prevent them from working from home and that internet speed is not fast enough for their family requirements (RTE.ie/news). From this, we can take it that a significant number of teachers do not have adequate access to www.curriculumonline.ie and to other web-based teaching and learning resources, which is likely to militate against their ability to undertake lesson planning at home in the evenings and at weekends.

There can also be difficulties in accessing the internet in some schools. Although the DES has indicated that all schools have been provided with the technology to enable them to connect with the internet, problems with broadband access remain. A survey of 60 Science and Mathematics education students in University College Cork, carried out in March 2016, found that only 10% of them taught in schools in which the access to the internet in their classroom teaching was very reliable. 60% reported that they frequently encountered difficulty with internet access and 30% reported that they rarely use online resources due to the great difficulty in accessing the internet in their schools. While this was not a representative sample, nor does it claim to be so, it is nevertheless indicative of the real-life, on the ground experience of student teachers in the southern part of the country (Kennedy, 2016).

PART THREE: CURRICULUM DEVELOPMENT: THE CURRENT SITUATION

This section of the paper will focus on the development of curriculum at all levels - early childhood, primary, Junior Cycle and Senior Cycle - since the adoption by the NCCA of its revised model of curriculum planning.

Aistear/ Síolta – the Early Childhood Curriculum

In October 2009, the NCCA published *Aistear: An Early Childhood Curriculum Framework for children from birth to six years*. (For further discussion of Aistear, see Chapter 2 of this report). Aistear can be used in a range of early childhood settings, including children's own homes, full and part-time day-care settings, and infant classes in primary schools. The framework uses four interconnected themes to describe the content of children's learning and development – Well-being; Identity and Belonging; Communicating and Exploring; and Thinking. The Framework has both implicit and explicit links with the *Primary School Curriculum* (Department of Education, 2009).

While the Framework is impressive, it requires its users to act as 'curriculum developers' in keeping with the revised approach to curriculum planning adopted by the NCCA (www.ncca.ie). For example, the first element of the document is entitled 'Developing your Curriculum and Curriculum Statement'. This document reminds staff that the curriculum is shaped and influenced by many different factors, and is affected by socio-economic and cultural factors, the type of setting, the physical environment and the philosophy, ethos, vision, principles, values, routines and policies of the setting. Developing a curriculum taking account of all these factors could prove quite a challenge for the average early childhood teacher, given the relatively low level of qualification required in the sector. Current guidelines relating to staffing of early childhood settings expect that each setting should be led by a person with a minimum of a Level 6 qualification. As indicated in Chapter 2, an increasing number of workers in the sector have completed a qualification at least at this level but this is not universally the case.

> " Aistear can be used in a range of early childhood settings, including children's own homes, full and part-time day-care settings, and infant classes in primary schools. "

The New Primary Language Curriculum, 2016

Research carried out by the NCCA in 2005, with particular reference to English, Mathematics and Visual Arts, identified some problems in the implementation of the 1999 curriculum (NCCA, 2005). Arising out of this research, it was recommended that the organisational framework for the

English Curriculum should be revised, that further support for implementing the writing strand unit should be provided and that detailed direction and guidance should be provided on spelling, phonics and grammar.

Following the introduction of the *Aistear/Síolta* curriculum for early years, work began on the revision of the Primary Language Curriculum for English and Irish in junior classes in primary schools. A draft curriculum prepared by the NCCA following wide-ranging consultation, espoused the principles and methodologies of Aistear (NCCA, 2009). It differs from the 1999 curriculum for English and Gaeilge in several respects. Firstly, it has the same curriculum structure and components for English and Gaeilge 'to support integration across the two languages'. It has far fewer outcomes (94) than the (268) objectives in the 1999 curriculum.

While the original specification for the Primary Language Curriculum consisted solely of topics and learning outcomes, it is interesting to note that the curriculum as set out on the DES website is now presented as having four 'interconnected parts' as shown below. These are Learning Outcomes, Support Material for Teachers, Progression Continua and Examples of children's language learning and development – all four of which will contribute to 'Planning, Teaching and assessing for learning in English and Irish'.

The four interconnected components of the Primary Language Curriculum (DES)

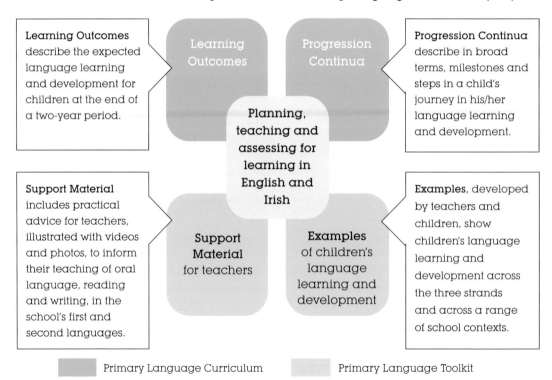

Learning Outcomes describe the expected language learning and development for children at the end of a two-year period.

Progression Continua describe in broad terms, milestones and steps in a child's journey in his/her language learning and development.

Support Material includes practical advice for teachers, illustrated with videos and photos, to inform their teaching of oral language, reading and writing, in the school's first and second languages.

Examples, developed by teachers and children, show children's language learning and development across the three strands and across a range of school contexts.

Planning, teaching and assessing for learning in English and Irish

Learning Outcomes · Progression Continua · Support Material for teachers · Examples of children's language learning and development

Primary Language Curriculum   Primary Language Toolkit

As shown in this diagram, documentation provided by the Department of Education and Skills (DES) includes a continuum (map) of significant milestones and detailed steps involved in children's language learning and development – referred to as Progression Continua. The Progression Continua illustrate progression in learning from Junior Infants to Second Class. Each progression milestone is characterised by a number of progression steps. These steps describe, in more detail, what children's learning and development look like as they move along the continuum. The outcomes and continua are complemented by examples of children's work and support material to help teachers to make professional judgements about, and to support children's achievement and progression across both languages (DES, 2015).

The new Primary Language Curriculum was approved by the Minister for Education and Skills and will be implemented on a phased basis starting in September 2016. In 2016/17, the Oral Language strand will be implemented for Infants to Second Class. In 2017/18, the Reading and Writing strands will be implemented along with the Oral Language strand. From September 2018, there will be full implementation of all strands from Junior Infants to Second Class and from September 2019, implementation of Primary Language Curriculum for Third to Sixth Class will begin.

In keeping with the new approach adopted by the NCCA, an interactive version of the new curriculum is available online. This includes an implementation 'Toolkit' to help teachers interpret the curriculum and to plan appropriately. A hard copy of the curriculum has been sent to schools and teachers will receive a USB stick containing 'an extensive sample' of the support materials and examples that are published online. The examples provided were developed by teachers and children, and show children's language learning and development across the three strands and across a range of school contexts. These examples are linked to learning outcomes and progression continua, and are presented as short videos.

Continuing Professional Development (CPD) to support principals and teachers in the implementation of the new curriculum will be made available, facilitated by the Professional Development Service for Teachers (PDST), over a three-year period. This will involve a combination of information seminars, workshops, classroom modelling, summer courses as well as website resources and publications.

Work is also underway to revise the primary Mathematics curriculum. Two research papers on Maths at primary level were published on the NCCA website in 2014. A Development Group (formerly comprising Syllabus Committees) will shortly begin work on redeveloping the Mathematics curriculum for Junior Infants to Second Class, which will be available to schools from autumn 2018.

While it is too soon to comment on the implementation of the revised Primary Language Curriculum, which was delivered in schools from autumn 2016, it is reassuring to see that final version of the curriculum which was disseminated to schools and teachers includes much more detail than had been made available by the NCCA in the original specification. It would be reassuring to know that similar detail will be made available for the revised syllabi for Junior Cycle and for the Leaving Certificate subjects as they are finalised.

The NCCA is also currently engaged in developing a syllabus for a new subject – Education about Religions and Beliefs and Ethics. The development of a curriculum in Education about Religions and Beliefs (ERB) and Ethics was one of the key recommendations of the Forum on Patronage and Pluralism in the Primary Sector (Coolahan et al, 2012). The Minister for Education asked the NCCA to undertake this task. In autumn 2015, the NCCA issued a consultation document on ERB and Ethics, and the consultation period closed in March 2016. It is understood from the NCCA that a 'consultation report' will be issued in early 2017. However, there is no indication as to what format this new syllabus will take or when it will be available for implementation nationally. The process of development has been slow. It has been four years since the Forum on Patronage and Pluralism recommended the development of this syllabus and it could be many more years before a new syllabus is available.

As this chapter was being finalised in December 2016, the NCCA issued a consultation document on "proposals for structure and time allocation in a redeveloped primary curriculum". The title of the document belies the radical and fundamental nature of the proposals. While two options for redeveloping the curriculum are suggested, either of the options are likely to have profound implications for teaching and learning in Irish primary schools for future generations. The proposals are based on recent research on children's learning and development in their early childhood and primary school years. They also attempt to address the demands for "more" to be included in the primary school curriculum by providing a more flexible approach to time allocation.

> " The development of a curriculum in Education about Religions and Beliefs (ERB) and Ethics was one of the key recommendations of the Forum on Patronage and Pluralism in the Primary Sector "

As regards the structure of the curriculum, two options are suggested – both of which move away from the existing model of four two-year stages (Infants; Junior; Middle and Senior). The first option would mean a move to a new three-stage model while the second option would use a two-stage model. The three stages of the first model would be (1) Pre-school (current Pre-school and Infant Classes); (2) First to Fourth Class; (3) Fifth and Sixth Class. In the first stage, the curriculum would be largely based on the Aistear themes; in the second stage, it would be based on curriculum areas and the third stage would be subject-based. Option 2 predicates two stages – (1) Pre-school to Second Class and (2) Third to Sixth Class. The first stage would be based on the Aistear themes and the second stage would be subject-based.

The issue of time allocation is also addressed in the consultation document. The framework includes three key elements: the time allocated to religious education; a suggested minimum time allocation for the six curriculum areas (or strands) of the 1999 curriculum, along with a period of discretionary curriculum time; and the time allowed for breaks and assembly time. A particularly important feature of the framework is the inclusion of a significant period of discretionary curriculum time (up to 40% of the total time). This time could be allocated to any of the six curriculum areas or to any of the subjects within them. The framework also allows for the inclusion of a modern language where this is available.

The consultation on the proposals will run through spring 2017 and the findings will inform more detailed work by the NCCA in preparing an overview of a redeveloped primary curriculum. As this overview will be the basis for further consultation in late 2017 and into 2018, it is likely to be some years before a new primary curriculum is ready for implementation. Nevertheless, the proposals contained in the consultation document must be seen as ground-breaking, and could well be at least as significant as the 1971 "new" curriculum was in its day.

Junior Cycle Curriculum

In spite of the obvious need and regular proposals for wide-ranging Junior Cycle curriculum and assessment reform dating back to the ICE report of 1975, no such reform had been implemented by the end of the first decade of the 21st century. While efforts had been made to introduce a revised curriculum with a broader range of assessment in the 1970s, 1980s and 1990s, and most recently between 2000 and 2010, the Junior Certificate examinations continued to dominate teaching and learning at Junior Cycle (see Chapter 1). Moreover, there was little continuity between the primary and the Junior Cycle curricula, an issue that had been a matter of concern for many decades.

Research undertaken by the Economic and Social Research Institute in the early 2000s provided new insights into the effect of the Junior Certificate on student participation and achievement. It noted that many students became disengaged at an early stage of Junior Cycle; it found a curriculum which was seen as inflexible and overcrowded with relatively little flexibility for teachers or students; it highlighted the dominating effect of the Junior Certificate examination on teaching and learning; it indicated the narrow range of assessment activity (Smyth, 2007 and 2011).

Towards a Framework for Junior Cycle – Innovation and Identity, 2011

In November 2011, a new framework for Junior Cycle was published by the NCCA, entitled Innovation and Identity. The new framework focused attention 'on the school as the site of innovation, and on teachers and school leaders as the agents of any change process'. The framework included curriculum and assessment change and proposed a balance between school-led change and system-wide change 'that will deliver a new Junior Cycle and a real difference in the learning experience of young people at this stage of their education'. What students would learn was described in 24 'statements of learning' and eight key skills, including literacy and numeracy. The statements of learning are broad generic statements – similar to the generic statements of the various levels of the European Qualifications Framework. They provide a basis from which learning outcomes for subject syllabi can be derived.

As well as providing the traditional Junior Cycle subjects, the framework allows for short courses, some developed by the NCCA and some developed locally by schools. The NCCA would continue to provide specifications (outline syllabi) for each subject but these specifications would be less detailed than before and teachers would be expected 'to ensure deeper learning, to focus on key skills and to monitor student progress'. Assessment would be a combination of external assessment by the State Examinations Commission (SEC) and internal assessment by the school (NCCA, 2011).

A year later, Minister for Education Ruairi Quinn launched the new framework for Junior Cycle. Under the framework proposed in 2012, a proportion of the marks for each subject were to be awarded for school-based components such as oral examinations, lab work, essays, or e-portfolios. Schools would be encouraged to develop short courses according to local needs and interests. The SEC would initially retain responsibility for setting and marking the final assessment for English, Mathematics and Irish. For all other subjects the SEC would provide assessment papers to be supervised and marked by teachers. The NCCA would provide support to schools in the form of assessment and moderation toolkits, syllabus specifications and exemplars of the standards expected. The new Junior Cycle curriculum would be phased in over a period of six years (DES, 2012).

This proposal was not acceptable to the teacher unions and, following discussion and negotiations, in May 2015 Minister for Education Jan O'Sullivan brokered a compromise agreement with the leaders of the teacher unions (TUI, ASTI et al., 2015). Following this agreement, a revised/new *Framework for Junior Cycle* (2015) was published by the Department of Education (DES, 2015). This framework reiterates the vision of the 2012 framework but makes significant concessions on assessment. Under this framework, the new Junior Cycle would be implemented in four phases – in September 2014, 2015, 2016 and 2017 (the revised specification for English had been introduced in 2014). Students can study between eight and ten subjects (from a list of twenty) as well as some short courses.

As regards assessment, the framework presents 'a dual approach to assessment that supports student learning over the three years of Junior Cycle and also measures achievement at the end of those three years'. Two structured Classroom-Based Assessments (CBAs) will be introduced – one in Second Year and one in Third Year. These assessments might include project tasks, oral language tasks, investigations, practical or designing and making tasks, field studies and artistic performance. After the second CBA, students will complete a written Assessment Task, to be marked by the SEC, on what they have learned and the skills and competences they have developed in that assessment. In addition, an externally-assessed, state-certified examination for every subject will continue to be provided at the end of Third Year. English, Maths and Irish will be provided at two levels – all other subjects will be provided at one (common) level. For each subject, the external examination will be two hours long. Slightly modified assessment structures will apply in Art, Craft and Design; Music; Home Economics and the Technology subjects.

It is disappointing that the Assessment Task will account for such a small proportion of the overall marks available for the Final Examination – according to DES circular 0024/2016, 'in the case of English, Business Studies and Science, the value assigned to the Assessment Task will not exceed 10% of the overall marks available for the Final Examination'. Had the 2012 framework been implemented, the proportion of marks for the Final Assessment would have been considerably higher.

However, it is significant that for the first time in the history of Irish education, timetabled time will be made available for teachers for professional in-school meetings, referred to as 'Subject Learning and Assessment Review' meetings (SLARs). At these meetings, teachers will 'share and discuss examples of their assessments of student work and build common understanding about the quality of student learning'. An additional two hours may be allocated by school management to a teacher for the co-ordination of the SLAR meetings for each individual subject. The two-hour allocation may be facilitated through the provision of paid substitution hours to the school. During the school year 2016/17, fourteen hours of professional time (six hours of school closure and the balance through paid substitution hours) will be made available for SLAR meetings for teachers of English. Similar meeting times will be timetabled for teachers of the other two proposed new subjects, i.e. Business Studies and Science. This will be in addition to 22 hours of professional time allocated within the timetable for each full-time teacher from 2017-18 onwards.

> " ...it is significant that for the first time in the history of Irish education, timetabled time will be made available for teachers for professional in-school meetings, referred to as 'Subject Learning and Assessment Review' meetings (SLARs). "

There will be a different grading scheme for the CBAs and for the SEC examined assessments. CBAs will be assessed using the following four-point scale:

- Exceptional
- Above expectations
- In line with expectations
- Yet to meet expectations.

The SEC final examinations at Junior Certificate level will use a five-point scale as follows:

Grade	Range (%)
Distinction	90 to 100
Higher Merit	75 to 90
Merit	55 to 75
Achieved	40 to 55
Partially Achieved	20 to 40
Not Graded	0 to 20

At the end of Junior Cycle, students will be awarded the Junior Cycle Profile of Achievement (JCPA) that will include the different assessment elements undertaken over the three years of Junior Cycle. This includes the results of the CBAs in subjects and short courses, assessed by teachers, and the grades achieved in the final examinations and the outcome of the Assessment Tasks, marked by the SEC.

The DES recognises the need to support teachers and school principals in implementing the new curriculum and assessments. CPD opportunities will be provided by the JCT (Junior Cycle for Teachers) support team, both off-site and on a whole-school basis as well as to school leaders. In addition to CPD, exemplar materials and complementary online support will be provided. Teacher feedback and requests for clarification will be collated on an ongoing basis through the JCT website and through social media mechanisms, and updated materials, resources and exemplars will be made available. It is hoped that this approach will promote professional dialogue and the sharing of experiences among school leaders and teachers.

Unfortunately, at the time of writing this paper, ASTI members are refusing to co-operate with the May 2015 proposal, in spite of the fact that ASTI leaders signed the revised Framework at their meetings with Minister for Education, Jan O'Sullivan, in May 2015 (TUI et al May 2015). Given the overwhelming evidence about the need for Junior Cycle reform, and the long and tedious efforts made over such a long period to accommodate the concerns of teachers, it is more than disappointing that more than 40 years after the need for Junior Cycle reform was first flagged, there is still no certainty about whole-scale reform of Junior Cycle curriculum. The proposed Junior Cycle framework and the new syllabi (now called subject specifications) are more than overdue and are very welcome. They focus on the knowledge, skills and attitudes that will be required by our young people in the future as well as providing exciting and creative new opportunities for students and teachers.

In June 2016, Minister for Education and Skills, Richard Bruton, confirmed that the implementation plan agreed in May 2015 would go ahead as planned, and that the revised specification for English (the first subject to be introduced) would be examined in 2017. In keeping with NCCA policy, the new specification, available on www.curriculumonline.ie, is much less detailed than previous syllabi. It is less than 20 pages long, including an introduction, rationale, and aims of the subject. An overview of the course covers just three pages, and 'Expectations for Students' (i.e. learning outcomes) take up four pages. Short assessment guidelines are also provided. A list of suggested texts is provided in a separate document. However, as promised in the 2015 DES Framework document, additional support material and resources are available on the JCT and DES websites and on www.curriculumonline.ie. In April 2016, the state Examination Commission issued sample examination papers for the 2017 examination (www.examinations.ie), which will no doubt be carefully studied by teachers and pupils alike.

One small criticism – it is difficult when navigating the various websites to find out exactly what curriculum and assessment changes are being introduced at Junior Cycle and how they are to be implemented. Documents relating to the changed syllabi, their delivery and assessment are to be found variously on the NCCA website (www.ncca.ie); on www.curriculumonline.ie; on the JCT website (www.jct.ie); on the PDST website (www.pdst.ie); on the SEC website (www.examinations.ie) and on the DES website (www.education.ie). Many of these documents are undated and it is difficult for the average reader to know whether they relate to the old or the revised syllabi. On its website, the NCCA's national curriculum framework provides minimal information and emphasises that teachers should customise the guidelines for their own particular students. The PDST website continues to provide guidelines and support materials, and the SEC website provides sample examination papers (which, unfortunately, may well be the sole determinant for some teachers of what will be taught and learned in classrooms!). The website of the Department of Education also includes further information on the proposed changes, including circulars to schools setting out the administrative arrangements for the changes. While the new and comprehensive JCT website (set up in March 2016) encapsulates all the information about the revised Junior Cycle curriculum in a single co-ordinated site, some of the other websites do not adequately emphasise the links to JCT. Nor is it always clear on some of the older websites whether their resources relate to the new specification or to the old syllabus. In order to counter some of the confusing misinformation about Junior Cycle reform that is currently being disseminated, this author suggests that an information campaign, highlighting the JCT website, and accessible to parents and students as well as to teachers, be mounted. The excellent online leaflet, entitled 'Information for Parents of Primary School Students' should now be re-titled 'Information for Parents of Post-Primary

School Students', and reissued for parents whose children have just enrolled in post-primary schools and widely distributed through schools, libraries, community centres etc. As indicated in an earlier section, it is important that hard-copy versions of support resources, as well as web-based versions, continue to be made available for the foreseeable future.

Senior Cycle

Ireland differs from a number of other EU countries in having a relatively undifferentiated Senior Cycle. When free education was introduced in Ireland in the late 1960s, and when vocational schools began to provide Senior Cycle education, it was envisaged that there would be a two-track system at Senior Cycle - with a technical Leaving Certificate provided by the vocational sector and an academic Leaving Certificate provided by the voluntary secondary sector (DES, 1972). A debate about a two-track system occurred again in the early 1990s following the publication of the *Culliton Report* (Sheehan, 1992) but following protracted discussion and consultation, Ireland decided not to adopt a dual technical/academic track at Senior Cycle (Gleeson, 2010). In practice, however, some differentiation does occur at Senior Cycle, as students can choose from a wide variety of Leaving Certificate subjects (both academic and technical) and they may opt to take these subjects at either Higher or Ordinary level.

When students complete Junior Cycle, they may take the Transition Year (TY) programme or proceed directly to the first year of a two-year Leaving Certificate programme. Thus, Senior Cycle is comprised of either two or three years, depending on whether or not students take TY.

TY provides students with access to a broader range of subjects, skills and experiences than otherwise provided in second-level education. It was first introduced as a pilot programme in the mid-1970s and expanded significantly following re-structuring in 1994. It is a matter for each individual school to decide whether they will offer TY and, if so, which students will engage with it. Smaller schools and those serving disadvantaged areas are less likely to provide TY than other schools (Smyth, Byrne and Hannah, 2004). Almost 60% of Senior Cycle students opt to enrol in TY - participation has increased from about 23,000 students in the year 2000 to about 30,000 in 2014.

There are three types of Leaving Certificate programme – the Leaving Certificate Applied (LCA) programme, the Leaving Certificate Established (LCE) and the Leaving Certificate Vocational Programme (LCVP). All three Leaving Certificate programmes are two-year programmes. The LCE is taken by the largest proportion of students (around 60%). Students taking this programme must take five subjects but usually take six or seven. There is a heavy emphasis on the terminal or end-of-cycle examination, which is marked and graded by external examiners. Most subjects are examined by one three-hour examination paper, with the exception of Irish, English and Mathematics, where students sit two three-hour papers. In some subjects, other modes of assessment are used in addition to the terminal written examination. In languages, a component of the marks is allocated for oral and aural tests; in Geography and History, students may submit a written project in advance of the examinations. There are also practical/performance assessments in subjects such as Music and Art. However, unlike other countries where a proportion of marks in national (or state) examinations are allocated for continuous school-based (and teacher-marked) assessment, the Irish Leaving Certificate is entirely marked by external examiners with no involvement in marking or grading by the students' own teachers.

The Leaving Certificate Vocational Programme was introduced in 1994 to help students develop business and enterprise skills as well as interpersonal, vocational and technical skills. Students must take at least five Leaving Certificate subjects, two of which must be from a specified list of vocational subjects. They must also take a modern European language as well as two so-called 'link modules' which focus on preparation for the world of work and enterprise education. The link modules are assessed based on a portfolio of coursework and the other subjects are assessed in the same way as the LCE. LCVP is taken by between 30% and 35% of students.

The LCA was introduced in 1995 for students who are not catered for by the LCE or LCVP and who might be at risk of early school leaving. It offers a combination of general education, vocational education and vocational preparation courses, and involves a cross-curricular approach rather than a subject-based structure. The programme is offered on a modular basis and assessment includes module completion, practical tasks and written examinations. The LCA is not recognised for direct access to higher education. About 6% of Senior Cycle students take the LCA and the number has been falling in recent years.

> " The Leaving Certificate Vocational Programme was introduced in 1994 to help students develop business and enterprise skills as well as interpersonal, vocational and technical skills. "

As over 90% of students take either the LCE or the LCVP, the vast majority are eligible for higher education entry. In practice, more than 60% of Leaving Certificate students proceed to higher education, which is one of the highest proportions in the EU. This contrasts with the situation in many other EU countries (e.g. Germany, the Netherlands) where an academic track leading to university is open only to a minority of the student cohort (OECD 2004, cited in Smyth, Banks and Calvert, 2011).

In 2009, the NCCA issued its revised framework for Senior Cycle education in the document *Towards Learning: An Overview of Senior Cycle Education* (NCCA 2009). The following diagram summarises the framework:

An Overview of Senior Cycle Education

Teaching and learning	**Planning**

resourceful
confident
engaged
active
LEARNERS

Teacher professional development	**School culture**

	PRINCIPLES	THE SENIOR CYCLE
	quality	**CURRICULUM**
	inclusive education	learning outcomes
VALUES	continuity	key skills
human dignity and respect	choice and flexibility	subjects
equality and inclusion	participation, relevance	short courses
justice and fairness	and enjoyment	transition units
freedom and democracy	well-being	assessment
	creativity and innovation	certificaiton
	lifelong learning	guidance

This framework recognises the need for greater emphasis on key skills. It states that

'the five key skills of information processing, being personally effective, communicating, critical and creative thinking, and working with others will be embedded in Senior Cycle curriculum and assessment, thus helping learners to think critically and creatively, to innovate and adapt to change, to work independently and in a team and to reflect on their learning'.

The Senior Cycle framework strives to produce learners who are 'resourceful, confident, engaged and active'. It also emphasises the values of human dignity and respect, equality and inclusion, justice and fairness, and freedom and democracy.

The National Council is currently reviewing the syllabi for some of the Leaving Certificate subjects for Curriculum and Assessment (NCCA) and, over the coming years, plans to introduce new syllabi for all Leaving Certificate subjects using the Senior Cycle framework.

The NCCA's process of review and revision of Leaving Certificate subjects involves the preparation of an outline specification of the various syllabi, focusing on topics and learning outcomes. The preparation of the outline specification is overseen by a 'development group', which includes representatives of the teacher unions, management bodies, the university sector, IBEC, the SEC; the DES Inspectorate; the relevant subject association and others with relevant expertise. The outline specification for the subject in question is then subject to wide consultation and includes opportunities for written submissions and meetings with subject associations, teacher networks, third-level students etc. Following consultation, the NCCA reconsiders the draft specification and, taking account of comments received, the specification is finalised and submitted to the Minister.

PART FOUR: SOME ISSUES OF CONCERN ABOUT THE REVISION OF LEAVING CERTIFICATE SYLLABI

Dissatisfaction with the process of reform of Leaving Certificate subjects has been expressed by some members of the development groups. Some of them were not aware that the framework for Senior Cycle, and the format in which the revised syllabi would be presented, were set in stone before the process of review and consultation started. They expressed particular concern about the format of the syllabus specification, consisting as it does only of topics and learning outcomes. Some higher education representatives, who are familiar for many years with a learning outcomes approach to programme planning in higher education, are aware of the limitations (and strengths) of a learning outcomes approach. They are particularly aware that the specification of syllabi solely in terms of learning outcomes could lead to what has been referred to as a 'dumbing down of standards', especially if the level and depth of the learning outcomes as well as higher order thinking skills (e.g. the skills of analysis, evaluation and synthesis) are not made explicit. Some representatives felt that they needed greater detail on implementation before they could recommend the draft specifications to their nominating body (e.g. the Irish Universities Association).

Their concerns are well exemplified in correspondence between the Irish Science Teachers Association (ISTA) and the NCCA in 2013. In a letter to the Chief Executive of the NCCA in October 2013, the chair of the ISTA stated that 'the essential problem with the proposed draft syllabi (for Leaving Certificate science subjects) is that they simply contain a list of learning outcomes with no indication re. depth of treatment and range of subject knowledge associated with these learning outcomes' (Mullaghy, cited in Hyland, 2014). She stated that 'even highly-experienced science teachers at the ISTA council meeting found problems with interpreting many of the learning outcomes'.

However, in spite of the concerns of the ISTA, the NCCA made it clear at the time that it did not intend to make any changes to the process or to the draft specification for physics, chemistry or biology, stating that

> 'in deciding to move to a learning outcomes approach to all primary and post-primary specifications in the future, the Council drew on research in teaching, learning and assessment and on international practice in the articulation of national curriculum'.

In a letter to the ISTA dated 25 October 2013, the NCCA stated that 'We don't intend to include 'depth of treatment' and/or 'range of subject knowledge' in the new specification for the sciences or for other subjects in Senior Cycle'. They indicated that they would include 'some examples of teaching, learning and assessment approaches that will support teachers in classroom planning'.

In view of the reference by the NCCA to 'international practice in the articulation of national curriculum', this author was asked by the ISTA to analyse the approach to the design of Senior Cycle syllabi in some other countries and to compare their approach to that taken by the NCCA (Hyland, 2014). Among the countries used by the NCCA to benchmark curriculum design were Australia and Scotland. Senior Cycle curriculum and assessment in these countries are similar to the Irish system - the examination system at the end of Senior Cycle is administered centrally (i.e. it is not school-based); the students sit an average of six subjects; and the examinations are high-stakes as they are used by universities to select students. The national curriculum authority in Australia is the Australian Curriculum, Assessment and Reporting Authority (ACARA) and in Scotland, it is Education Scotland. Both authorities have recently revised their national curriculum frameworks. However, as indicated earlier in this chapter, in both of those countries, detailed syllabi and examination 'intermediate' bodies provide guidelines. In Scotland, detailed and specific examination syllabi for Scottish Highers (the equivalent of the Irish Leaving Certificate) are provided by the Scottish Qualifications Authority. In Australia, the examination syllabi (also detailed and specific) are provided by individual states e.g. in the state of Victoria the relevant body is Victoria's Curriculum and Assessment Authority. Centrally-administered high-stakes examination syllabi in other English-speaking jurisdictions (e.g. India, England and Wales, Canada), and the International Baccalaureate examination, all provide detailed and specific syllabi for their end of Senior Cycle examinations.

While school-based curriculum development and teacher-led syllabi may well be appropriate at primary school level and at Junior Cycle in second-level, as far as this author is aware, all centrally-administered national examination systems at the end of Senior Cycle schooling, especially in those countries where universities accept the final-year national examination for selection and admissions purposes, provide detailed subject syllabi and assessment guidelines which are not confined merely to topics and learning outcomes. This author holds that it is not sufficient to describe the requirements of a national high-stakes examination syllabus in terms only of topics and learning outcomes. More detailed information about the depth of treatment of subjects and the requirements for examination will need to be provided at national level to bring the new Leaving Certificate curriculum into line with international good practice and to ensure that it will be of a sufficiently high standard to be acceptable to the university sector.

It would be desirable that the NCCA development groups for the various subjects continue to be actively engaged in the detailed development of the subject specification, including clarification of the level and depth at which topics should be taught; providing exemplars of good practice in the teaching of the subject; drafting of sample examination questions etc. It makes little sense to bring together a highly expert development group to draft the (minimal) subject specification, and not to use their expertise to oversee the follow-on development of the specification. While suggestions and resources provided by classroom teachers regarding implementation of the subject specification are undoubtedly valuable, the expertise of the higher education sector and of researchers who are at the cutting edge of developments in the subject is essential to ensure that revised Leaving Certificate subject syllabi are up-to-date and take account of the most recent research in the subject.

Under the current approach, the process of reviewing and revising Leaving Certificate syllabi is long-drawn out and protracted. In the case of the revised Leaving Certificate syllabi for Physics, Chemistry and Biology, for instance, the process began in 2007 and is not yet complete. It is likely to be at least another three years before the new syllabi are approved and implemented nationally. The new Politics and Society syllabus has been in gestation for almost a decade and is being implemented (for the first time) in a selected number of schools this year (2016-17). While precipitated and overly-rushed reform of syllabi is clearly undesirable, it is important that the process is not so protracted as to militate against regular modernisation and updating.

> " Under the current approach, the process of reviewing and revising Leaving Certificate syllabi is long-drawn out and protracted. "

PART FIVE: CO-CURRICULAR INITIATIVES

No discussion of curriculum in Ireland would be complete without reference to the many co-curricular initiatives and opportunities that exist throughout the country. Many schools facilitate extra-curricular classes and activities, often provided by teachers on a voluntary basis, and availed of by large numbers of pupils. A wide range of out-of-school educational activities are also provided, both formally and informally, for children and young people by various organisations and agencies – some of which are supported from public funds. Some initiatives provided by non-school-based organisations, are provided both in school and out of school.

Public libraries, various museums and art galleries offer a wide range of educational opportunities for children from birth to late teens, as well as providing books and other educational resources. Arts organisations, locally and nationally, provide facilities and tuition, individually and in groups and organise exhibitions and performances for young people in the Visual Arts, Drama, Music etc. Youth organisations (e.g. Foróige) and Scout and Guide organisations, as well as a vast range of sports organisations, nationally and locally, work in and out of schools to provide personal development, sports and recreational opportunities for children and young people. There are close links between many of these organisations and the school system. Education Centres also provide support for educational activities and for networking between schools and various out-of-school organisations.

An example of collaboration between relevant agencies is the establishment, in 2015, of Encountering the Arts Ireland (ETAI), an organisation of over thirty agencies. The National Cultural Institutions' Education, Community and Outreach (ECO) grouping, now has a new policy framework document, agreed in 2015. The grouping is making available a wide range of imaginative and high quality arts and cultural experiences for children and opening up for them the richness of these great cultural institutions. The Association of Teacher and Education Centres of Ireland (ATECI) has established a network for arts partnerships, with valuable opportunities for the regions. The Arts Council has produced a new strategy for 2016 to 2020. Objective 8 of this strategy is focused on arts for children and young people, and makes a number of strong commitments in this regard. Ireland's first Arts in Education Portal, the key national digital resource for arts education in Ireland, was launched in May 2015. The portal allows for two-way involvement, as contributors and receivers, with a key focus on quality. The Ark Cultural Centre for children is celebrating its 21st anniversary and its new strategic plan aims to have greater impact for arts in education. Youth Theatre Ireland supports voluntary youth drama groups throughout the country and provides training, support and advice for these groups. Creative Engagement, the NAPD arts scheme, has involved up to 100 post-primary schools each year in grant-aided arts projects. There is also evidence of renewed energy and activity in many other children's arts organisations throughout the country. The Arts in Education Charter, launched in 2013, has been a landmark development in relation to the culture change that is afoot. The Charter is an initiative of the Department of Education and Skills, the Department of Arts, Heritage and the Gaeltacht, working in association with the Arts Council.

Out-of-school science and technology activities and interactive exhibitions are also very popular with children and young people. The Young Scientist of the Year Exhibition, held annually in the RDS, attracts tens of thousands of young exhibitors, competitors and visitors. It recently celebrated the 50th anniversary of its inauguration. Another very popular initiative is SciFest – which encourages a love of Science, Technology and Mathematics through active, collaborative, inquiry-based learning. It provides a forum for students at local, regional and national level to display their scientific investigations through a series of one-day science fairs hosted by third-level institutions for second-level students. An initiative that has gained great success, nationally and internationally, is Coder Dojo, which provides free tuition in computer programming for young people. It was set up about five years ago by a young Cork-based entrepreneur, James Whelton, supported by investor Bill Liao. It is community-based and self-led, staffed entirely by volunteers providing peer-mentoring, project-based learning and youth leadership. A further resource that supports the sciences is the Science Gallery at Trinity College Dublin, which offers a diverse range of educational programmes for young people aged 15-25, providing them with the opportunity to pursue creative ideas that interrogate and explore the boundaries of Art and Science. Its education programmes aim to ignite a passion for science, technology and innovation, highlighting the rich network of interconnections between science, the arts, culture, design, business and innovation. An exciting proposed new educational facility for children up to 15 years of age is the new Children's Science Museum (Exploration Station), which is due to open in 2018/19 in the refurbished north wing of the National Concert Hall Building on Earlsfort Terrace in Dublin. The initiative is an excellent example of collaboration between public and private funders. The museum is being designed and refurbished by the Office of Public Works and will provide opportunities for children and young teenagers to engage in STEM activities which will complement the school curriculum.

> " Creative Engagement, the NAPD arts scheme, has involved up to 100 post-primary schools each year in grant-aided arts projects. "

The above are just some examples of the wide range of co-curricular activities which are available for children and young people and which complement school-based education. They are also indicative of the very significant level of volunteerism and pro-bono engagement that epitomises so much of the out-of-school educational activities that are available in Ireland. While public funding for many of these educational activities is scant, especially in comparison with some other OECD countries, the range and quality of out-of-school educational activities in Ireland compares more than favourably with those provided at much higher public cost in other jurisdictions.

CONCLUSION

This chapter has outlined curriculum policy in primary and second-level schools since publicly-funded schooling was first provided in Ireland in the nineteenth century. It has traced the development of the curriculum at primary and second level through the generations, identifying how the curriculum was used at various times to achieve political, cultural, religious and economic aims.

It traced the changes at primary level from a prescriptive, exam-led curriculum (from 1871 to 1900 and from the mid-1920s to the late 1960s) to a more child-centred, discovery-based curriculum (from 1900 to 1922 and from 1971 to date). It referred to the changing role of the primary teacher from that of a purveyor of knowledge to that of a guide and a facilitator of learning. It recognised that at primary level, in spite of the many demands on teachers and school principals, especially those in schools where the principal teaches on a full-time or almost full-time basis, there has been a long tradition of school-based curriculum planning. Both the 1971 and the 1999 primary curriculum were designed to encourage school-based curriculum planning. The curriculum designers in the Department of Education in 1971 recognised that teachers would require support and guidance to develop and implement the curriculum – and the Teachers' Handbook and ongoing in-service courses provided that guidance and support. The revised primary curriculum of 1999 provided guidelines that are even more extensive and exemplars for teachers. Given the many other demands facing principals and teachers, not least their heavy teaching timetables, it was recognised that there would be limitations to the extent to which practising teachers could be curriculum developers and innovators.

The documentation which the DES has made available for the new Primary Language Curriculum appears to have achieved a reasonable balance, providing as it does, a practical 'Toolkit' which encompasses learning outcomes, progression continua, support material for teachers and examples of children's learning and development. The web portal provides opportunities for sharing lesson plans and exemplars. While the richness and potential of the web is recognised, the importance of ensuring that no teacher or pupil is excluded from accessing the curriculum because of inability to access the web is also recognised by making all materials available in hard copy and/or on a USB stick. It will continue to be necessary to provide alternatives to web-based resources for as long as broadband coverage in Ireland is inadequate, to ensure the widest possible engagement by teachers and pupils.

Curriculum development at second level is also traced in this chapter, and various efforts at Junior Cycle reform since the ICE report of 1974 are identified, in particular the efforts of the (Interim) CEB between 1984 and 1987 as well as the NCCA from 1988 to the present day. The attachment of second-level teachers to a prescribed, exam-led syllabi and an overdependence on textbook-based teaching and learning is chronicled as well as the continuing reluctance of ASTI members to assess their own students for certification purposes. It points out that, since learning for certification has been assessed almost solely by end-of cycle examinations, with only limited practical or other assessments, the emphasis in second-level education has tended to be on linguistic and logical intelligences, to the detriment of other important skills and intelligences.

The breakthrough achieved in the Junior Cycle Framework document signed by the leaders of the ASTI and the TUI in May 2015 is welcomed. It is noted that for the first time in the history of Irish education, the Junior Cycle curriculum has the potential to be flexible, with short school-based courses, and a dual approach to assessment – both classroom-based assessments and end of cycle examinations. The chapter recognises the support which is being provided for teachers through the JCT (Junior Cycle for Teachers) team, and lauds the decision of the DES to allow for timetabled time for meetings at which teachers can discuss syllabus and assessment issues with their colleagues (SLAR meetings). All these developments herald a new and welcome era in second-level education whereby the professionalism of teachers will be recognised and the learning environment will be more engaging for students.

The approach adopted since 2009 by the NCCA in designing curriculum at all levels – from early childhood to Leaving Certificate – is analysed and discussed. While a policy of encouraging teachers to be curriculum developers and innovators is laudable, such a policy assumes a well-educated and experienced professional body, as well as the provision of expert advice and support on an ongoing basis. In the case of Aistear, the curriculum framework for early childhood education, the question is raised as to whether the majority of staff in this sector have the capacity and expertise to be curriculum innovators and developers.

> " The breakthrough achieved in the Junior Cycle Framework document signed by the leaders of the ASTI and the TUI in May 2015 is welcomed. "

In relation to the current curriculum and assessment changes at Junior Cycle, reference is made to the difficulties that can be encountered in navigating the various official education websites in order to build up an accurate picture of the changing curriculum landscape. The new user-friendly JCT website is welcomed but to ensure that all teachers can benefit from the new resources that are becoming available, it is important that hard-copy teaching and learning resources continue to be made available for the foreseeable future. It is also suggested that a publicity campaign be mounted to ensure that Junior Cycle students, their parents and teachers have accurate information about the new Junior Cycle curriculum.

CHAPTER FOUR ● ● ● ● ● ● ● ● ● ● ● ● ● ● ● ● ●

Assessment: Primary and Junior Cycle

INTRODUCTION

Up to the late 1960s, assessment policy and practices in Ireland were mainly limited to externally devised and administered terminal examinations. What happened in relation to in-school assessments was in the main undocumented and at post-primary level, school-administered end-of-term tests were mainly a mirror image of the public examinations. The experience in Ireland in this area was not very different to that in most developed countries at this time. However, policy changes introduced in Ireland from the mid-1960s onwards led to widespread debate on curriculum development and assessment. The decision to introduce comprehensive schools in 1964 threw up new challenges for the provision of programmes in the new schools, the first of which were opened in 1966 (Randles, 1975; Coolahan, J, 1981). A sharp division existed at this time between the voluntary secondary and vocational schools, each having its own distinctive programmes and examinations, with limited opportunities for cooperation or sharing across the two sectors. As the new comprehensive schools fitted neither of these curricular models, it became necessary to review the existing programmes. After a lengthy and protracted process, this ultimately resulted in the replacement of the existing Intermediate and Day Group Certificate programmes with a unified Junior Cycle curriculum and examination system in 1989. Although it was planned to introduce more varied modes of assessment in addition to the terminal examinations at this level, thus extending the range of skills being examined, oral tests in languages and practical tests in technology-based subjects were initially introduced on a voluntary basis and were devised and examined centrally.

At primary level, the abolition of the Primary Certificate examination in 1967 at the end of this cycle and the introduction of a new primary curriculum in 1971 opened up new opportunities for schools to develop assessment policies free from the demands of a centrally-devised examination system. With this newfound freedom also came the introduction of standardised tests in literacy and numeracy aimed at monitoring standards across the system (Department of Education and Skills, 2012). This scenario created a basis for renewed discussions on assessment and standards, especially in the light of hitherto unsubstantiated claims that the abolition of the external examination would inevitably lead to falling standards in literacy and numeracy.

This chapter is organised as follows. The first section briefly outlines the nature, scope and purposes of assessment. The development and implementation of assessment in the primary and Junior Cyclesectors are then outlined and this is followed by a summary of the main findings of a number of standardised assessment surveys conducted at both levels. A review of performance patterns at primary and post-primary is presented in the section that follows. Some general suggestions for further developments in this area complete the chapter.

NATURE, SCOPE AND PURPOSES OF ASSESSMENT

Internationally, following the downturn in the economy in the early 1970s, arising mainly from the oil crisis and resulting in large-scale unemployment, schools came under increasing scrutiny mainly because, it was contended, that they were not producing students with employable skills. Questions were raised as to whether schools were making a difference to the advancement of their pupils, above that already conferred on them by their home and social background. There followed a wave of research studies into school effectiveness and school improvement, and a new emphasis on assessment (Cheng Cheong, 1996; Macbeath, 1999; Madaus et al., 1980; Rutter et al., 1980; Smyth, 1999). This became evident in some countries in the competency testing movement, the introduction of standardised testing and the publication of school league tables based on examination results.

Assessment involves the use of a range of techniques aimed at capturing the achievement of students across a wide span of knowledge and competences. It is defined by the NCCA (2007, p.7) as:

> **The process of gathering, recording, interpreting, using, and reporting a child's progress and achievement in developing knowledge, skills and attitudes.**

While the emphasis is generally placed on the assessment of cognitive and psychomotor skills, it is also important not to lose sight of the role of key skills in the 'affective domain' that can have a significant influence on the motivation and development of learners. Thus, such skills as the ability to work alone, to work in groups, to participate in classroom discussions, etc., although possibly not appropriate for certification purposes, indicate important areas of development and can form part of the agenda for discussions with parents on the progress of their children. These form part of the informal observations that teachers make on a daily basis in classrooms.

Assessment forms an integral component of the curriculum development process. Its fundamental purpose is to promote and support high-quality teaching and learning, to serve the curriculum but not to dominate it. In the past, assessment policies have frequently been developed in isolation from the aims, objectives and content of the curriculum. In such a scenario, assessment can unwittingly dominate the teaching and learning process and thus frustrate the intentions of developers by narrowing the focus of instruction to that which is measured. This can be especially so in the case of 'high stakes' testing and has been described as 'teaching to the test'. What gets tested gets taught and gets learned. Ensuring that assessment policies and practices are congruent with curricular aims and objectives requires the use of a range of techniques, especially in the case of terminal tests that are used for certification purposes. Matching the objectives of the subjects on the curriculum with appropriate techniques can be a major challenge for test designers. Designing tests of this nature requires specialist skills in both the theory and design of appropriate test instruments and in the interpretation and analysis of outcomes.

Assessment policy, practice and outcomes, each for its own particular reasons, can frequently be highly controversial. This can arise for a number of reasons. Firstly, teachers and schools can sometimes fear that they will be judged, unreasonably so, by the achievements, or more so the lack of achievements, of their students in public examinations. Secondly, difficulties can arise in informing parents on the achievements of their children. Such difficulties can be due to problems in understanding and interpreting the outcomes of tests and also to unrealistic expectations on the part of parents and their children. Thirdly, difficulties can arise due to the wide constituency that has an interest in the outcomes of assessment. Teachers, pupils, parents, school management, the Department of Education, further education institutions, employers and the general public all have an interest in the outcomes. Matching the findings of assessment and communicating them to the different interest groups can be problematic. Finally, difficulties can arise from the manner in which the findings of assessment can be presented, for example, by the media, and for political purposes. Policy and practice in this area have changed significantly over the past half-century. As already mentioned, the downturn in the economy led to an increased emphasis on the outputs of the school system and a renewed emphasis on examination performance. At the same time, increased participation levels by students in the school system up to the end of the post-primary cycle led to the need to provide a wider range of curricular and assessment practices, so as to cater for the broader range of student abilities and interests entering schools.

Assessment has many purposes. The findings are of interest to a wide range of audiences, each having its own particular interest in the outcomes. Its main purpose is to support teaching and learning by providing feedback to pupils and teachers on the progress of the students and to assist in planning the next stages of teaching and learning. This is generally known as 'formative assessment' and is based on various combinations of observation of pupils' performance in the classroom setting, homework, projects and short classroom tests. Thus, it can be seen as being contiguous with regular classroom activities. For the teacher, it requires well-developed skills in the areas of observation, test design and interpretation, record-keeping and reporting. For the pupil, it provides immediate feedback and, hopefully, motivation to tackle the next phase of learning. Assessment in this case is flexible both in its timing and in its focus, which can be on the individual pupil, specific groups in the class, or on the class as a whole. One of the main advantages of this form of assessment is its closeness to the teaching and learning activity, thereby affording the opportunity to provide immediate feedback to the learner and to chart the way forward for the next phase of learning, and, where necessary, to adapt pedagogical practices.

'Summative assessment' takes place at specific stages such as at the end of a course, term, school year or the end of a programme cycle. It can be based on a combination of teacher/class-based tests, projects, portfolios and externally-administered examinations. Unlike formative assessment, summative assessment typically occurs at the end of a programme and thus too late to provide feedback which can inform the teaching and learning for the students in question. However, the two forms are not mutually exclusive as classroom-based, teacher-led assessments, such as projects, practical work, oral and aural assessments, can also contribute to the final assessment, especially in the case of terminal examinations, while summative assessment data can inform both teaching, learning and programme development.

> " Assessment has many purposes. The findings are of interest to a wide range of audiences, each having its own particular interest in the outcomes. "

Assessment should not be an end in itself. Its main benefit lies in the uses that are made of the findings. A main purpose of assessment, particularly in the case of routine classroom assessment, is not just in observing students and administering tests but also in using the findings to provide meaningful feedback to learners and ensure that it is understood and acted upon in a manner that informs future learning. Monitoring trends in the achievement of students, particularly in the case of individual students, requires excellent record-keeping systems, not just for the benefit of the students concerned but also for their teachers as they advance through the system. Assessment outcomes not only provide feedback to students and their teachers; the findings also form an important source of information for school administration in building whole-school policies for sharing assessment data among school classes and year groups, and as a source for the development of school-improvement strategies. School policies and the outcomes of assessment are also of interest to the Inspectorate and to the DES in evaluating the effectiveness of the wider education system. Parents have an immediate and direct interest in the performance of their children and in this case, the reports of their school assessments form a basis for linking home and school in the learning progress. Elsewhere, assessment results, particularly summative assessments, are used as a basis for planning further study and by further education institutions in planning admission policies and programmes. Employers also have an interest in the certification provided on the basis of terminal examinations for employee selection purposes, while prospective parents use assessment findings as part of a strategy for the selection of schools for their children.

Although it may seem obvious that any one mode or technique of assessment cannot adequately capture the range of achievements of students, assessment reports are of interest to so many audiences that it can sometimes be difficult to change policies in this area, even when it is demonstrated that these changes are designed to improve the quality of education and the quality of the information which can be provided to the various audiences, particularly the students.

ASSESSMENT AT PRIMARY AND JUNIOR CYCLE

The abolition in 1967 of the Primary Certificate examination, which had had a significant negative influence on the implementation of the curriculum (Madaus, G. and Greaney, V, 1985), and the introduction of the new primary school curriculum in 1971, later updated in 1999, were significant policy decisions that supported new initiatives in teaching, learning and assessment. Up to this stage, assessment practices at primary level, apart from the terminal examination, were largely informal. As assessment practice was no longer dominated by a terminal external examination in Irish, English and Mathematics, schools were provided with greater latitude to concentrate on assessment strategies more closely geared to the on-going development of their pupils.

Assessment of this nature is described as having four main features: formative, summative, diagnostic and evaluative (NCCA, 2007, p.3). The discussion here is mainly limited to formative and summative assessments, as these are the forms more commonly used by teachers across the system. Formative assessment is defined by Black and William (quoted in Constant and Connolly, 2014, p.34) as:

> all those activities undertaken by teachers, and/or by their students to be used as feedback to modify the teaching and learning activities in which they are engaged.

It encompasses a wide range of techniques including teacher observation, discussions in the class, performance on homework, projects, portfolios, pupil self-assessment, and teacher-designed tests that are usually administered at the end of a section of a programme or at the end of the year. Formative assessment is an umbrella term embracing all those methods used in classrooms by teachers, and with this emphasis a new focus on two distinct but related concepts of assessment has come into focus: Assessment of Learning (AoL) and Assessment for Learning (AfL). The former relates to monitoring the on-going achievement of pupils throughout their schooling and the latter summing up the attainment reached at particular stages in the system (NCCA, 2007; Lysaght and O'Leary, 2013).

This new emphasis on assessment can be seen in the publication of guidelines on *Assessment in the Primary School Curriculum (NCCA, 2007)*, inspectors' reports on whole-school evaluations, and a number of surveys conducted at regular intervals by the INTO as well as other related publications. These have generated informed discussions on the implementation of assessment in schools. The NCCA publication mentioned above provides guidelines on all aspects of classroom assessment and, together with exemplars of related activities, forms an excellent resource for teachers and schools in framing policy and practices in this area. It also contains an important explanatory section on standardised testing which will be discussed hereunder. The INTO (1997, 2001, 2005, 2008, 2011, 2013) has also issued an important range of informative reports on various aspects of assessment, as well as teacher surveys of the implementation strategies being adopted in their classrooms.

Data derived from inspection reports and from the *Chief Inspector's Report 2010-2012* (DES, 2013a) confirm that post-primary schools use a range of assessment formats to monitor the progress of their students. Examples of good practice included setting regular homework, having common assessment tests where appropriate, administering written tests at various stages of the programme such as end of term and end of year, analysing stateexamination results, and keeping good records of students' progress (DES, 2013a, p. 77). Assessments based on subject inspections were reported as unsatisfactory in 23% of schools, while in some cases there was little evidence of assessment for learning and of providing formative feedback on students' work. The *Chief Inspector's Report* concluded (p.77) that there was a need for schools to make planned systematic provision for assessing students' learning and to use the findings to inform their teaching approaches.

The major focus on assessment at the Junior Cycle has been on the terminal examination that takes place at the end of the programme. This examination has been the subject of a number of official reviews and subsequent debates, although it might also be considered as the less important of the two terminal examinations that are administered at post-primary level in relation to decisions arrived at on the basis of the outcomes achieved. The Junior Certificate, which is currently being phased out, is assessed mainly by means of terminal written tests, and is externally designed, administered and analysed. These written tests can be supplemented by oral tests, practical tests, journals, reports, investigations; portfolios, project work and performance tests as appropriate for the subjects in question. However, practice is almost entirely based on the externally-administered written tests. A total of 60,247 candidates took this examination in 2016.

Madaus and McNamara (1970) conducted research on the validity and reliability of the ten most popular subjects at Leaving Certificate. They reported that the examination across all the subject areas mainly tested the recall of knowledge to the neglect of all other important skills and also had poor reliability. The findings had equal relevance for the Intermediate Certificate examination. Subsequent to the publication of this report, a grading system for reporting results was introduced, thus acknowledging the virtual impossibility of making such fine distinctions as those involved in reporting percentages.

Almost in tandem with the publication of the above report, a committee was established to examine the Form and Function of the Intermediate Certificate Examination. Initially, it was intended to review the examination system in isolation from the programme it was intended to assess. It was widely believed, though not officially stated, that the intention was to replace the essay-type examinations with the widespread use of objective tests, essentially on the basis of their reliability in scoring. Soon after it began its deliberations, the Committee incorporated a review of the curriculum

> " It was widely believed, though not officially stated, that the intention was to replace the essay-type examinations with the widespread use of objective tests, essentially on the basis of their reliability in scoring. "

structure in its discussions, as well as the other examination at this level - the Day Group Certificate. The report, which was published in 1975, recommended the abolition of the existing terminal examinations and their replacement by a system of school-based, teacher-led assessment, supported by a system of moderation, based on consortia of schools. Despite the fact that the Committee was established by the Department of Education and had conducted detailed research into the curriculum and examination system, the Department accepted the report with notable reluctance and its findings were never seriously considered.. The proposals for school-based assessment, together with the abolition of the public examination, were viewed by some of the stakeholders as being too elaborate and would lead to the diminution of existing standards. Nevertheless, a glorious opportunity was lost in not initiating a wider debate on the recommendations contained in the report. This could have brought to the fore many of the structural issues around the curriculum and assessment now being discussed and perhaps have resulted in at least some of the less controversial proposals being adopted. How much further on we could now be if that debate had taken place!

The Committee also recommended the establishment of a research project, The Public Examinations Evaluation Project (PEEP), with the brief of designing examinations that would test higher-level skills, exploring the potential of the large-scale use of objective tests rather than essay-type examinations, and involving teachers and school authorities in the assessment of their own pupils. This was to be accomplished through two subjects, History and Mathematics. An extensive programme of in-service education on the principles and techniques of assessment was organised for the teachers who volunteered to engage with the project. Thereafter, the respective subject teachers, having examined the objectives and content of the subjects, designed pilot tests that were later administered to pupils in the teachers' schools. This involved the application of a model of multiple-objective examining whereby appropriate assessment techniques were selected to match the objectives of the respective subjects. Combinations of objective tests, short-answer and long-answer items were used in each case, in addition to a project/personal topic in the case of History. Objective tests were limited to the testing of knowledge and comprehension, short-answer items to the testing of application, and essay type questions to testing analysis and synthesis.

Ideally, a project of this nature would require specially-designed programmes that would facilitate the development of the higher-level skills the project was expected to test and which it was believed were not being currently developed. However, this was not forthcoming and thus the potential impact of the project was limited. Nevertheless, a number of important outcomes were identified, not least in the provision of a comprehensive programme of in-service education on all aspects of assessment for the teachers, matching tests to specific objectives, and the involvement of the teachers in all aspects related to the design, administration and examining of the pilot tests. Although the project was established at the request of the ICE Committee in order to research some of the issues relating to the new system they were proposing, it did not wait for the findings of the research project before submitting its own report. The PEEP report suffered the same fate as its predecessor in that the Department reluctantly accepted the report but did not seriously engage with the findings (Heywood, McGuinness, and Murphy 1980).

> " The next phase in the reform process was the establishment of the Curriculum and Examinations Board (CEB) in January 1984. In this phase, the curriculum and examination systems were to be reviewed in tandem. "

The next phase in the reform process was the establishment of the Curriculum and Examinations Board (CEB) in January 1984. In this phase, the curriculum and examination systems were to be reviewed in tandem. This offered great promise. The CEB issued a number of key reports on a rationale and structure of a unified curriculum and an assessment system to match, involving the use of a broad range of assessment techniques and an element of school-based assessment with the involvement of the teachers in this process. The Board, through its publications and engagement in discussions with interested groups, generated lively interest and debates across the system on its proposals, and the feedback was both supportive and critical, especially in relation to the structure of the curriculum. However, the CEB was abolished in 1987 and replaced by the National Council for Curriculum and Assessment (NCCA) which, unlike its predecessor, was given an advisory role (Coolahan, B, (2014); Heywood, J. (2012); Hyland, A (2014b). Subsequently, both the Day Group and the Intermediate Certificates programmes and examinations were abolished in 1989 and replaced by a new Junior Certificate programme.

The NCCA undertook a review of the new Junior Certificate programme in 1993 and again reiterated the view that a system of assessment based solely on terminal written examinations served neither the curriculum it was intended to support, nor the students who took the examination. The narrow range of assessment modes and techniques, it was contended, discouraged the changes in methodologies required for the successful implementation of the curriculum objectives. However, little change emanated from this review (NCCA, 1993). The publication of *The Junior Cycle Review* (NCCA, 1999) again outlined the inadequacies of the current system of assessment, with its reliance on a narrow range of assessment techniques and terminal written examinations. However, this time the review did not fall on deaf ears. As Coolahan, B. (2014, p. 24) observes, a change of approach became evident on the part of the DES with the publication of a report on the Junior Certificate, in which the mismatch between the curriculum objectives and the system of assessment was acknowledged, and the use of a broader range of assessment techniques was proposed (DES, 2000). NCCA submitted its proposals for the reform of the programme to the DES(NCCA, 2011). Heywood (2012, p. 90) draws parallels between the ICE proposals and those of the NCCA, adding that the NCCA proposals were "a small step in the direction recommended by the Intermediate Certificate Committee". Based on his own experience as Director of PEEP and other projects, he concludes that the proposals "should raise the level of professionalism among teachers, and lead to the development of higher-order thinking."

Following on from the NCCA report, the DES published its own proposals, *A Framework for Junior Cycle* (DES, 2012c), in October 2012. In the introduction to the document, Minister Ruairi Quinn stated that a school-based model of assessment would replace the Junior Certificate Examination. While the Framework was based on the NCCA report *Towards a Framework* (NCCA, 2011), it proposed a somewhat different model of assessment that, it states (p.vi), "will include formative and summative assessments and involve schools and teachers in ongoing assessment and reporting of students' progress and achievements." In addition to the school-based model of assessment, the introduction from 2014 of standardised testing in English reading, Mathematics, and Irish reading in Irish-medium schools towards the end of second year, and of Science by 2016 was also proposed (p. vi). Certification would be limited to a minimum of eight subjects and a maximum of ten, with some minor modifications for students with special educational needs. Schools would be free to offer up to a maximum of four short courses, each equivalent to half a subject, in place of full subjects. Schools would also be provided with an assessment and moderation toolkit, and would be assisted by both the State Examinations Commission (SEC) and the NCCA in both the planning and assessment processes. In the initial years, it was proposed that the final assessment of subjects at the end of the cycle would be set by the SEC but administered and marked by the schools, while final assessments in the case of English, Mathematics and Irish would be administered and marked by the SEC. The school-based component (comprising a range of tasks including assignments, projects, performances, oral and aural skills, and practical tasks as appropriate for each subject) would receive a weighting of 40% and the final assessments 60%. The teachers in the school would mark the short courses.

The Framework represented a radical shift in policy by the DES, from dismissing all previous reviews dating back to the ICE report of 1975, to proposing a reform that embraced both the curriculum and assessment, and recognition of the limitations of terminal written examinations. The reform proposals could be said to represent a reasonable response to addressing the well-articulated and universally-agreed limitations of the existing system of assessment and at the same time a major change to an assessment system that had largely remained unchanged for decades. It was almost certain to be resisted. A move from a centrally-administered public examination system, in which teachers traditionally have had little or no involvement, to one in which they would play a major role in the assessment of the work of their own students for certification purposes, was more than likely to face stern opposition. Perhaps, it was a step too far, too soon, for a system that was unprepared for such a major overhaul of the assessment system. It could be argued, on the other hand, that the approach presented in the Framework at least alerted those concerned to the serious intent of the Department in implementing a long-overdue reform of the system and in this sense captured their engagement with the proposals. Perhaps, a more nuanced approach in which a phased introduction of the proposals leading to the end stage outlined by the DES might have had a better chance of acceptance. In effect, this is what emerged.

Following long and protracted discussions between the Department and the teacher unions, a way forward was agreed. Minister Jan O'Sullivan outlined "five immutable principles which must underpin any reform of the Junior Cycle." These included:

- The need to recognise a broad range of learning
- A requirement to considerably reduce the focus on one terminal examination as a means of assessing our students
- The necessity of giving prominence and importance to classroom-based assessment
- Greater professional collaboration between teachers to be a feature of our schools
- Both parents/guardians and students to get a broader picture of students' learning throughout the whole of Junior Cycle.

These principles were endorsed by the Department and representatives of the teacher unions in May 2015 and formed a basis for a ballot of trade union members (Teachers' Union of Ireland et al., 2015).

A revised and significantly modified plan, based on the outcome of the discussions with the teacher unions and endorsed by both parties, was published by the Department – *Framework for Junior Cycle 2015* (DES, 2015b). This radically reduced the involvement of the teachers and schools in the assessment process. "A dual approach to assessment, involving classroom-based assessment across the three years and a final externally-assessed, state-certified examination" (p. 35) in each subject was proposed. Two classroom-based assessments (CBA) are specified in the document, the first to be taken towards the end of the second year and the second in the third year. The tasks to be covered are the same as those in the original proposal. Following the second CBA, the students will be required to prepare an Assessment Task (AT), a reflective exercise linked to the second CBA and demonstrating an acknowledgement of the knowledge and skills developed during the second CBA. This will be submitted to the SEC for marking and will account for 10% of the final assessment, with the external examination accounting for the remaining 90%.

Plans for the phased introduction of the new system were also included in the Joint Statement by representatives of DES and ASTI in May 2015, as well as the provision of a significant allocation of additional professional time for schools and teachers to support them in the implementation of the new system. The timetable for phasing in the new system, as well as details on the supports to be made available to the schools, were included in Circular 0024/2016 titled *Arrangements for the Implementation of the Framework for the Junior Cycle with particular reference to the school years 2015/16 and 2016/17,* (DES, 2016a). In addition to the above, a new mandatory Well-being programme, which will include short courses in SPHE, PE and CSPE, wasincluded in the Junior Cycle programme. The new system was introduced in 2016, when the first phase of classroom-based assessments was implemented.

> " While the 2015 Framework is a major deviation from the original 2012 proposals, it can also be seen as a more realistic way forward in the short term and hopefully representing a phased approach directed towards a more comprehensive reform of the examination system as outlined in the 2012 proposals. "

While the 2015 Framework is a major deviation from the original 2012 proposals, it can also be seen as a more realistic way forward in the short term and hopefully representing a phased approach directed towards a more comprehensive reform of the examination system as outlined in the 2012 proposals. Following a ballot conducted by the two post-primary teacher unions, the proposals were endorsed by one union and rejected by the second. A further ballot of ASTI members in January 2017 brought a further rejection. The impasse continues, leaving doubts whether a large number of students will have the opportunity to complete the Junior Cycle assessments in 2016-17.

STANDARDISED ASSESSMENTS AT PRIMARY AND JUNIOR CYCLE

Introducing standardised assessments to a system can be controversial and, in the main, this depends on the purposes for which they are used. According to Shiel et al. (2010, p. 67), they can serve three main purposes: to support teachers' assessments of the work of their students; to provide information on standards of achievement nationally; and to provide information on standards of achievements internationally. When, however, the results of such tests are used solely for accountability purposes, such as in developing and publishing league tables of schools and consequent competition, they can have detrimental consequences in narrowing teaching and learning to what the tests purport to measure. Ireland participates in a range of standardised tests, both nationally and internationally, and happily, the findings reported are used to best effect to support and promote the achievement of students and to consider any strengths or weaknesses identified in the programmes being offered.

There is a long-standing practice in Ireland in conducting national surveys of attainment at primary level in English reading and Mathematics (INTO, 2001, DES, 2012a). Four surveys of reading standards in English were conducted by the Teachers Study Group among a sample of Dublin primary school pupils between 1964 and 1974 (INTO, 2001. pp. 25:26). The Curriculum Unit in the Department of Education, in conjunction with the Educational Research Centre (ERC), Drumcondra, also conducts surveys of Reading

> " Introducing standardised assessments to a system can be controversial and, in the main, this depends on the purposes for which they are used. "

Literacy and Mathematics at primary level on a regular basis. International assessments of Reading Literacy, Mathematics and Science at both primary and post-primary levels have been conducted. The *Progress in International Reading Literacy Study* (PIRLS) survey takes place every five years and is conducted under the auspices of the International Association for the Evaluation of Educational Achievement (IEA). Ireland took part in PIRLS for the first time in 2011. *Trends in International Mathematics and Science Study* (TIMSS), also conducted under the auspices of IEA, surveys achievement in Mathematics and Science every four years and was first conducted in 1995. The *Programme for International Student Assessment* (PISA), conducted under the auspices of the Organisation for Economic and Cultural Development (OECD), assesses achievements in Reading

Literacy, Mathematics and Science every three years since 2000. The ERC, in addition to managing the administration of the various surveys, also provides a most valuable and professional service in preparing and issuing detailed reports on how students in Ireland perform on the various assessment surveys. In considering the findings of standardised tests, or indeed any other tests of achievement, it is important to bear in mind that any single test result only provides a limited picture of achievement and needs to be interpreted against other test findings and the context in which they are conducted. However, analysing the outcomes of assessments conducted over a number of cycles of the same survey programme can be useful in tracing trends in achievements over time. In the interests of coherence and in order to facilitate comparisons between studies, assessments conducted at primary level are grouped together, and similarly those at post-primary level. In so doing, differences in all aspects relating to the design and administration of the various assessment programmes should be borne in mind when comparing outcomes.

(a) Standardised Assessment at Primary Level

In this section, we explore the main findings of national assessments in Reading Literacy and Mathematics (Shiel et. al., 2014; Kavanagh et. al., 2015); DES, 2016f), international assessments in Reading Literacy, PIRLS, (Eivers et al., 2012), and Mathematics and Science, TIMSS, (Clerkin et al., 2016).

(a1) Reading Literacy Attainments at Primary Level

The National Assessment conducted in 2014 reported improved outcomes in Second Class compared with the previous assessment in 2009. Significant improvements were reported in reading vocabulary, reading comprehension and on 'retrieve, infer, integrate and interpret process' subscales, while improvements were also noted at both the lower level (Proficiency Level 1) and the higher levels (Levels 3 & 4). A similar pattern emerged at Sixth Class. Compared with the 2009 findings, improvements were noted across all proficiency levels and content areas, with the exception of the 'examine and exclude' subscale, where less progress was reported.

Significant improvements were also reported in DEIS schools, but no reduction in the gap between these schools and other schools. With the exception of Second Class in Band 2 schools, a large number of struggling readers was noted in DEIS urban schools, with 44% in Second Class and 47% in Sixth Class performing at or below Level 1. In the overall study, girls in Second Class significantly outperformed boys and in Sixth Class, but not significantly so in this case.

The PIRLS 2011 assessment of reading in South Class showed Ireland performing very well, with a mean score significantly above the international average and in 10th place overall. While Ireland's score was only marginally lower that of the four countries immediately above it, it was significantly lower than that of the top five countries. Ireland also performed well on the benchmarks set for the study, with more than half reaching the higher benchmark and a lower percentage falling below the lower benchmark. As in the national assessment, girls outperformed boys.

(a2) Mathematics Attainments at Primary Level

In the 2014 National Assessment, performances at both Second and Sixth Classes were higher than in a previous assessment in 2009. Significant increases at Second Class were found on three of the four main content areas and all five process areas. No significant improvement was found on the 'data content' area. Improvements were also noted across all proficiency levels. Significant increases at Sixth Class level were noted across all content areas and all proficiency levels. In the case of DEIS schools, while improvements were noted, especially in Second Class in Band 2 schools, improvements have only kept pace with those of pupils in other schools. Boys in both classes outperformed girls, but in neither case was the difference significant.

In the most recent TIMSS survey conducted in 2015, Fourth Class primary pupils achieved a score of 547, which was significantly above the TIMMS centre point average, and ranked ninth among 49 countries. This was a significantly higher score than that recorded in 1995 or 2011, and an improvement in ranking from 17th out of 50 countries in 2011. Improvement in performance has also been made across the three assessment cycles among the 'below-average' and the 'above-average' range, with much of the improvement appearing to have occurred since 2011 and among the 'lowest-achieving' pupils. Relative strengths were noted in the content area of Number and relative weaknesses in Geometric Shape and Measures. In the cognitive domain, strengths in Knowing and Weaknesses in Reasoning were recorded. No significant gender differences were noted.

(a3) Science Attainments at Primary Level

A score of 529, significantly above the centre point average, was recorded in the 2015 TIMSS survey, and ranked Ireland's pupils 19th out of 47 countries, significantly higher than reported in 1995 and 2011. Substantial improvement was found among the 'lowest-achieving' group and a small disimprovement among the 'highest-achieving' pupils. Earth Science was a particular strength in the 'content' area, and Physical Science a weaknesses, while broadly similar performances were found across the three cognitive domains of 'knowing, applying and reasoning'. No significant gender differences were noted.

(b) Standardised Assessments at Junior Cycle

Ireland has participated in two international standardised surveys of achievement - TIMSS and PISA - at Junior Cycle level over a number of cycles. TIMMS, already referred to in the context of primary assessment, conducts surveys of achievement in Mathematics and Science among students mainly in the Second Year of the Junior Cycle. Ireland participated in the first international survey in 1995. The most recent survey was conducted in 2015 and the findings presented here are based on a report published by the ERC (Clerkin et al., 2016).

The aim of PISA is to measure how well students at age 15 are prepared to meet the challenges they may encounter in future life. PISA conducts an international assessment of the skills and knowledge of

15-year-old students in Mathematics, Reading Literacy and Science. It is conducted under the auspices of the OECD and takes place in three-yearly cycles beginning in 2000. In each cycle, one subject area/domain becomes the main focus of the assessment; the other two are 'minor domains'. Reading Literacy was the main focus in 2000 and 2009, Mathematics in 2003 and 2012, and Science in 2006 and 2015. In reviewing PISA surveys, it should be noted that the 2009 survey differed considerably from all other cycles in finding significant declines in achievement in both Reading Literacy and Mathematics, most notably in Reading, both in Ireland and in other participating countries. A number of aspects of that survey have been extensively analysed by Perkins et al., 2012; Cosgrave et al., 2010, and Cosgrave, 2015, in which it is stated that the extent of the decline has been exaggerated. These include demographic and curricular changes, administration issues, lower engagement by students, changes in assessment specifications, and issues concerning the estimation of PISA achievement scores within and across cycles.

> ❝
> The aim of PISA is to measure how well students at age 15 are prepared to meet the challenges they may encounter in future life.
> ❞

The most recent analysis of the performances of Irish students in PISA surveys is based on the 2015 assessment. In that year, Science was the main domain assessed and Reading and Mathematics were minor domains. In 2015, PISA changed from print-based to computer-based testing. The ERC conducted an analysis of the performances of students in Ireland and this summary of findings is based on its report authored by Shiel et al., 2016.

(b1) Reading Attainments at Junior Cycle

In the 2015 PISA assessment, Ireland achieved a mean score significantly above the OECD average and was ranked third out of 35 OECD countries and fifth among all participating countries/economies. Only Singapore had a significantly higher score than Ireland. Just one in ten of students in Ireland compared with one in twenty across the OECD performed at the lowest level of reading proficiency (Level 2), while the proportion performing at the highest level (Levels 5 & 6) was marginally higher than the corresponding OECD average. As with the two other domains, the range of achievement was significantly narrower than the OECD average. Further gains in Reading Literacy in Ireland can be achieved through improvement in the proportion of students performing at the highest level.

Female students significantly outperformed males. The difference of 12 score points is among the lowest across comparison countries. The gap in gender differences in Ireland in favour of females narrowed from 28.5 score points in 2012 compared with 12.0 in 2015 as a result of fewer female students performing at Levels 5 & 6.

(b2) Mathematics Attainments at Junior Cycle

In the 2015 TIMSS survey of achievement a score of 523, significantly above the TIMSS centre point average, was recorded and ranked Ireland's students ninth out of 49 countries. The performance of the 'lowest-achieving' students improved between the two cycles of 1995 and 2015, while that of the 'highest-performing' students showed a small dis-improvement. Relative strengths in the Content areas of Number and Data and Chance and weaknesses in Algebra and Geometry were noted. In the Cognitive domain, a relative strength was recorded in Knowing and a weakness in Applying. Ireland's performance in Mathematics has not significantly changed since 1995. Compared with 1995, a slight increase of three percentage points was noted at the Lower and Intermediate benchmarks and no change at the Higher and Advanced benchmarks. In all cases, the changes were not statistically significant. No significant gender differences were found.

In the 2015 PISA survey, students in Ireland achieved a mean score of 503.7, significantly above the corresponding OECD average and ranked 13th out of 35 OECD countries and 18th out of all participating countries/economies. Singapore significantly outperformed all other countries, while fourteen countries significantly outperformed Ireland. The range of achievement in Ireland is significantly narrower in comparison with the OECD average. In Ireland, the performance of students at the lower level (Level 2) was greater than that of the corresponding OECD average (15.0% v. 23.4%), while at the higher levels (Levels 5 & 6), the corresponding proportions were 9.8% and 10.7%. In short, lower-performing students do well relative to their OECD counterparts, while higher-performing do less well.

> " In the 2015 PISA survey, students in Ireland achieved a mean score of 503.7, significantly above the corresponding OECD average and ranked 13th out of 35 OECD countries and 18th out of all participating countries/economies. "

Male students in Ireland significantly outperformed females by 16.1 points. This is a larger difference than the corresponding OECD average, which is also in favour of male students. The performances of males and females below Level 2 are broadly similar (14.1% and 15.8%) and much lower than the OECD averages of 23.0% and 23.7%, while that of male students in Ireland at Levels 5 & 6 is higher than that of females (12.4% and 6.5%).

(b3) Science Attainments at Junior Cycle

In the TIMSS 2015 survey, a mean score of 530, significantly above the centre point, was recorded and placed the performance of Ireland's students 10tham among 39 countries. In the Content areas, relative strengths were noted in Biology and Earth Science and weaknesses in Physics and Chemistry.

Performances were relatively similar across the three Cognitive areas except for a small weakness in Knowing. Increases in the percentages of students across all four benchmarks were noted compared with 1995, but these were only statistically significant at the Intermediate level. As in other subject areas, 'lower-achieving' students performed relatively well and 'higher-achieving' students somewhat poorer when compared with their counterparts in other countries. No significant gender differences were found.

Science was a major assessment domain in the PISA 2015 survey. Students in Ireland achieved a mean score of 503, significantly above the OECD average, and ranked Ireland 13th among all OECD countries and 19thamong all 45 participating countries. This represented a small but non-significant drop of six score points compared with 2006, the last year in which Science was a major domain, and compares with an OECD drop of five points. Ireland's mean score dropped by 19 score points between 2012 and 2015, compared with an OECD average of eight points. Twelve of the top countries in 2012 also had significantly lower scores in 2015. The introduction of computer-based testing and the inclusion of new items, including those linked to interactive visual experiments have been suggested as reasons for this decline.

The range of achievement of students in Ireland is much narrower than that of the corresponding OECD average. Ireland has fewer lower-achieving students at 15% students (below Level 2) compared with the OECD average of 21%, while the percentage of higher-achieving students is the same as the OECD average but well below that of the a number of higher-achieving countries. Ireland's mean score on all three competency subscales and on the Content Knowledge and Procedural and Epistemic subscales were all above the corresponding OECD averages. Male students outperformed females by 10.5 score points. The corresponding OECD average was 3.5 points. This represents a reversal of performances in 2006 when female students outperformed males by a non-significant 0.4 score points. While similar proportions of both male and female students performed below Level 2 in 2015, a greater percentage of males than females performed at or above Level 5. Possible reasons for this decline have already been noted.

REVIEW OF PERFORMANCE PATTERNS AT PRIMARY & JUNIOR CYCLE

(a) Performance Patterns at Primary Level

As already stated, the abolition of the Primary School Certificate examination and two revisions of the curriculum (with another in prospect) have re-focused attention on the role of assessment in schools, with considerable emphasis now being placed on linking instruction, learning and assessment policies into a coherent process, and monitoring pupil outcomes at every stage in the system. In-school assessment practices incorporating both Assessment of Learning (AoL) and Assessment for Learning (AfL), and the increasing use of standardised testing both by the schools themselves and through involvement with PIRLS, TIMSS and the National Assessments in Reading Literacy and Mathematics conducted at regular intervals by the ERC on behalf of the DES, ensure that primary schools have access to a large body of achievement data upon which to guide both their teaching and learning practices. However, conducting assessment should not be seen as an end in itself; it is merely a means to a much more important consideration. The real benefits arise when assessment findings are used to provide meaningful feedback to the learners, and to improve teaching and learning both within the school and across the wider system. For all of this to happen, as has been noted in the *Chief Inspector's Report 2010-2012* and other inspection reports, teachers need to be supported with regular in-career development opportunities on all aspects of assessment theory and practice.

Research conducted by the INTO would indicate that teachers use a variety of assessment tools, including traditional classroom observation, questioning of pupils, participation in class by pupils, homework, teacher-designed tests and a range of standardised tests (INTO, 2001). Lysaght and O'Leary (2013) trialled an instrument designed to audit teachers' use of Assessment of Learning (AoL) among a sample of primary school teachers. They found that AoL practices were at an early stage of implementation and required further development before they are embedded in classrooms. Constant and Connolly (INTO, 2014) also conducted research on the introduction of formative assessment practices in a mainstream primary school over an eight-week period. An important feature of the research was that the students were formally introduced into formative assessment instruction, a factor that may have had a significant positive impact on the outcomes reported. The authors concluded that the students benefitted significantly from the experience, becoming more engaged, autonomous and motivated learners.

Inspection reports indicate that the majority of schools have policies on assessment that influence and encapsulate the approaches taken by the teachers at individual classroom level. However, some concerns were raised about practices in a number of schools. More generally, the communication of assessment data within the school as pupils move upwards in the system is a feature that, it is stated, could be strengthened. An Inspectors' report (DES, 2010, pp.1, 9,12) on the teaching and learning of English and Mathematics in primary schools found that the learning experiences and learning outcomes were satisfactory in the vast majority (85%) of lessons evaluated (803 lessons in English and 527 in Mathematics were evaluated). Serious issues were identified in assessment practices in one third of the lessons (ibid, pp. 6, 9). What is even more striking and more serious is the strong link found between assessment practices and pupil learning outcomes. In three quarters of classes with satisfactory pupil outcomes, assessment practices were also judged satisfactory. On the other hand, in over three quarters of classes with unsatisfactory pupil outcomes, assessment practices were also unsatisfactory. In effect, it would seem that a significant proportion of pupils were doubly disadvantaged. The report concludes (p.16) that there is scope for the development of assessment practices in primary schools. Similar findings on assessment are included in the *Chief Inspector's Report 2010-2012* (DES, 2013a) where it is stated that the use of assessments to guide instruction was also found to be particularly challenging in one third of the Irish lessons observed (p.51).

Participation in both national and international surveys of attainment provides another perspective on achievement at this level. These surveys confirm that there are positive indicators of improvements in both Reading Literacy and Mathematics at primary level as evidenced in the most recent National Attainment survey of Second and Sixth Classes. Significant improvements were reported in Reading Vocabulary and Comprehension for both class groups and in all the process areas, but less so in the case of Examine and Evaluate. A similar pattern emerged for Mathematics where significant increases were reported for Second Class in all areas except for the Data content area, and for all content and process areas at Sixth Class. On the basis of the above findings, the targets set for 2020 in literacy and numeracy for both Second and Sixth Classes

> " Inspection reports indicate that the majority of schools have policies on assessment that influence and encapsulate the approaches taken by the teachers at individual classroom level. "

have already been met. However, Shiel et al. (2014, p. 40) add a note of caution in relation to the relatively large increases reported in this survey and add that the norms for the existing tests may overestimate pupil performances and may not be suitable for setting targets. They suggest that tests at this level may need to be re-normed. A follow-up report examining factors associated with the main findings of the assessments raises issues with the broad range of purposes for which standardised test results are currently being used. It is also recommended that there is a need to separate the evaluative purposes of the tests, such as in submitting aggregated results to the DES,and the use of the same test results to monitor progress and plan future teaching. In addition to re-norming current tests, separate tests need to be developed for monitoring progress and guiding future teaching (Kavanagh, et. al, 2015, pp. xxii–xxiii).

In the 2015 TIMSS survey, a significantly higher mean score and an improvement in ranking was recorded in the case of Mathematics. An improved performance among the 'below-average' and 'above- average' pupils was noted in the case of this subject. Improvements have also been noted in the case of Science, with again substantial improvement among the 'lowest-achieving' pupils and little change in the performance of the higher-ranking group. There is still some scope for improvement in both subjects in the case of higher-achieving students and in the content areas, particularly in Geometry and Physics. There was no equivalent PIRLS reading survey conducted in Ireland prior to 2011 on which comparisons could be made. Equally impressive performance was also noted for Science, with students performing significantly above the international average on the overall test.

Primary schools are also required to conduct standardised assessments at Second, Fourth and Sixth Classes, and to submit the findings to the Inspectorate. We are informed that there is total compliance with this request. Inspectors consult the findings as part of the background data when conducting school evaluations. In this way, shortfalls in policy and practice are identified and appropriate action advised. Follow-up inspections then can find if the appropriate action has been taken. An improvement in the transfer of assessment data at the transition phase to post-primary school (with the support of guidelines provided by the NCCA) has been reported. This should enable a smoother transition to this level, although there is little evidence to indicate how well the data are used to ease the transition and plan instruction at this early stage in the new schools.

(b) Performance Patterns at Junior Cycle

At post-primary level, assessment practices were judged to be satisfactory or better in the majority of schools. Examples of good practice included the maintenance of good records, ongoing monitoring of pupils' progress, and analysis of state examination results. However, practices were deemed unsatisfactory in almost one quarter of the schools (DES, 2013a, p.77).

The main focus on assessment at Junior Cycle level has largely been on the public examination held at the end of the programme. Over the period under review, some success has been achieved in broadening the range of assessment modes and thereby reducing total reliance on the end-of-cycle terminal written examinations, and with this, a redistribution, if not a reduction, in the stress experienced by the candidates. However, these changes have been modest and the terminal written examination has remained the dominant mode of assessment. For many years, going back to the mid-1970s, the Department of Education was reluctant to entertain change proposals, even though it established the Intermediate Certificate Examination Committee, the Public Examinations Evaluation Project, and the Curriculum and Examinations Board to examine the system of assessment and propose reforms. It is interesting to speculate the benefits that could have been gained if the current reform proposals were taken on board and seriously considered at a much earlier stage. Now, when the DES is actively promoting and supporting reforms, resistance has emerged from other sectors, more especially from representatives of those with ultimate responsibility for implementation. As a result, in the case of the Junior Cycle, progress has been painfully slow and revised reform proposals, after protracted negotiations, are modest and far removed from those originally proposed by the NCCA and thereafter by the DES. It is generally accepted that reform is necessary if congruence is to be established across the curriculum, and a range of assessment modes, including various forms of coursework assessment

> " The main focus on assessment at Junior Cycle level has largely been on the public examination held at the end of the programme. "

as befits each subject specification, is to be incorporated into a revised system of assessment. However, obtaining agreement on the implementation of reforms has proved a stumbling block, with teachers reluctant to accept a greater role and responsibility in assessing the work of their own students for the purposes of certification. This has resulted in an almost total reliance on the centralised administration of the examination and much less emphasis on school-based, teacher-led assessment.

The overall performance of Irish post-primary students in PISA surveys of assessment is quite impressive. Students consistently score at or above the international averages. This is especially so in Reading Literacy where the students are ranked high in the upper ranges in the respective surveys. A consistent finding across all PISA surveys in the case of Ireland is the narrow range of achievement across the entire distribution of scores. This is a consistent finding across the various surveys and compares unfavourably with the performances of the highest-achieving countries. While the performance of the lower-achieving students in Ireland is commendable and significantly above the relevant OECD averages, that of the highest-achieving students is only marginally above the comparable OECD averages. There is considerable scope for improvement in raising the achievement of students at the highest levels. The narrowing of the gender gap in Reading Literacy compared with earlier PISA surveys is to be welcomed, although the drop in the proportion of female students performing at the higher levels may explain some of these gains. The situation in Mathematics, although impressive, is somewhat more problematic when compared with Reading Literacy, with performance at the higher levels proving to be particularly challenging, as well as some specific areas of content. The findings for Science have been more encouraging and have been consistently positive ever since 2000 but more especially in later surveys. However, considerable scope exists for improving performances at the higher levels and in some content areas such as Physics and Chemistry.

A recently-published *Action Plan for Education: 2016-2019* (DES, 2016j) has set targets to be achieved between now and 2025. At primary level, these include reducing the gap with the top European countries in areas of Numeracy and Science, as well as that between lower-achieving students in DEIS and non-DEIS schools in Numeracy and Literacy. At post-primary level, the main focus is centred on improving achievements at the higher levels in Reading Literacy, Science and Mathematics and decreasing the proportions at or below level 2 in the case of Mathematics and Science. While these targets are consistent with the various survey findings, a note of caution is added in relation to the possible consequences of competing for the top-rank places in international assessment surveys. Pressures to compete at this level could unwittingly lead to an undue focus on the narrow range of skills included in these surveys, to the exclusion of other equally important areas of development that schools seek to promote. In this context, Professor Klenowski, at a recent Education Forum in Maynooth University (Klenowski, 2016), noted that Singapore, which consistently scores among the top five countries in PISA assessment surveys, has now found that the development of key skills beyond those included in the surveys has been neglected in their system, due to the pressures to remain competitive at the top level, and is now tending to reverse this trend.

Despite the reservations that may be held about the potential negative impact of standardised assessments, the evidence shows that they can identify particular strengths and weaknesses in the programmes provided in schools, as well as international comparisons of the standards being reached in the system. Happily, policy in Ireland in relation to participation in such tests and to the uses being made of the findings has ensured that they do not unnecessarily dominate the work in schools, while at the same time providing a valuable external perspective on the achievements of our students. The primary system is adequately served with appropriate programmes of standardised assessments but the same cannot be said for the Junior Cycle. A National Standardised Assessment in English reading and Mathematics at this level, so as to monitor trends in achievement, has been proposed (DES, 2012a, p, vi), but so far has not implemented. This has particular relevance in view of the changes proposed for the Junior Certificate, as Shiel et al. (2010, pp.98: 99) indicate that possible grade inflation has been evident in the Junior Certificate examination when compared with relevant PISA findings. How much more likely is this to happen when the Junior Cycle reform proposals are fully implemented? Looking to the future, it is hoped that the decision to launch the literacy and numeracy initiative in 2011 (DES, 2011a), and which already may be making an early impact, will make a significant contribution towards further progress in these areas.

LOOKING AHEAD

Debate and reform of assessment policy and practice has become increasingly common across education systems. Considerable emphasis is now being placed on linking instruction, learning and assessment policy into a coherent process. This forms an important dimension in the formation of school planning policies. Certain basic principles, supported by developments in the theory and practice of assessment, emerge from these reforms and should be borne in mind when developing assessment policy and practices. In the first instance and most importantly, every effort should be made to assess that which we really value in our students rather than that which can be more easily measured. Assessment policy and practices should be congruent with the subject/curriculum aims and objectives. Assessment should serve the curriculum, not dominate it. Assessment findings are defined in time, in that they provide an estimate of performance at a particular juncture and in a specific context. This does not define the achievement beyond the particular time the test has been taken and should not be deemed as a final judgement on the ability and potential of the learner.

The two most important considerations in framing policy in this area are validity and reliability. Achieving absolute values in these variables is neither realistic nor possible. Yet, every effort should be made to achieve the highest measures in both cases. Of the two, validity is the more important, for a test that has poor validity, in that it does not adequately sample the content and objectives of a subject, has no relevance and its findings should be dismissed. On the other hand, a test that has poor reliability should also be discarded, as performance will fluctuate over repeated administrations of the test and thus fail to provide a reliable estimate of performance. As course specifications become more detailed, it is apparent that no one mode or technique of assessment can adequately capture the essence of intended outcomes. Rather, a combination of modes, each designed to test specific outcomes, is necessary in order to match learning experiences with appropriate assessment techniques. The limitations involved in total dependence on written, end of programme/cycle examinations are well documented, especially in the case where a range of outcomes, particularly higher-level skills, is included. It is at this stage that the advantages of a variety of forms of coursework assessment come into play.

Conducting assessments should not be seen as an end in itself. The most important benefits derive from the decisions that are made on the basis of the findings. These should be communicated to the various groups who have a direct interest in the outcomes. Assessment findings should be seen first and foremost as a service for the learner. The results should be communicated to the learner in a manner that will indicate strengths and weaknesses and help direct future learning. However, provision of feedback is not unproblematic. It is important to ensure in the first place that the feedback provided is valid, understood and accepted, and that appropriate action is taken by the learner to implement the findings. There is some evidence in inspectors' reports to indicate that the outcomes of assessment are not being shared widely enough and used to best effect to improve student learning and promote school and system effectiveness.

The involvement of the teachers in the assessment of their own pupils is widely confirmed and accepted. This is based on the belief that the classroom/subject teacher is best placed to observe and record the achievements of their students over an extended period of time and in their natural settings. An important advantage of teacher-led assessment is its closeness to the teaching/learning activity and thereby the opportunity to offer immediate feedback so that, where necessary, corrective action can be taken and the next phase of learning planned.

> " Conducting assessments should not be seen as an end in itself. The most important benefits derive from the decisions that are made on the basis of the findings. "

Primary schools are well served with a variety of complementary assessment modes, combining the advantages of internal-led assessment with a variety of standardised assessments. Various inspectors' reports indicate that the majority of primary schools have good assessment systems in place. Both the NCCA (2007) and the INTO (1997; 2001; 2005; 2008; 2011; 2013) have provided a range of excellent publications on assessment for the teachers, while the INTO also provides periodic surveys of teachers' practices in conjunction with their annual conferences. In addition, reports by the Inspectorate provide valuable data on the implementation of policy across the system. Evidence based on a range of standardised tests of achievement confirm that the standards in Reading Literacy, Mathematics and Science in Irish primary schools compare favourably with their international counterparts, consistently scoring at or above the international averages. However, pupils tend to underperform at the higher levels.

It is reported that a significant number of the primary school classes inspected have deficiencies in the implementation of assessment policy, and it is shown that in over three quarters of these classes unsatisfactory pupil outcomes were also noted. This vividly illustrates the interrelationship between teaching, learning and assessment so that where one component is found to be unsatisfactory the probability is that all three are problematic. We are informed, on the basis of follow-up inspectors' reports, that these deficiencies have now been rectified. We are, however, largely dependent on inspectors' reports on the functioning of assessment policy in schools. Apart from some small-scale research, much of which is conducted by post-graduate students, there is a notable dearth of more extended long-range, detailed investigations into the practices engaged by teachers in schools. Such research can provide examples of good practice that can be shared more widely, as well as issues surrounding implementation. The need for continuous upgrading of teachers' skills on all aspects of conducting assessments, as emphasised both in inspectors' reports and by the INTO, is also essential in order to ensure that the teachers are adequately supported in this crucial area of curriculum development and implementation.

Different challenges and opportunities arise at post-primary level. The demands of the terminal examination at the end of the Junior Cycle have understandably, if unfortunately, to a large degree influenced the range of assessments in use at this level. Inspectors' reports would indicate that the main techniques in operation include various tests, largely influenced by the techniques used in the state examination, and administered at various stages throughout the year, at the end of a section of a programme, at the end of term and

> " It is now generally accepted that the Junior Certificate examination in its current form no longer serves the curriculum. "

at the end of the year. Standardised tests of achievement are also administered as part of the PISA international surveys of attainment.

It is now generally accepted that the Junior Certificate examination in its current form no longer serves the curriculum. Moreover, it has also been generally acknowledged, as far back as the ICE report of 1975, that this is not a high-stakes examination as very few, if any, critical decisions are made on the basis of the outcomes. The need to introduce a range of coursework assessments as appropriate for each subject specification is also acknowledged. Unfortunately, reluctance is evident in situations where teachers are required to accept responsibility for assessing the work of their own students for the purposes of certification. Thus, as the current reform proposals indicate, the terminal written examination remains as the main mode of assessment. The allocation of a mere 10% to a school-based assignment is unlikely to capture the serious engagement of many of the students, particularly those less motivated, who may deem it a minor contribution to the overall grade in a subject. Achieving a more substantial element of a school-based, teacher-led assessment system remains one of the main challenges to be addressed in reforming the system.

Reform of the Junior Certificate examination has its own unique challenges. As policy moves away from total reliance on terminal written tests to a more balanced system, as suggested in the DES 2012 reform proposals, the requirement to maintain the integrity of the examination system is paramount, and this depends in no small degree on the systems put in place to ensure the validity, reliability and practicality of the assessment process. Devolving the main responsibilities for the administration of the examination to the teachers in the schools requires putting in place a robust system of external moderation so that standards can be monitored across the system. This is also important for the overall credibility of the system for all intended users, and for the protection of the teachers who are involved in the process. The engagement of the teachers in external moderation procedures can also form a very important component in sharing their experiences and in the continual updating of their skills in assessment.

Credibility also depends on the competence and commitment of those charged with conducting assessment. To a certain degree the reluctance of teachers to accept responsibility for assessing the work of their own students for certification purposes is understandable, if account is taken of the inadequate preparation of teachers, until recently, both at pre-service and in-service levels, on all aspects of assessment policy and practice. Appropriate development opportunities in this area can give teachers the expertise, the experience and, equally important, the confidence to play a more significant role in the assessment of their own pupils, up to and including certificate level. It can also give them the confidence to share the outcomes with other groups and, where appropriate, to defend, as befits their professional status, the judgements they make.

For this reason, it is important that appropriate and regular development opportunities be made available for the teachers on all aspects of assessment theory and practice, as well on the application to specific subject areas. This is an essential requirement for the success of the reforms. The extension of initial teacher education programmes offers additional opportunities to provide student teachers with the appropriate skills in assessment theory and practice, while the extended period of school experience will also enable them to observe and to contribute to the formulation and application of school policies in this area. Elsewhere, institutes of teacher education, education centres and subject associations are all well placed to make a substantial contribution to the provision of appropriate in-service programmes for teachers already in the system. The introduction of an appropriate system of moderation, together with adequate in-service support, should also enable teachers to gain the competence and confidence required to undertake a more central role in the examining process.

Designing new models of assessment and planning for their implementation in schools is an important first stage in the reform process. How well schools and teachers understand and adapt their practices to accommodate the new requirements can vary, both within and across schools. It is at this stage that policies can succeed or fail. For this reason,it is important that a range of research initiatives, both small- and large-scale, be planned in order to monitor on a regular basis the implementation and impact of assessment policies across the system. In the context of any reform of the assessment system, the earlier proposal in 2012 to introduce national standardised assessments in Reading Literacy and Mathematics should, for the reasons already stated, be activated so as to monitor trends in achievement standards.

> " "
> The introduction of an appropriate system of moderation, together with adequate in-service support, should also enable teachers to gain the competence and confidence required to undertake a more central role in the examining process.
> " "

A public information system needs to be put in place for parents, parent councils and the general public outlining the rationale and structure of the new assessment policy so that the innovation can be understood and supported across the system by all interested groups. Boards of Management, in particular, have an important role in supporting change proposals.

While current proposals for the introduction of the new assessment system are very modest, they at least represent an important first stage in the reform process. Hopefully, as experience of the new forms of assessment grows, will lead to the full implementation as outlined in the Department's initial reform proposals in 2012, albeit with the addition of adequate external moderation. This will finally bring into play an assessment system that can better serve the aims of the curriculum and the needs of the students.

CHAPTER FIVE ● ● ● ● ● ● ● ● ● ● ● ● ● ● ● ● ● ●

Transition from Second Level to Higher Education

INTRODUCTION

This chapter will focus on the transition of students from second to third-level education. It will outline the processes used by higher education institutions in Ireland to select school leavers and will discuss the central role of the Leaving Certificate in the process. It will trace the growth of the Central Applications Office (CAO) and the development of the Points system, and will discuss possible alternative selection mechanisms, taking account of international experience.

TRANSITION TO HIGHER EDUCATION

The proportion of school leavers who proceed to higher education in Ireland is high by international standards. The number of new entrants to higher education in 2015 was 45,000, or over 60% of the relevant age cohort. This is a tenfold increase since the mid-1960s when fewer than 4,500 per annum entered higher education annually. The number of new entrants is projected to grow during the next decade to at least 53,000 in 2025 (DES, 2014).

Not all those in higher education come directly from second-level education. About 20% of higher education entrants either are mature students, or come from further education with Quality and

Qualifications Ireland (QQI) Level 6 qualifications. In addition, quotas of places are set aside in all Higher Education Institutions (HEIs), under the Higher Education Access Route (HEAR) and Disability Access Route to Education (DARE) schemes, for students from disadvantaged backgrounds and for students with disabilities (HEA, 2016). In the case of these students, contextual factors such as special educational needs, educational history, home circumstances etc. are taken into account in selection. This chapter will focus on the transition of students from second-level to higher education and will not address the selection of mature students, international students, or those entering the system with QQI further education (formerly FETAC) qualifications.

Irish HEIs focus almost entirely on student performance in the Leaving Certificate when selecting applicants, unlike HEIs in some other countries, where factors such as performance on Standardised Aptitude Tests (SATs), school references, applicants' involvement and success in extra-curricular activities, personal achievements and motivation, performance at interviews etc., are also taken into account. In countries which have national assessment and certification at the end of second-level education, applicants' results in national examinations are usually taken into account for third-level selection, but these results are often just one of a number of factors taken into consideration (Kellaghan, 1995).

There is a heavy emphasis in the (established) Leaving Certificate in Ireland on the terminal or end-of-cycle examination, which is marked and graded by external examiners. Most subjects are examined by one three-hour examination paper, with the exception of Irish, English and Mathematics, where students sit two three-hour papers[1]. In some subjects, other modes of assessment are used in addition to the terminal written examination. For example, in languages, a component of the marks is allocated for an oral exam; in Geography and History, students may submit a written project in advance of the examinations. There are also practical/performance assessments in subjects such as Music and Art. However, unlike other countries where a significant proportion of marks in national (or state) examinations are allocated for continuous school-based (and teacher-marked) assessment[2], the Irish Leaving Certificate is entirely marked by external examiners with no involvement in marking or grading by the students' own teachers.

> " There is a heavy emphasis in the (established) Leaving Certificate in Ireland on the terminal or end-of-cycle examination, which is marked and graded by external examiners. "

---

1. In practice, three hours and 20 minutes are allowed for examination papers that have a high linguistic component, e.g. English and History.
2. However, there is an increasing tendency in other countries to reduce the element of internal marking and to increase the proportion allocated to external marking.

In spite of empirical evidence that has shown consistently over the past fifty years that that the Leaving Certificate is a reliable predictor of student performance in higher education (Hyland, 2011)[3], there has been persistent criticism of the Leaving Certificate as a mechanism to assess the range of skills and abilities which are required in higher education. Critics of the Leaving Certificate allege that students are rewarded for rote learning and regurgitation of facts, rather than for critical analysis and higher-order thinking (Hyland, 2011). As far back as 1970, an analysis of the Leaving Certificate criticised both the curriculum and the way it was assessed (Madaus and Macnamara, 1970). The authors of the report stated that subject syllabi emphasised content to the detriment of skills and 'intellectual functioning'. The report was critical of the extent to which the Leaving Certificate examination influenced the student learning experience and stated:

> For too long the cart has been before the horse; final marks (i.e. the marks achieved in final examinations) have been treated by society as the ultimate goal of education. Intellectual curiosity, the joy of discovery, involvement in intellectual issues – in a word, all these activities and responses which contribute to true learning have been subordinated to, often sacrificed to, a public examination.

In 1986, a report by the Curriculum and Examinations Board (CEB) on Senior Cycle was again critical of the Leaving Certificate and pointed out that the 'backwash effect' of the points systems on teaching and learning at second level was detrimental and harmful to the quality of learning, not only of those progressing to third level, but also of those students who might wish to leave the education system on completion of Senior Cycle. The report stated that Senior Cycle education should instil 'a sense of confidence, enterprise, creativity and achievement in students, as well as the capacity for self-directed learning and the ability to identify problems and to propose and implement solutions to them' (CEB, 1986).

In 1999, the Report of the Points Commission also referred to the negative impact of the Leaving Certificate on students and on their Senior Cycle school experience (Commission on the Points System, 1999). Issues raised in that report included high levels of student stress (Hannan et al., 1996); its negative impact on students' personal development; choice of subjects by students to attain the highest levels of points for entry to third-level education; a narrowing of the curriculum arising from the tendency to teach to the examination rather than to the aims of the curriculum; and an undue focus on the attainment of examination results.

In 2003, the NCCA published a paper on Senior Cycle and engaged in a series of meetings and seminars, as well as establishing an online survey (NCCA, 2003). Drawing on the views elicited during the consultation, the NCCA submitted proposals for the future of Senior Cycle education

---

3.   This echoes the findings of international research that student performance in second-level education, as measured by examinations, is the best predictor of subsequent performance in higher education.

to the Minister for Education in June 2004 (NCCA, 2004). The proposals included a strong emphasis on key skills and reform of assessment whereby 'a greater variety of modes of assessment will be available, including written examinations, oral and aural assessments, project assessment, assessment of the performance of students in completing tasks and portfolio assessment'. The document made the point that '(t)he current concentration of assessment into one event at the end of Senior Cycle is unacceptable and unproductive in relation to meeting many of the desired aims and principles of assessment and of Senior Cycle education'. It pointed out that the demand to spread assessment over the two or three years of Senior Cycle, bringing it closer to the point of learning, was consistent throughout the review process. The NCCA proposals of June 2004 envisaged radical reform of the Leaving Certificate programme and its assessment. But the proposal was not accepted by the then Minister for Education and Science, Mary Hanafin, who regarded it as a 'Rolls Royce' model of reform. The current situation in relation to the reform of Senior Cycle curriculum and assessment and of individual Leaving Certificate syllabi has been outlined in Chapter 3 of this report.

Given the high-stakes nature of the Irish Leaving Certificate examination, it is certainly true to say that at Senior Cycle 'assessment is the tail that wags the curriculum dog' (Hargreaves, 1989). Even when the written syllabus emphasises higher-order thinking and the skills of application, analysis, critical engagement, synthesis and evaluation, such skills are unlikely to be prioritised by teachers or students, unless they are assessed for certification purposes. An analysis of current syllabi indicates that in many subjects, critical and analytic thinking is emphasised but in some cases, such thinking and skills are not being assessed, because the tools of assessment of the current Leaving Certificate are limited to end-of-cycle written examination (Hyland, 2011). For example, how can the ability of a student to carry out a science experiment be assessed if there is no practical examination? Moreover, how can a student's ability to engage in a debate on a topic in the English syllabus be assessed if there is no oral assessment of English? Even when the mode of assessment is congruent with the learning outcomes of a subject, an analysis of examination papers and of marking schemes in some subjects (carried out by this author) suggest that there is an undue emphasis on knowledge and accuracy, to the detriment of higher-order thinking such as critical analysis and evaluation[4].

Subject textbooks for Senior Cycle are largely based on the Leaving Certificate examination, rather than on the syllabus, and most teachers and students in Leaving Certificate classes, are more familiar with textbooks, past examination papers, and marking schemes than they are with the actual written syllabus of a subject. With the setting up of the State Examinations Commission a decade ago, a policy of transparency and openness in relation to all aspects of the public examination system was adopted. Today, marking schemes for all subjects are published after the examination results are issued and are publicly available on the SEC website, as are examiners' reports, which include an analysis of examination scripts. These reports include advice and recommendations to students and teachers

---

4. See for example the examination papers and the marking schemes for the higher Leaving Certificate Paper in Religious Education for 2015.

about improving examination performance. When the results are issued in August every year, any student who so wishes may view his/her marked script or scripts. This gives further information on how marks are allocated.

As a result of this transparency, students and teachers are now acutely familiar with how examination scripts are marked and they know what types of answers are likely to result in high grades. As they approach the examination period, they focus more and more on exam techniques and are reluctant to engage with any form of learning which will be not be rewarded in the examination.[5] (See Chapter 1 of this report).

Another source of debate among students, teachers and the media each year is the variability in the marking/grading of different subjects. There is a perception that some subjects are marked more leniently than others are and that, by taking these subjects, students are more likely to get higher grades. (Kellaghan and Millar, 2003 and MacAogáin, E, 2005). Some students base their subject choice for Leaving Certificate on the perceived likelihood of getting a high grade, rather than on their aptitude for the subject or its relevance to their higher education course of choice.

More than fifty years ago, Benjamin Bloom suggested a taxonomy (classification) of educational objectives, which for many generations of educationalists has proved to be a useful and relatively simple tool for defining and assessing the various levels of thinking skills and educational outcomes. The following diagram summarises the different levels of thinking skills as set out in Bloom's Taxonomy:

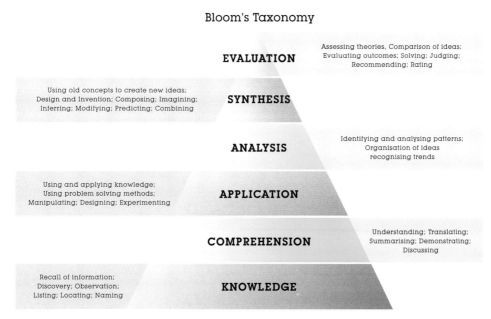

Bloom's Taxonomy

EVALUATION — Assessing theories, Comparison of ideas; Evaluating outcomes; Solving; Judging; Recommending; Rating

SYNTHESIS — Using old concepts to create new ideas; Design and Invention; Composing; Imagining; Inferring; Modifying; Predicting; Combining

ANALYSIS — Identifying and analysing patterns; Organisation of ideas recognising trends

APPLICATION — Using and applying knowledge; Using problem solving methods; Manipulating; Designing; Experimenting

COMPREHENSION — Understanding; Translating; Summarising; Demonstrating; Discussing

KNOWLEDGE — Recall of information; Discovery; Observation; Listing; Locating; Naming

5. A research study carried out in Cork in the 1990s found that second-level teachers and students were willing to engage in creative and innovative teaching and learning methodologies in First and Second Years and in Transition Year and Fifth Year but were not willing to get involved in such activities during the Junior Certificate or the Leaving Certificate years (i.e. the final year of schooling) as they were of the view that such activities would not be recognised or rewarded by the Junior or Leaving Certificate examinations (Hyland, 1999).

Bloom's Taxonomy is sometimes used (implicitly or explicitly) by curriculum and examination designers to ensure that a broad range of thinking skills is included and assessed. For example, the template used by the Indian Board of Secondary Education authorities for the marking of the national end of Senior Cycle examination in that country – an examination that is taken by millions of students, is based on Bloom's Taxonomy (Central Board of Secondary Education, India, 2015).

The following matrix[6] was suggested by Professor Áine Hyland at an NCCA/HEA conference in 2013 as an aid to ensuring that both lower and higher-order skills are assessed and rewarded and that there is broad consistency of marking across different subjects (Hyland, 2013). While recognising that there would have to be flexibility in applying this matrix, such a matrix could be useful in drafting examination questions, developing subject marking schemes for the Leaving Certificate, and devising rubrics for defining grades.

Assessment Grid Framework

GRADING THE LEAVING CERTIFICATE

During the first fifty years of the existence of the Leaving Certificate (from 1924 to the 1970s), candidates received the actual mark which they were awarded by examiners for each subject. In the 1970s, a grading scheme was introduced and candidates' results were subsequently made available on a seven-point scale – A, B, C, D, E, F and No Grade. In the late 1980s, a more refined grading scheme was introduced and

6   The authors are indebted to Dr. Jennifer Murphy, Admissions Officer, University College Cork, for her work in developing this matrix.

since then, a 14-point scale has been used: (A1, A2, B1, B2, B3, C1, C2, C3, D1, D2, D3, E, F). From 2017 onwards, a less detailed grading scheme (based on eight grades) will be used to indicate a candidate's results. However, there will be no change in the way in which examiners will return results to the SEC – examiners will continue, as they have always done, to return results as raw scores.

Is the Leaving Certificate fair and equitable?

One of the often-mentioned attributes of the Leaving Certificate is its fairness. All candidates, whatever their social, cultural or economic background, follow the same syllabi and are assessed in the same way. No student, teacher or examiner has access to the examination papers in advance of the examination. Candidates' scripts are anonymous from an examiner's perspective – the examiner does not know whose scripts s/he has marked, what school they attend or what part of the country they come from. As the examinations are taken in rigorously-supervised conditions, the public can be confident that the scripts are entirely the candidate's own work, that no assistance has been given and that no plagiarism has occurred. The penalties for cheating are very severe and only a tiny number of candidates have been found cheating over the years.

However, not all students fare equally in the examination stakes. Students who excel linguistically and logically are at a significant advantage. The terminal written examinations place a very heavy emphasis on two of Gardner's Multiple Intelligences – the logical/mathematical and the linguistic – often to the detriment of other intelligences (Gardner, 2006)[7]. A better alignment between the syllabus aims and their assessment would require more varied modes of assessment, which in turn would encourage the development, and application of other skills and intelligences.

Students from higher socio-economic backgrounds achieve better Leaving Certificate results than their less socially-privileged peers. In schools with a high concentration of students from lower socio-economic backgrounds (e.g. DEIS schools), overall examination results are generally poorer than in schools where there is a broader social mix of students. This can be due to the fact that such schools have a higher proportion of students with literacy and numeracy problems; or that student motivation may be lower or that the expectations of parents and teachers might be more limited. These factors may also be exacerbated by the fact that some schools in less advantaged areas sometimes offer fewer Leaving Certificate subjects at higher level, especially in the STEM area. In addition, students from lower socio-economic groups are less likely to be in a position to pay for additional out-of-school coaching or grinds, which can enhance a student's confidence and their performance in the Leaving Certificate examination (Smyth et al., 2015).

---

7   Gardner posits that each individual possesses at least eight intelligences: - linguistic, visual, logical/mathematical, musical, bodily-kinaesthetic, interpersonal, intrapersonal, and naturalist.

Should Leaving Certificate Assessment be reformed?

There seems to be an increasing consensus among educationists and the public at large that the Leaving Certificate needs to be reformed, to ensure greater congruence between the stated learning outcomes of the curriculum and the various syllabi, and the modes and techniques of assessment.

There is a long history in Ireland of teachers objecting to assessing their own students for certification purposes, especially in a high-stakes examination like the Leaving Certificate. Given the difficulties encountered in the past decades in reforming Junior Certificate assessment, it is unlikely that this objection will be overcome in relation to the Leaving Certificate in the foreseeable future. However, some actions could be taken to reduce the pressure created by a single terminal examination and to ensure greater congruence between the desired outcomes of the subject syllabi and their assessment. The existing examination system could be supplemented with a greater variety of modes and techniques of assessment to ensure that the syllabi and the examinations are more closely aligned and that the skills which have been identified as necessary for lifelong learning, such as analytic reasoning, critical thinking, the ability to generate fresh ideas, the practical application of theory etc., will be recognised and rewarded by the assessment system. Supplemental modes of assessment could include projects, portfolios and other assignments completed in supervised but non-examination conditions. Essays and open-book questions answered in supervised classroom conditions and externally marked could also be considered. Instead of requiring students to sit one written examination at the end of the final year, two or more sittings at different points throughout the two-year Senior Cycle could be an option. New and different forms of assessment might also reduce the current reliance on pen and paper tests and provide for greater use of new technologies, which might include online submission of essays (written under supervision) and computer-marked multiple-choice questions.

Ireland has a lot of experience of assessing student performance by modes other than terminal examinations. The SEC could build on the experience gained in the assessment of the Junior Certificate School Programme, Leaving Certificate Applied, Youthreach, as well as the Further Education and Training Awards Council (FETAC)[8].

HIGHER EDUCATION SELECTION – THE HISTORY OF THE POINTS SYSTEM

Under legislation governing higher education in Ireland, universities and institutes of technology are responsible for their own policies in relation to the selection and admission of students. Until the 1960s, there was no need for a selection system in Irish universities as demand for places was broadly in line with the number of places available. Following the introduction of free second-level education and a

---

8   See for example, A, Hyland (ed.) *Innovations in Assessment in Irish Education* UCC 1998.

university grants system in the late 1960s, demand began to exceed the number of places. The Central Applications Office (CAO) was set up as a limited company in January 1976 by the universities to administer a central system of selection and a common application system was put in place for universities for the first time in the academic year 1977/8. Initially, the CAO acted only on behalf of the universities but, in the early 1990s, it was expanded to include colleges of education and regional technical colleges (now called institutes of technology). Since the mid-1990s, a number of private or partially publicly-funded third-level colleges have also used the services of the CAO (Hyland, 2011).

Different selection systems were used by different universities in the early years of the CAO. For example, while UCD accepted the best six subjects as the basis for points, Trinity College accepted five and UCG accepted seven. Similarly, different colleges gave different weightings to different subjects. NIHE Dublin (now DCU) initially used an aptitude test in addition to Leaving Certificate results. Some colleges continued to interview students within the CAO framework and some required applicants to provide a portfolio of work. For the first few decades of the existence of the CAO, both the NUI and Trinity College continued to provide their own matriculation examinations, which students could take either in addition to or instead of the Leaving Certificate. From a technical perspective, the CAO system has shown that it can accommodate a wide range of different criteria set by different institutions and programmes.

Successive studies carried out before and since the introduction of the CAO indicate that the Leaving Certificate is a reliable predictor of student performance in higher education (Coolahan, 1979; Commission on the Points System, 1999). In general, students who perform well in the Leaving Certificate obtain higher grades on graduation. Results in Mathematics in the Leaving Certificate are a particularly good predictor of subsequent academic performance, regardless of the discipline chosen. Most recently, a study carried out by the HEA on progression in Irish higher education in 2009/2010 confirmed earlier findings (HEA, 2011).

The process of application and selection for higher education has been refined over the decades. School leavers who wish to apply for a place in higher education are required to submit an application to the CAO by 1 February of their final year in school. They can choose a maximum of ten courses at Level 8 and ten courses at Levels 6 and 7, which they identify in order of choice. There are two separate lists, Level 8 and Levels 6 and 7, and the system is designed so that students are offered the top choice for which they are eligible on each list. They can change their mind about their course(s) of choice until 1 July – except in the case of a small number of courses where criteria in addition to the Leaving Certificate (e.g. interviews, portfolios etc.) are taken into account.

Applicants must satisfy the minimum requirements for their course of choice, and when demand for places exceeds the number of places available, places are allocated based on the rank order of students on a points scale. The points scale is based on an applicant's results in six subjects of the Leaving Certificate examination, the maximum number of points for most courses being 625. (This includes an additional 25 points for higher-level Mathematics).

A small number of courses require candidates to satisfy other criteria in addition to the Leaving Certificate results. For example, courses in Art, Visual Communication, Design or Architecture require the submission of a portfolio of student work. Applicants for Music courses are usually required to undergo a performance test. Courses in Drama or Theatre Studies include an interview and, since 2009, applicants for Medicine are required to sit an additional test called HPAT-Ireland (Health Professions Admission Test). The HPAT is designed to measure a candidate's logical reasoning and problem-solving skills as well as non-verbal reasoning and the ability to understand the thoughts, behaviours and/or intentions of people. Candidates can gain a maximum of 300 further points in this test and these points are added to the points gained in the Leaving Certificate. In an effort to reduce the pressure on students to gain maximum points in the Leaving Certificate, the Irish Medical Schools agreed to reduce the maximum number of points gained by applicants to 585 points instead of 625 points[9]. Applications for Medicine are therefore scored out of a maximum of 885 points.

From 2017 onwards, the common points scale will be revised to take account of the new Leaving Certificate grading scale. The following is the proposed revised scale (DES, 2015):

New Grades and Common Points Scale for Leaving Certificate 2017

HIGHER		ORDINARY	
GRADE	POINTS	GRADE	POINTS
H1	100		
H2	88		
H3	77		
H4	66		
H5	56	O1	56
H6	46	O2	46
H7	37	O3	37
H8	0	O4	28
		O5	20
		O6	12
		O7	0
		O8	0

9 Each additional five points gained above 560 points is calculated as one point, thereby reducing the maximum number of points which it is possible to gain from 600 to 560.

The scale is non-linear – which will reduce the use of random selection in the admissions process – by minimising the number of candidates presenting with identical points scores. The new scale was drawn up following extensive mathematical analysis and modelling of the distributions of points scores that would result from different non-linear scales.

When applying for a place in higher education through the CAO, students can choose from over 1,500 courses in universities, institutes of technology, colleges of education and private colleges, about 1,000 of which are Level 8 courses. The number of courses has increased steadily over the past 20 years. The HEA report on a *National Strategy for Higher Education to 2030* noted that the number of Level 8 courses on the CAO list doubled between 1998 and 2008, with many of these courses being very narrowly-specialised (HEA, 2011). It noted that one Institute of Technology offers 14 separate specialised Business programmes. On the other hand, other HEIs offer one generic First Year course in Arts or Business or Engineering and students are not required to specialise until after First Year.

In 2013, the universities agreed to work together to reduce the number of undergraduate entry routes 'to the minimum number necessary for academically appropriate and efficient allocation of places to applicants', while at the same time maintaining the number of student places. It was hoped that this would simplify the process of choice for applicants and the level of competitiveness driving the system. This approach would also offer a broader First Year experience for students with specialisation to follow later. In the university sector, it was planned to reduce the number of entry routes by 20% by 2017. (DES et al, 2013).

However, in a recent media interview, the President of Maynooth University, Professor Philip Nolan, expressed disappointment that instead of reducing the number of courses, some higher education institutions, especially in the institute of technology sector, had increased the number of courses – many of which accepted only a very small numbers of students. There is now a 'bewildering array' of more than 1,400 CAO courses, as against 1,286 five years ago (Donnelly, *Irish Independent* 15/08/2016). 20% of these admit 10 students or fewer, and almost 60% have fewer than 30 students (*Irish Times*, 15/08/2016).

A key question arises here: Can the points system be changed? It is important to bear in mind that the Points System was created and is owned by the higher education institutions and that it can be changed at any time by those institutions. As its history shows, the system can and has been adjusted from time to time to take account of different selection criteria. It is open to the higher education institutions, together or separately, to change their selection criteria. If the institutions believe, either individually or collectively, that the current selection system is no longer appropriate, they have the authority, the power and (arguably) the responsibility to change it.

The points system is merely one of many possible selection mechanisms for selecting students for higher education. Its key purpose is to allocate scarce third-level places. If there were sufficient places on every course for all qualified students who applied, there would be no need for a points system. The issue of points arises only when demand exceeds the number of places available. Some countries in the European Higher Education Area, which have a national public examination at the end of second level, use a similar points system, while other countries such as France and Italy allow all students who pass the Baccalaureate examination to transfer into higher education. In those countries, for courses where places are limited, *de facto* selection is based on the results of First Year examinations. Selection for higher education in England has some similarities to the Irish system in that A Level results are an important element of the selection criteria, but many English institutions use supplemental criteria, such as personal statements, interviews and/or school references, when selecting students. In the US where there is no centralised examination or certification at the end of high school, candidates' performance in American College Tests (ACTs) or SATs are used in addition to high-school results, personal statements, school references and interviews. Many U.S. universities also take account of non-academic achievements in sports, the arts, community endeavours etc. For example, the ten campuses of the University of California use a system called 'comprehensive review' to assess its applicants. The following factors are taken into account in assessing applications (University of California, 2016):

- Academic grade points
- Scores on ACT or SAT tests
- Number of, content of and performance in academic courses
- Number of, content of and performance in UC-approved honours and advanced placement courses
- Being ranked in the top 9% of the applicant's high-school class
- Quality of a student's senior year programme
- Quality of their academic performance relative to the educational opportunities in their school
- Outstanding performance in one or more academic subject areas
- Outstanding work in one or more special projects in any academic field of study
- Recent marked improvement in academic performance
- Special talents, achievements and awards in a particular field such as visual and performing arts, athletic endeavours, leadership, significant community service etc.
- Completion of special projects undertaken in the context of the high-school curriculum
- Academic accomplishments in light of a student's life experiences and special circumstances
- Location of a student's secondary school and residence.

While the above list of criteria is impressive, the challenge of applying such a comprehensive list to each application must be extremely time-consuming and resource-intensive. The self-reported aspects of every application would have to be checked for truth and accuracy and qualitative criteria would require individual scrutiny and professional judgement. Given the demands on the time and resources of admissions and academic departments in Irish higher education, it would be unrealistic to expect that Ireland could afford to introduce such a wide-ranging selection system.

DEVELOPMENTS IN IRELAND SINCE 2011

In a paper prepared for the NCCA and the HEA in 2011, Áine Hyland suggested some alternative and/or additional selection mechanisms for Irish higher education institutions. The paper advised that any proposed change to the current system would need to be carefully considered and the advantages and disadvantages carefully weighed against each other (Hyland, 2011).

Building on the 2011 report and an NCCA/HEA Seminar on transition from second to third level which was held in September 2011 (HEA 2011), a Transitions Committee was set up, consisting of representatives of the Department of Education and Skills, HEA, NCCA, SEC, Irish Universities Association (IUA), QQI, and Institutes of Technology Ireland (IoTI). The committee, which is chaired by the Secretary General of the Department of Education, has met regularly since 2012. Issues relating to selection and admission are discussed and analysed by this committee, and various alternatives to the Points system are considered.

A Task Group on Reform of University Selection and Entry (TGRUSE) has been set up by the IUA and its programme of work has three major elements: (a) Broadening Entry Routes; (b) Improving the Existing System, and (c) Decoupling university entry from the Leaving Certificate. A wide range of options was considered under each heading, the Task Force developed principles, and criteria against which proposals were tested (IUA, 2014). For example, any new proposal should promote positive educational values, outcomes and personal development at second and third level; it should reward student merit, achievement and potential; promote equity of access; ensure reliability, validity, transparency and simplicity; maintain integrity, incorruptibility and a high level of public trust etc.

Among the possible alternative approaches to selection considered by the Task Force were supplementary student submissions, e.g. personal statements; portfolios of work and e-portfolios; interviews; supplementary assessment tests, such as aptitude tests or other tests of intellectual ability; school references and school reports; and adjusting for difference in school performance, by using contextual information to reduce socio-economic bias in points scores.

The options were researched and analysed by sub-groups reporting to the Task Force. Each subgroup reviewed available evidence and summarised the positives and negatives of the options. Having considered the research reports, the Task Force supported the recommendation that Leaving Certificate assessment should focus more on higher-order skills, including a suggestion to have a special paper set and marked by the SEC, which would focus specifically on skills such as problem-solving, analytic thinking etc. – skills that are deemed essential for successful engagement in higher education. The Task Force also supported proposals for reducing the number of grades in the Leaving Certificate and a concomitant revision of the points system. The Task Force also supported the suggestion that First Year courses should be more generic and should avoid undue specialisation too soon. As regards alternative selection systems or supplemental approaches, it concluded that great care would need to be taken in the use of personal statements to avoid socio-economic bias and fraudulent submissions.

While the potential of portfolios and/or e-portfolios was recognised, it was felt that any assessment of general portfolios would best be done in partnership with NCCA and the SEC. The Task Force discussed a variety of supplementary assessment tests, some of which are already in use in Irish higher education institutions, and referred in particular to the Irish experience of HPAT, to which there have been mixed reactions. For example, there is compelling evidence that applicants can improve their score on the HPAT tests by attending special classes or through individual coaching. This militates against those who cannot afford to pay for grinds or for coaching and adds yet another obstacle to higher education entry for those from less advantaged backgrounds. An interview system did not get much support from the Task Force and is unlikely to be introduced in the foreseeable future. However, recent reports suggest that the introduction of bonus points for subjects that are relevant to the course applied for is still under consideration.

> "
> While the potential of portfolios and/or e-portfolios was recognised, it was felt that any assessment of general portfolios would best be done in partnership with NCCA and the SEC.
> "

There was widespread support among Task Force members for the HEAR scheme, whereby quotas of places are set aside on courses in all higher education institutions for students from educationally and socio-economically disadvantaged backgrounds. The scheme has been in place for over a decade and its success is widely acknowledged. While it has not removed all the barriers to participation and retention of under-represented minorities, it has gone some way towards alleviating some of the obstacles (HEA, 2013).

The Task Force was of the view that a feasibility study into an alternative method of selection for a small number of its courses, currently being carried out by Trinity College Dublin, would provide interesting and useful information. Under the terms of this feasibility study, which was introduced in autumn 2013 and is now in its third year, 25 students are selected each year (Heaphy et al, 2016).

Selection is based on three scales: (a) Leaving Certificate results; (b) Relative Performance Rank (i.e. the performance of the applicant relative to other applicants from his/her school; (c) Personal and contextual data, gleaned from a personal statement submitted by applicants. According to the architect of the study, Professor Patrick Geoghegan, all three criteria were weighted equally for the first two years (Geoghegan, 2014). In 2015 and in the coming year, the weighting has been refined, with less weighting currently being allocated for personal and contextual data. A rigorous analysis of the data collected so far is currently being carried out by a research group in the School of Education in Trinity College and the findings of the analysis are eagerly awaited (Geoghegan, 2016).

In the meantime, as indicated in the report on '*Supporting a Better Transition from Second to Higher Education*', launched by Minister for Education Jan O'Sullivan in April 2015, a number of changes have been agreed by the higher education institutions to date. A new grading structure for the Leaving Certificate; a revised common points scale for entry to higher education; broader undergraduate entry; and addressing issues relating to predictability in the Leaving Certificate. The first three of these changes will come into effect in autumn 2017 and, hopefully, issues relating to predictability in the Leaving Certificate will be addressed without delay by the SEC.

Before concluding, it is worth noting that Ireland is not unique in questioning, reviewing and reforming its higher education admissions system. Their current systems have been reviewed and sometimes revised in a number of eastern European countries, Australia, some universities in the UK and in the US. In 2011, the Group of Eight (a coalition of leading Australian universities) commissioned a report that examined criteria and strategies in student selection and their implications for equality of opportunity in higher education. (Palmer et al, 2011). That report offered an analysis of the strengths and weaknesses of criteria for prior academic achievement, tests of aptitude and preparedness and broader criteria used in university selection. The aim of the report was to support informed discussion regarding the development and improvement of university selection criteria and practices, recognising the common challenges universities face in fostering diversity of participation and student success in an expanding tertiary education environment.

A recent report produced by a consortium of universities in the US, co-ordinated by the Admissions Office in Harvard University, made the point that 'today's culture sends young people messages that emphasise personal success rather than concern for others and the common good' (HGSE, 2015). The report expressed concern that 'too often the college admissions process … contributes to this problem'. It went on to state:

> **As a rite of passage for many students and a major focus for many parents, the college admissions process is powerfully positioned to send different messages that help young people become more generous and humane in ways that benefit not only society but students themselves.**

The report was critical of the fact that colleges were perceived as simply valuing students' achievements, not their responsibility for others and their communities. The report addressed what it refers to as 'three challenges'. First, it described how college admissions could promote more meaningful contributions to others, community service and engagement with the public good. Secondly, it discussed how the admissions process could more accurately and meaningfully assess young people's contributions to others and their communities. Thirdly, it attempted to redefine achievement in ways that level the playing field for economically diverse students and reduce excessive achievement pressure.

The report is helpful in that it emphasises the importance of community engagement rather than personal advancement and brings to the fore a commitment to equality of access. However, the report is less helpful in providing practical suggestions as to how college admissions offices might assess the desired qualities, while at the same time ensuring that the system of selection is reliable, fair, and transparent and is implemented with integrity. While the report recognises that some candidates and their parents will continue to 'game' the system, no matter how carefully it is designed, it fails to provide solutions for this 'gaming'.

An examination of the development of higher education selection in Ireland and an analysis of selection systems all over the world show that there is no perfect system of selection, nor is a 'one size fits all' solution possible. As long as demand exceeds supply, either in an aggregate sense or for individual programmes, some system of selection has to be put in place – and there will be winners and losers. The winners will tend to be happy with the system - since they were among the chosen ones – and the losers will, understandably be critical of the system that rejected them, again understandably. Having said that, it is important that every system is reviewed and if necessary reformed, from time to time, if and when the evidence points to a more successful system.

CHAPTER SIX • • • • • • • • • • • • • • • • •

Educational Leadership & Governance

INTRODUCTION

Until the mid-1990s, educational leadership was not regarded as a priority in Irish educational policy, or in the management and the daily work of schools and colleges. In the aftermath of the 1991 OECD report on Irish educational policy, however, a greater awareness grew of the importance of good leadership for the health of an education system in a rapidly-changing society. The beginnings of this new awareness are evident in the 1992 Green Paper *Education for a Changing World*, particularly Chapter 5, which illustrated the need for new forms of management. A major stimulus was then provided by the wide-ranging deliberations of the National Education Convention (1993-94). Based largely on policy pathways identified in the *Report on The National Education Convention* (1994), the 1995 White Paper *Charting our Education Future* devoted three chapters to matters that had major implications for leadership – Ch. 10: Governance of Schools; Ch.11: In-school Management; Ch.12: School Plan. As yet, however, leadership was largely seen as something contained within management, as distinct from an issue that required analysis and action in its own right. As the decade of the '90s progressed, however, new research on educational leadership began to make a strong impact internationally, including in policy-making quarters. In its early days, this research was associated with scholars like Thomas Sergiovanni, Michael Fullan and Robert J. Starratt in North America, but the field soon grew to be one of the larger domains within international educational research.

In Ireland, the growth of a new engagement with educational leadership can be seen in a number of developments over the last two decades. These developments range across policy-making, organisational changes and the provision of educational courses. They include the following:

- The growth of post-graduate courses in educational management during the nineties – at Master's level and more widely at post-graduate diploma level
- The establishment of the In-career Development Unit within the DES in 1994, reorganised and expanded as the Teacher Education Section (TES) in 2004
- The setting up of NAPD in 1998 and of IPPN in 2000
- The provision of a more secure basis for the Education Centres by the Education Act 1998
- The establishment of the School Development Planning Initiative (SDPI) in 1999
- The establishment of the Leadership Development for Schools service (LDS) in 2002
- The development of designated educational leadership courses at post-graduate level in the later part of the new century – including the PGDEL /Tóraíocht course under the joint auspices of LDS and National University of Ireland Maynooth, and further educational leadership courses by other universities
- The establishment of the Centre for School Leadership (CSL) in 2015, resulting from joint efforts by IPPN, NAPD and DES.

In the pages that follow, some important issues that are specifically concerned with educational leadership are selected for consideration. Arising from a review of these issues, some possibilities for further developments in leadership policy and practice are put forward.

CLARIFICATIONS

In view of the background sketched out above, it is important at the start to distinguish between administration, management, leadership and governance in education. It is worth noting in passing here that management and leadership are mentioned as separate functions of the school principal in Section 23 of the 1998 Education Act. While acknowledging that the everyday use of the term 'management' is generally taken to include administration, management and leadership, and sometimes governance, clarifying the difference between the terms helps to identify what is particular to each and to prevent any confusion of purposes:

- **Administration –** taking care of the daily, weekly, monthly and annual tasks that have to be completed to keep the school functioning
- **Management –** 'getting things done through people' – some of the 'things' being matters of administration and some being matters of leadership

- **Leadership –** discovering and pursuing initiatives that enhance the quality of learning and teaching in the school
- **Governance –** discharging responsibilities at a corporate level so as to ensure the best use of resources and to provide the best opportunities for leadership to be productive.

From these distinctions, it will be seen that the particular concern of educational leadership is with enhancements in learning environments that yield a higher quality of educational experience for the students. Educational leadership initiatives then will normally result in changes in the practices of students *and* of teachers. Leadership initiatives that affect other aspects of a school's work, but have little ultimate influence on the quality of teaching and learning, would fall largely outside of educational leadership, as understood here. There are two further important consequences of defining the terms in this way. Firstly, pedagogical initiatives taken by teachers who are not themselves school principals or deputy principals would count centrally within educational leadership. This lesser-known dimension of educational leadership is termed 'teacher leadership' by Ann Lieberman & Lynne Miller (2004), whose research has done much to disclose the promise of this domain. The second consequence concerns the relationship between governance and leadership. Good governance structures that are well used at a corporate level enable school leadership at an everyday level to be more purposefully engaged and more fruitful. Following a review of some leadership issues there is further consideration of governance matters later in this chapter.

THE QUALITY OF EDUCATIONAL LEADERSHIP IN SCHOOLS

The quality of educational leadership in a school or college is largely influenced by the values, attitudes and practices that have become embodied in established custom and routine. If such custom and routine does not include a lively traffic in visionary educational ideals, the school's management culture is likely to be resistant to movements for change. Educational leadership in such circumstances is unlikely to have a high profile in that management culture. Neither are new pedagogical initiatives taken by teachers likely to receive the recognition or support that they might expect from the school leadership. On the other hand, where a receptivity to meaningful innovation has itself become habitual, the momentum of custom and routine itself provides a stimulus to genuine educational leadership (Hargreaves & Fink, 2006, Ch.2; Hogan et.al, 2008, Ch. 2).

A school can continue to function where educational leadership is largely absent – where everything important is decided by the way 'things have always been done'. Fullan calls this 'losing sight of the 'why' question and getting lost in the 'how to' question' (2003, p.61). It is important to note that such a school might still be efficiently run from an administration perspective, and that the management might pride itself on its effectiveness in the handling of students, staff and parents. When confronted by new expectations that challenge this equilibrium, a characteristic response can be 'If it's not broken, why fix it?' That mentality was common enough at managerial level in Ireland until the late 1980s. In a reflection paper on the role of religious congregations in education published in 1997 by the Conference of Religious of Ireland (CORI), the point was made that religious-run schools largely acquiesced in this mentality:

> **'No longer were they running schools which were in some way counter-cultural; instead, their schools were now some of the principal agents of socialisation into the values and outlooks of the new establishment.'**
> (CORI, 1997, p.15)

In this regard, the OECD report of 1991 had helped to unsettle an established equilibrium. It had also brought to the fore the need for some major changes in structure and management. That report's comments on educational leadership itself, however, were more implicit than overt.

OECD research reports are now more likely to give quite explicit recognition to the importance of educational leadership and the OECD itself has been involved in an ongoing international research programme called *Improving School Leadership* (OECD, 2008). In one of its larger publications from this programme, the OECD provides a summary of findings from the international research literature. The following extract identifies key departures from traditional patterns promoted by fruitful educational leadership:

> **Providing intellectual stimulation, supplying professional development and other support, developing a vision of and focus on learning with others, creating a strong professional learning community through team commitment to learning and achievement – these are key ways that leaders have exerted their effects on learning, achievement and performance among students.**
> (OECD 2008, p.71)

In Ireland, the tenor of such departures is echoed strongly in the NCCA Discussion Paper of 2009, *Leading and Supporting Change in Schools*. That paper argues for 'seeing schools as centres of innovation and learning and powering them through investment, support and knowledge management to realise that role' (p.21). It notes in particular the success of forms of professional engagement cultivated and led by the Project Maths initiative (p.9). It is worth pointing out that these forms of engagement arose mainly from research projects here in Ireland, tailoring international research ideas and home-grown ones to Irish workplace circumstances. Specifically on the issue of leadership, the NCCA document states:

> Reports of pilot projects and implementation initiatives published during the past twenty years in Ireland commonly conclude that change happens most effectively when it is supported by those in positions of leadership, such as school principals, and when leadership is evident at every level of the project or initiative
>
> (NCCA 2009, p.14)

Bodies like IPPN and NAPD have kept abreast of developments in the research literature on educational leadership. Their regular publications over the last few decades have acted as valuable communication channels to disseminate such developments among their own members, and to promote informed professional debate on educational leadership issues. This is also true of the conferences, seminars and other professional development events organised by both bodies. Such events occurred in a more small-scale way, also a more fragmented way, before the setting up of IPPN and NAPD during the nineties. They are now, however, an established part of the annual educational calendar and an important support to school principals and deputy principals nationwide.

THE 'EDUCATIONAL' IN EDUCATIONAL LEADERSHIP

Most of the research literature on educational leadership stresses the importance of things like mission, vision and moral purpose. Nevertheless, the literature is less articulate on what constitutes an *educational* vision, or what is to count as moral purpose in *educational* leadership, as distinct from vision more generally, or leadership more generally, or even moral purpose more generally. For instance, as a business leader, I could believe strongly in moral purpose, seeking ethically acceptable ways to build a collaborative vision in the company around agreed goals. But these goals themselves might chiefly be ones like maximising returns to shareholders (as distinct from stakeholders more widely), or increasing the company's market share: goals that in turn secure better bonuses for those who sign up to sharing the vision. Variants of this familiar picture from the business world have been increasingly common in education internationally. This is especially so where school leaders are keenly aware of the consequences of any underachievement, as measured by the performance management systems which policy reforms may have mandated for their schools.

Therefore, some basic clarity is necessary on what constitutes the 'educational' in educational leadership, and on what kinds of moral purpose would be appropriate here. Most of the literature on educational leadership is not sufficiently clear on these points, including the work of central figures like Fullan, 2003, Hargreaves & Fink, 2004, and Hopkins, 2008. Despite insightful critiques of policy reforms and explorations of more constructive reform pathways, the research literature tends to associate high quality in educational leadership with conceptions of performance and underperformance that remain unexamined. Performance is all too often described merely in terms of test scores and examination results. There are some notable exceptions to this pattern, including the work of Starratt, 2011, or Duignan, 2011, which bring a fuller view of the personal, ethical, cultural and social purposes of education into the analysis of educational leadership.

The 'educational' in educational leadership has plenty to do with vision and with moral purpose, as the research literature rightly stresses. However, what needs more emphasis is the unique kind of challenge involved in this particular form of leadership. Educational leadership needs to take its bearings from the most promising and most defensible conceptions of education itself as a distinct human good. It needs to remain focused on the challenge of finding the best ways of promoting high quality *in the experience of learning itself*, including what this might mean for the full diversity of students. It needs, moreover, to invite criticisms of its own best efforts. Chapter 1 above explores this issue in relation to teaching as a practice in its own right. If educational leadership neglects this specifically educational challenge, or largely acquiesces in marching to another's drum (e.g. political, ecclesiastical, commercial), it becomes from the start burdened by ambiguities of purpose and by expectations it should not have to meet. In such ways can practitioners of educational leadership lose sight of the priorities that are properly theirs. In such ways, moreover, can they come to follow beaten paths that lead elsewhere than to taking practical initiatives to enhance the quality of educational experience in schools.

PROFESSIONAL LEARNING COMMUNITIES & COMMUNITIES OF PRACTICE

A well-known Irish proverb says '*Níl neart go cur le chéile*' (there is not strength until efforts are put together), which is an obvious motto for leadership in school settings, one might say. Yet, despite its social nature, teaching is a practice that has long been marked by the professional isolation and insulation of teachers – from each other and from school leadership (Lieberman & Rosenholtz, 1987, p.94; DuFour & Marzano, 2011, Ch.3; Smith, 2012, Ch.10). Against this insular background, goals like those of collaboration, shared vision, intellectual stimulation and team commitment, recommended by the international research on educational leadership, take on a practical priority. Questions that now come to the fore include: How are such goals to be realised in practices of leadership in a school? How is progress toward such goals to be sustained? How can the pursuit of such goals become the prevalent pattern in schools more widely? Such questions are implicit in the NCCA publication *Leading and Supporting Change in Schools*, but to advance matters further, the questions need to be identified explicitly and then pursued in constructive and concrete ways.

In tackling such questions, some researchers on educational leadership have, for a decade or more, been exploring the potential of professional learning communities (Hord & Sommers, 2007; DuFour & Marzano, 2011). Hord & Sommers (p.9) describe such communities in schools as having five following characteristics:

■ Shared beliefs, values and vision among the staff, focused consistently on students' learning
■ Shared and supportive leadership where decision-making is concerned
■ Collective learning and its application among the teaching practitioners
■ Supportive conditions, including time for sharing, mutual respect, openness to others' views
■ Shared personal practice, particularly the giving and receiving of feedback among colleagues.

Promoting a professional learning community in a school calls firstly on the principal and deputy principal to take initiatives to create conditions of dialogue, including, in particular, the time and opportunities needed for professional dialogue to develop. Teachers are thus enabled to talk about what they really value in their work and about the significance of what they do. Where such dialogue becomes a regular feature of teachers' working lives, new energies are released in unforced ways and new initiatives are forthcoming from teachers themselves. This process cultivates an enhanced sense of professional identity among teachers, even a transformed one (Lieberman & Miller, 2004, pp. 24-31). Teachers become more open to new approaches and more active in taking ownership of them. Equally important, professional learning communities cultivate a more informed and more authoritative voice among teachers in reshaping and enriching the practice of teaching itself. In Ireland, such advances would have major implications for current issues of concern - the moves toward school self-evaluation, the induction and probation of new practitioners and, not least, the reform of curriculum and assessment at post-primary level.

The notion of a community of practice is largely similar to that of a professional learning community. The notion has been developed and refined largely through the practical researches of Etienne Wenger and Jean Lave (Lave & Wenger 1991). In a community of practice, however, leadership is chiefly associated with the actions of members of the community themselves. In other words, 'distributed leadership' has already become embodied in everyday practice. As a form of workplace learning, a community of practice lies at the other end of the spectrum from the hierarchical notion of apprenticeship. It also sits uneasily with notions of 'delegated' responsibility, particularly if these are uncritically accepted. Members of a community of practice are keenly conscious of their practitioner identity and of their need to learn from each other, including from newcomers to the practice. While not rejecting the idea of mentoring, members of a genuine community of practice readily allow that a newcomer might in some particular respects be a valuable mentor to longer-serving colleagues. They are keenly aware that fresh possibilities for developing the practice arise from sharing the evolving expertise of practitioners. On this understanding, practice and the leadership of practice are not something purely – or even mainly – guided by theory. Rather, as some central sources in leadership research readily acknowledge, many of the best insights for educational leadership spring from new departures that have arisen and proven fruitful in challenging but reflective workplaces. Action research and case study research are particularly significant in this regard. (Duignan, 2011; Lieberman & Miller, 2004; MacBeath 2012; Starratt, 2011).

The *Action Plan for Education issued* in September 2016 (DES, 2016j) makes a number of welcome references to educational leadership and its importance. These references specify actions like the following: expanding the range of supports available through the Centre for School Leadership; provision of a post-graduate course for aspiring school leaders; provision of coaching for school principals (pp. 31-35). The *Action Plan* states that one of the more major actions to be undertaken is to 'change the middle management structure and functions carried out in schools by the holders of posts of responsibility' (p.36). This last action could have long-term beneficial effects. In this context, however, it is important that if terms like 'posts of responsibility' and 'middle management' are to be retained, they need to be thoroughly reviewed and re-conceived. Both terms look back to 20th century management patterns that included two important flaws. Firstly, the widespread acceptance of the notion of 'delegation' in such patterns tended to obscure the more promising notion of shared leadership, and of collaborative leadership. In fact, the strong growth in the new century of research on shared leadership sprang mainly from recognition of the many limitations of a 'delegation' model. Secondly, important distinctions such as those outlined at the beginning of this chapter – e.g. between responsibilities of management and those of leadership – were frequently overlooked. It is no accident that terms like 'middle management' and its cognates have largely disappeared from research on educational leadership and from international reports on developments in leadership practice. (Duignan, 2011; Harris & Jones, 2016; Spillane, 2015; OECD, 2009, Ch.6).

EDUCATIONAL LEADERSHIP BEYOND THE SCHOOL

Yet, creating the conditions conducive to the growth of professional learning communities may sometimes fail the best efforts of school principals. This can happen if the timetabling constraints within which schools work are so rigid as to rule out finding non-teaching time on a regular basis, and if there are industrial relations difficulties in working outside normal school hours. The 'Croke Park hours' of recent years were an effort to create such non-teaching time. These 'hours' were ingeniously used for constructive purposes by many school leaderships. However, the fact remains that in teachers' minds they were widely regarded as a much-resented imposition, directly linked to a government austerity regime. Anything resembling a 'Croke Park hours' concept is unlikely to have a bright future where the leadership of Ireland's schools is concerned. What might hold more promise is a re-conceiving of the work of Ireland's teachers that takes account of 21st century circumstances and needs. The provision for non-teaching hours in the recently-issued circular 0024/2016 from the DES (DES, 2016a) represents an important new development here. From a leadership perspective, however, what is called for is a clear recognition by all parties of the manifold responsibilities that now constitute teaching as an occupation, reaching well beyond the classroom-based elements of the job. A negotiated settlement arising from such a re-conceiving might lay the ground for some very worthwhile developments in the years and decades ahead. The McCrone settlement in Scotland offers some instructive insights here, though not a panacea, or a ready-made model (Scottish Government, 2001). No less productive as a source of ideas might be some of the resourceful arrangements made internally within schools during the austerity period: the in-house leadership wisdom that developed in a new key when necessity gave birth to more than a few inventive solutions.

Fullan makes a provocative point, but also a thought-provoking one, in declaring that 'the moral imperative will never amount to much unless school leaders also take it on the road' (2003, p.47). For Fullan this primarily means school leaders taking their leadership insights beyond the school to work together in school districts and regions in 'closing the performance gap beyond their own narrow bailiwick' (p.47). For a smaller country like Ireland, with national associations of school leaders at primary level (IPPN) and post-primary level (NAPD), educational leadership beyond the school would have a national scope as well as a regional one. This arguably gives a more concentrated potential to the work of both bodies than would be possible for national associations in much larger countries. As suggested earlier, moreover, the work of educational leadership beyond the school would include a richer conception of moral purpose than that of closing performance gaps. A research-informed agenda that would do more justice to the view of leadership being advanced here would embrace actions like the following wider ones, in addition to taking development initiatives within schools:

- Encouraging the profession to take ownership of the induction and probation of newly-qualified practitioners (e.g. *Droichead* – primary schools mainly)
- Working actively with policy initiatives which seek to redress the inequities and other shortcomings of a misshapen assessment system (post-primary schools mainly)
- Promoting professional learning communities between schools as well as within schools, including web-based communities
- Articulating and promoting new ideas for policy and practice on how time in school might best be spent (including examples from other jurisdictions)
- Contributing ideas to Teaching Council, Education Centres, DES/TES and other bodies on new forms of CPD and its accreditation
- Engaging proactively with national support agencies and the Inspectorate to enhance the learning environments of formal education.

In the Irish context, the establishment of the Centre for School Leadership in April 2015 on a partnership basis between IPPN, NAPD and the DES augurs well for the advancement of ideas and actions like those considered above. Crucial to the success of the Centre is the provision of high-quality leadership courses for established and aspiring school leaders. No less crucial is the building up of a strong research dimension, informed by the most promising leadership developments at home and internationally. Fundamental to the longer term-success of such a Centre, moreover, is its freedom to speak fearlessly for and with school leaders.

GOVERNANCE AND EDUCATIONAL LEADERSHIP

The governance structures in our primary and post-primary education clearly bear the stamp of Ireland's 19th century educational history. This is especially evident in the prominence of the role of patron, or patron bodies – a concept that is not common in governance structures in education internationally. The roles and powers of the patron were acknowledged and specified in the 1998 Education Act, so any developments in governance structures or policies have to take place within the legal framework established by that Act. The various patron bodies in Ireland are keenly conscious of their own traditions and distinct identity. There are cases, however, where the lack of a statutory governance tier within some patron bodies can have negative consequences.

It is widely acknowledged that too much of the time of school leaders at present is taken up with activities that leave only limited opportunity to deal with the primary concern of promoting high-quality learning in the school. It is important to recognise that changes in some governance structures in recent years have allowed significant inroads into this problem to be made in some schools. For instance, the reorganisation of VECs into ETBs has lessened the burden of administration on school principals, thus enabling a more successful and sustained engagement of educational leadership at school level with priorities such as the following: school self-evaluation, mentoring of student teachers and newly-qualified teachers; new initiatives in assessment and in feedback to students; and inventive use of 'Croke Park hours' for professional development purposes. ETBs are 'patron bodies', but what has empowered them here is their function as statutory governance authorities. There has been notably less progress made in situations where the patron body is not such an authority. All too frequently here, school leaderships have been hampered by a plethora of tasks that might be handled by the governance authority, or have otherwise lacked the capacity or opportunity to identify and take educational leadership initiatives.

> " The governance structures in our primary and post-primary education clearly bear the stamp of Ireland's 19th century educational history. "

On governance more generally, it is instructive to compare, or rather to contrast, the changes promoted in England & Wales after the 1988 Education Reform Act with those that have taken place in Finland since 1990. Schools in Britain were encouraged to leave Local Education Authorities, thus becoming more autonomous. However, autonomy here was linked to a more centralising thrust: government-mandated performance targets on which individual schools could be ranked in league tables, and then rewarded or penalised through funding mechanisms. Meanwhile, in Finland, long-term measures were being enacted to entrust governance more decisively to federated municipalities.

These measures promoted a light but capable central administration and a strong local leadership that was well-resourced and professionally supported (Aho et al, 2006, p.118ff).

The kinds of powers given to patrons in the Irish legislation make Finnish-type reforms to governance difficult to accomplish here. Nevertheless, while working within the current statutory governance framework, it is still possible for gains of the kind mentioned above to be made in sectors other than the ETBs. For instance, clustering of small and medium-size schools could enable many leadership responsibilities, that are currently daunting, to be carried out with less difficulty, including the probation of newly-qualified teachers and the sharing of expertise in school self-evaluation and in professional development. Where the heavy burden of administration on individual schools is concerned, moreover, there is much to recommend co-operative efforts by boards of management to explore how and where joint efforts might help to lessen that burden. In any event, to continue with a situation where very many schools – often quite small schools – have to work alone on resourcing and administration is to curtail the growth of a strong leadership capacity within the schools.

EDUCATIONAL LEADERSHIP AND THE NOTION OF PARTNERSHIP

We all recall the era of social partnership - between 1997 and 2007 - that brought major advances in Ireland's economic development. During that period, the notion of partnership was not just that of a formal agreement to be negotiated and renewed between the government and the main social partners. It was also an idea that became influential outside of such formal agreements. Within the field of education, it was a notion that found a new realisation during the deliberations of the National Education Convention of 1993-94. The Convention was itself a major educational leadership initiative. The degree of shared understanding it accomplished made possible the publication of the 1995 White Paper *Charting Our Education Future*. This landmark policy document was accepted by all of the main interested parties – a marked contrast to the 1992 Green Paper, *Education for a Changing World*. The five underlying principles of *Charting our Education Future* provided the rationale for the 1998 Education Act, and are included in the preamble to that Act: partnership, plurality, quality, equality, and accountability. Although overshadowed by acrimonies stoked by the recent recession, these five principles, together with the provisions of the 1998 Act, still provide the foundations for educational policy-making in Ireland.

The experience of the Convention and its aftermath reveals the kind of strength-in-unity that becomes possible when partnership is taken seriously enough to enable the more sectional concerns of different groups to be lowered in the order of priority. This brings home the need for a vision of educational effort, and more particularly of educational leadership, that can be shared among the different parties. Moreover, it underlines the importance of a clear and succinct concept of educational leadership such as that offered at the beginning of the chapter: discovering and pursuing initiatives that enhance the quality of learning and teaching in the school.

School principals and deputy principals have a central role to play in building such partnerships anew, and sustaining them. This is the real significance of 'taking the moral imperative on the road.' The work involves sustaining a dialogue with a range of bodies that have themselves a proper role to play in educational leadership, but who are often preoccupied by other concerns, normally administrative and managerial ones. Partners to such a leadership dialogue would include: the DES, particularly the Inspectorate and the Teacher Education Section; national support agencies like PDST, JCT; the Teaching Council; the NCCA; Education Centres; parents' bodies; student representative bodies; teacher educators and educational researchers in higher education. The educational leadership voice of bodies like IPPN and NAPD has a particularly valuable contribution to make here.

Where such a dialogue on educational leadership becomes a lively and central part of a country's educational life, the balance of influence in policy-making shifts dramatically. In an inclusive and energetic to-and-fro such as this, the initiative comes to the hands of those who move to take it when the right opportunity arises, and who use it well. It may move over, back and around, as the lead does in an accomplished set-dance. One of the main positive consequences of such a dialogue is that the discourse of educational policy-making now tends to become marked more by fertile ideas with a research-informed backing than by bureaucratic ideas or ideologically inspired ones. This allows a 'virtuous circle' to arise (viz. the reverse of a vicious circle) and enables educational leadership voices to come to the fore. Where our own country is concerned, this wouldn't mark the end of acrimony in debates on educational policy-making and implementation, but it could do much to promote a more promising vista and to redress the negative and frequently misinformed character of much that has passed for debate in educational reform in recent years. It might even cultivate the conditions that would make the exploration of a new and necessary contractual deal for teachers possible. The fact that such a new deal for teachers has yet to appear on the horizon illustrates that a clear and convincing vision of educational leadership urgently needs to be taken on the road in Ireland.

The School System: Equality, Inclusion and Rights

'The educational system is shaped by public policy, criteria of selection for different tracks, the way it is financed, the cost of study for students and their families, and the availability of continuing education…To sum up: the best way to increase wages and reduce wage inequalities in the long run is to invest in education and skills'.
(Piketty, 2014, pp. 305 & 313)

'Although good schools make a difference, the biggest influence on educational attainment, how well a child performs in school and later in higher education, is family background…More unequal countries and more unequal states have worse educational attainment'
(Wilkinson and Pickett, 2009, pp. 103 & 105)

INTRODUCTION

The focus on equality and inequality in education has been a significant feature of educational research. This is because of the marked variation in educational experiences and outcomes of a number of social groups. Research on equality and inequality poses questions. These questions are vital to successful policy-making, concerning the capacity of schools to foster social solidarity, inclusion, academic achievement and personal growth, on the one hand, and to assess the impact of power and inequality on the outcomes for different groups, on the other. In this chapter, we will review the evidence on equality, rights and inclusion in the Irish educational system in order to assess the gains, achievements and remaining challenges, and to highlight potential directions for policy and improvements.

Equality is a concept about which there is sometimes a lack of clarity. It does not mean that the ambition is to make everyone the same. On the contrary, equality involves respecting and valuing diversity. Nor does it mean treating all individuals exactly the same. Sometimes trying to achieve equality necessitates giving additional resources to disadvantaged groups. As the Educational Disadvantage Committee (2005) pointed out, equality of opportunity, access and participation has been the focus of many previous policy interventions in Ireland. However, equality of outcomes is the more challenging aim insofar as research has consistently found that even when improvements in access and participation occur in the school population as a whole, there are still persistent inequalities between the different sub-groups.

> " Equality is a concept about which there is sometimes a lack of clarity. It does not mean that the ambition is to make everyone the same. On the contrary, equality involves respecting and valuing diversity. "

In defining equality, Baker et al. (2009) endorse the concept of equality of condition, which, in the area of education, would involve providing educational and occupational options that give everyone the prospect of self-development and satisfying work. Baker et al. (2006: pp. 413-414) argue that material inequalities - sexual orientation. Therefore, inequality in education is the obvious 'elephant in the room' in any discussion on education. Inclusion is also a key concept at national and European levels. Finally, the various obligations arising from human rights covenants and treaties place great obligations on education systems, schools and teachers to maximise the participation and achievement of all children. We will now look at the evidence on gains and challenges in the above-mentioned areas and will start by looking at the findings relating to social class/socio-economic disadvantage.

SOCIAL CLASS/SOCIO-ECONOMIC DISADVANTAGE

A glance at the statistics on educational participation from primary to third levels from 1965/66 at the time of the Investment in Education Report (1965a) to the present day illustrates the enormous increase in participation. In 1965/66, the participation numbers were 504,865 at primary, 142,983 at second level and 20,698 at third level. In 2014/15, the numbers were 544,696 at primary, 372,296 at second level and 173,649 at third level. These represent proportionate increases of 8% at primary, 160% at second level and 739% (more than eight fold) at third level, while the population increase was 61% over the period (CSO, 2016). This is undoubtedly one of the great successes of the Irish state and of generations of educators. Nevertheless, in spite of these considerable achievements, the issue of inequality relating to social class/socio-economic disadvantage is still very evident and is a matter of concern to educationalists. Research evidence from Ireland, and from around the world, shows that investment in education yields very significant economic and social benefits for society at large (Smyth and McCoy, 2009).

So, what does the evidence tell us about contemporary social class/socio-economic inequality? Ireland, by the end of the so-called 'Celtic Tiger' 'boom' period, ranked well above the Organisation for Economic Cooperation and Development (OECD) average on the overall poverty rate and on measures which indicated poverty among children (OECD, 2009, pp. 91-93). The country was on the lower end of the range on the indicator of average public social spending and of net social spending (ibid., pp. 97-99), partially due, perhaps, to the dominance of neo-liberal, pro-market policy philosophies. Ireland had made relatively poor progress at the time of its highest prosperity on measures of social cohesion.

Social class inequalities in society are closely interlinked with educational inequalities. Indeed, it has been argued by many sociologists that education both maintains and reproduces social class and socio-economic inequalities. The failure of education as a social institution to eliminate social-class-related inequalities is well documented in Ireland and elsewhere (Lynch and Lodge, 2002). The persistence of educational inequalities relating to socio-economic background is also well documented and persisted right throughout the period of Ireland's apparent economic prosperity (Lynch and Moran, 2006). For example, recent figures on the economic status of school leavers (Byrne et al., 2008) show that school leavers from professional backgrounds have a high share of further and higher education places relative to those from other socio-economic backgrounds. Those from manual and non-manual backgrounds were more likely to go straight into employment. Those from unemployed backgrounds had similar labour market participation levels as these manual and non-manual groups, but a greater share of these young people were themselves unemployed (ibid.).

The findings of the largest cohort study ever conducted in Ireland are continuing to provide valuable insights into the impact of socio-economic inequality on children's education. *Growing Up in Ireland*

(GUI) is a government-funded study of 18,000 children and follows their progress from infancy (10,000 nine month olds originally visited by researchers in 2007 and 8,000 nine year olds selected randomly through the primary school system). The children have been followed up as they developed: the nine-year-olds at age 13, the infants at ages three and five. Further information is to be gathered at ages seven and nine from the infant cohort and at 17 and 20 for the child cohort. Already information on a wide variety of dimensions of the children's lives has been analysed and published and further results will emerge over the coming years (www.growingup.ie) The anonymised *Growing Up in Ireland* data from the child (13 years and nine years) and infant (nine months, three years and five years) cohorts are available for request for bona fide research purposes by professional and postgraduate researchers through the Irish Social Science Data Archive (ISSDA).

Children from unskilled manual backgrounds and economically inactive households were much more likely to spend time on sports and watching television. Nearly half of children from economically inactive households were in the TV/sports group. Children from working-class backgrounds were somewhat more likely to be involved in sports/computer games (accounting for typically one-quarter of these children) than children from more advantaged backgrounds. Participation in cultural activities was strongly differentiated by social class; one in three children from professional backgrounds were engaged in cultural activities compared to less than one in 10 of the most disadvantaged children. The study points out that these types of structured activities have been found to enhance school engagement and academic performance. Clear differences were evident in reading and Mathematics performance according to the types of out-of-school activities in which the children engaged. Even taking account of a wide range of background factors, children who engaged in cultural activities and social networking performed better in reading and Mathematics than other groups. Those taking part in sports/computer games also had higher Reading and Mathematics scores. The lowest test scores were found among those who spent their time on TV/sports and among those with 'busy lives' – i.e. a diversity of activities. The results also suggested that low income operates as an additional barrier to participation by children because of the paid nature of many out-of-school activities (Ibid.). We concur with the recommendations of McCoy et al. that greater collaboration with, and financial support for, non-governmental organisations could play an important role in developing greater and more diverse leisure and cultural facilities and infrastructure for children, particularly for those from disadvantaged backgrounds. We agree also that during the school day, principals and teachers should encourage children's learning in the broadest sense, facilitating access to a wide range of enrichment activities for all children and moving beyond a narrow academic focus.

As well as out-of-school activities, we must also consider the importance of early education. Research from a variety of studies shows that high quality early pre-school education is essential to improve educational outcomes and to combat disadvantage, such as early leaving and unemployment (Pascal and Bertram, 2013 – also see Chapter 2 of this report for an analysis of the development of Irish policy on early education). Ireland has one of the lowest rates in pre-school enrolment in the OECD for three year olds. In 2013/14, the enrolment rate in Ireland for children aged three was 46%, the sixth lowest of all countries shown (OECD, 2016a, p. 308) but because so many Irish children begin primary school at age four or five this pushes up the figure for four and five year olds above the OECD average. By primary school, socio-economic disadvantage is already very evident. For example, regarding the literacy of educationally-disadvantaged children, a report by the Irish school Inspectorate has shown, *inter alia*, that despite some good practice and initiatives, nearly half the primary school children in disadvantaged schools evaluated had very low scores in reading, while almost two-thirds of children scored poorly in Mathematics (Department of Education and Science, 2005a). Most of these disadvantaged schools come under the DEIS (i.e. Delivering Equality of Opportunity in Schools scheme) and receive additional resources. Lower scores in Reading and Mathematics in the most disadvantaged DEIS primary schools were observed in a study of student outcomes over the period 2007-2013 (Smyth et al., 2015).

> " By primary school, socio-economic disadvantage is already very evident. "

The DEIS schools experienced an improvement in planning for teaching and learning, and in setting targets for achievement during the period (ibid.). Previous evaluation studies had indicated a significant improvement over time in the literacy and numeracy test scores of students in DEIS primary schools, with greater increases for literacy than for numeracy. The ESRI study found some mixed and varied results on student outcomes at primary level and that, overall, the achievement gap between urban DEIS and non-DEIS schools did not show any marked improvement over time, albeit in the context of worsening economic conditions for disadvantaged families over the recession. No doubt, the high concentration of children with multiple disadvantages was a factor here. However, at post-primary level, the study showed a slight but significant narrowing of the gap in average Junior Certificate grades as well as in English grades between DEIS and non-DEIS schools over the period 2003 to 2011 (ibid.).

Another important factor in assessing the impact of social class and socio-economic inequality on educational performance has been the level of segregation or stratification of the different elements of the school system (see Drudy and Kinsella, 2009). The results of the OECD's Programme for International Student Assessment (PISA) show that, in a number of different countries, the effect on student performance of a school's average economic, social, cultural status is very substantial, and that socio-economic differences at student level are much less predictive for performance than the school's socio-economic context (OECD, 2004b, pp. 189-190). One of the key features of the Irish second-level system is that it is divided into a hierarchy of four main strata. Fee-paying voluntary schools are at the 'top', followed by non-fee-paying voluntary secondary schools, then community and comprehensive schools and lastly the schools in what was the vocational education sector, now the Education and Training Board (ETB) sector. ETB schools have the highest proportions of students from poor and unemployed family backgrounds (Smyth, 1999). In line with their relatively privileged positions, fee-paying schools have the highest proportions transferring to higher education. On the other hand, reflecting their more socio-economically disadvantaged intakes, ETB schools have the lowest (ibid.). These, of course, are overall patterns and there are many exceptions – such as particular ETB schools, which have very high levels of transfer to higher education. Nor do these patterns provide an indication of the quality or effectiveness of schools in any particular sector. Some of the most effective schools are those who raise the achievement of children with great challenges in their backgrounds but who do not necessarily transfer to higher education.

Nevertheless, the status hierarchies between different types of schools make it difficult for schools to become more inclusive or egalitarian. The PISA report argues that those more inclusive schooling systems have both higher levels of performance and fewer disparities among students from differing socio-economic backgrounds (OECD, 2004, p.197). Thus, a more inclusive school system has to be part of the solution to Ireland's economic difficulties and to increasing social cohesion.

The need for an integrated public policy approach to educational inequality, involving a range of government departments, has long been signalled as essential - for example, in the 1992 Government Green Paper *Education for a Changing World* (p. 45) and more recently in the Department of Education and Skills' (DES) *Statement of Strategy 2015 – 2017* (p. 6). This integrated public policy has yet to be fully implemented. For example, the income inequalities indicated above are reflected in residential patterns in Ireland, which in turn place barriers to the capacity of the school

> " The PISA report argues that those more inclusive schooling systems have both higher levels of performance and fewer disparities among students from differing socio-economic backgrounds "

system to be fully inclusive (Drudy and Kinsella, 2009). Over the years many Local Authorities have, perhaps unwittingly, pursued a housing policy of 'segregation' by concentrating low-income families in particular geographical areas (Drudy and Punch, 2005, p. 140). On the other hand, particularly in urban areas, élite residential areas are ring-fenced from the poor or other 'undesirable' groups on the grounds that they might 'downgrade' the area or adversely affect house prices (ibid., p. 142).

Research on the Irish school system has shown that, when it comes to second-level schooling, those who have resources can exercise choices and those without resources generally cannot, or have relatively restricted choices, depending on where they live (Lynch and Lodge, 2002: 48). Schools can, by the way they profile themselves, or by the criteria they choose for admission, indirectly exclude students from particular social backgrounds (ibid.). If certain social classes are excluded from a school through these kinds of sociological mechanisms, it is difficult to see how they can be inclusive, or how greater equality can be achieved. Indeed, exclusionary practices, of whatever kind, have no place in the system if the DES is to achieve the inclusive system envisaged as a goal of its current strategy (DES, 2015a).

While social class has a very strong influence on educational outcomes, school social mix is found to have a very significant impact on post-school outcomes, with those who attended middle-class schools having particularly high levels of participation in higher education (McCoy et al., 2014). In contrast, young people who had attended working-class schools are much more likely than those in middle-class or socially-mixed schools to enter the labour market directly upon leaving school, even taking account of their Leaving Certificate grades (ibid.). However, in recent decades general school completion rates and transfer to higher education have improved very significantly. For example, Central Statistics Office data show that 38% of Irish 25-64 year olds had attained a third level qualification in 2011 and 48% of 25 – 34 year olds had a third level qualification (www.cso.ie). This places Ireland very favourably in the matter of attainment levels in comparison to many European countries. Nevertheless, in spite of these undoubted gains, there are still substantial inequalities relating to social class.

The impact of a range of austerity measures brought into effect in all Budgets since 2008 is very likely to be a negative one in the area of social class inequality. These Budgets introduced substantial cuts in public expenditure, which impacted disproportionately on the poor. The effects are already evident. In 2008, 6.3% of all children aged 17 and under were living in consistent poverty. By the year 2014, the most recent *Survey on Income and Living Conditions* (SILC) shows the proportion had risen to 11.2% (CSO, 2015). A recent UNICEF (2016) analysis points out that in Ireland, the household income of the child at the 10th percentile is 41.5% lower than that of the child in the middle of the income distribution – the median. Such is the level of child poverty in Ireland that the Children's Rights Alliance in its annual Report Card (2016) awarded the government an E-grade on this area. This report points out that the children at high risk of poverty include children in lone parent families, children in jobless households, Traveller and Roma children, children living in direct provision centres, children with a disability, and homeless children. A range of recommended actions to address child poverty is included in this Report Card.

While cultural and social capital plays a key role in educational achievement, there is ample evidence from Ireland and other countries that children from poor households are much more likely to do poorly in school and to have lower levels of achievement than others. An increase in child poverty will aggravate existing levels of educational inequality and will increase the risk of socially destabilising factors such as early school leaving, future unemployment, juvenile crime and early parenthood.

In the 1998 Education Act, an Educational Disadvantage Committee was established to advise the Minister on policies and strategies to be adopted to identify and correct educational disadvantage. The first Educational Disadvantage Committee presented its final report in 2005, with a comprehensive, evidence-based range of recommendations and strategies to address educational disadvantage arising from a range of circumstances, including of course socio-economic disadvantage. This Committee took an approach to educational inclusion and equality based on fundamental principles of human rights and social justice. It adopted six principles underpinning the proposed strategy: a rights-based approach to equality; the inclusion of diversity; integration of strategies, structures and systems; coherence of provision; focused target-setting and measurement; monitoring of outcomes and results (p. 27). Although the Educational Disadvantage Committee was established by statute under the 1998 Act and was clearly intended to have an ongoing advisory role in relation to disadvantage, it has not been replaced since 2005. Indeed, on the contrary, Section 32 of the 1998 Education Act, which established the Committee, was repealed under the 2012 Education (Amendment) Act. Such a Committee, were it to be re-established, could clearly play an important role in advising the Minister on evidence-based policy development and implementation.

It is now widely acknowledged that a proportion of children (albeit a minority) continue to suffer from some form of abuse – either physical, emotional or sexual. Such abuse is not related to social class, per se, but in some cases can certainly lead to educational disadvantage because of its profound psychological effects. Thus, all schools must have a child protection policy. The DES has produced guidelines for schools, the most recent of which are *Child Protection Procedures for Primary and Post-Primary Schools* (2011b). These guidelines and procedures are based upon those in Children First (Department of Children and Youth Affairs, 2011) and provide substantial detail and guidance for schools and teachers. It is therefore a matter of concern that research has found that a significant proportion of newly-qualified (primary) teachers are unaware of the national child protection guidelines for teachers and the policies of their own schools (Buckley and McGarry, 2011). Half of the respondents in this study did not know whether their school had a child protection policy or not. Of those who were aware of their school's child protection policy, only just over half had read it. Well under half of the respondents knew whether there was a Designated Liaison Person (DLP) with responsibility for child protection in their school. Furthermore, nearly two-thirds of respondents reported uncertainty or lack of confidence in being able to identify suspected child abuse. A significant number were also unaware of whom to contact if they encountered suspected child abuse. The study has also shown that the training received during teacher education has made very limited impact (ibid.). These results indicate a need for greater input on child protection in initial teacher education and in continuing professional development.

DISABILITY/SPECIAL EDUCATIONAL NEEDS

At the time of the 2011 Census there were 595,335 persons (of all ages), or 13% of the population, who declared that they had a disability (CSO, 2012). It is important to point out in a discussion on education that not all people with a disability have a special educational need (SEN). Likewise not all people with a special educational need will have a diagnosed disability. Thus, the numbers of persons in these two categories at any one time may differ.

When the Irish state was founded in 1922 there were only eight institutions, all charitable, private and voluntary, dedicated to serving the needs of people with disabilities and special educational needs (Griffin and Shevlin, 2007). It was not until 1952, when the schools for the blind were allowed a special pupil-teacher ratio of 1:15 and financial aid towards the purchase of specialised equipment that state intervention became a reality (ibid.). After this, state provision for special education expanded slowly, including the establishment of post-graduate programmes for teachers such as the Higher Diploma for the Teaching of the Deaf (1956), the Higher Diploma in Remedial and Special Education (1984) in University College Dublin and the Diploma in Special Education in St Patrick's College of Education, Dublin (1961). However, state provision for special education remained segregated (mainly in special schools) to a very substantial degree until the 1990s.

> " It is important to point out in a discussion on education that not all people with a disability have a special educational need (SEN). "

For the first time a policy of integrated education in the EU was endorsed in 1990 concerning integration of children and young people with disabilities into ordinary systems of education (Council of the European Union, 1990). This was proposed by the Irish Minister for Education during the Irish presidency and was adopted unanimously by the EC Council of Ministers for Education (Government of Ireland, 1992, p. 61). This was followed by the establishment of the Special Education Review Committee, which reported in 1993. This was a comprehensive report which is still influential and which provided a blueprint for the development of special education – with one major exception, that of the area of autism spectrum disorder (ASD). A number of court cases (initiated by parents) and court judgments followed, the most important of which was the landmark High Court judgement in the O'Donoghue case which underlined the state's responsibility to provide appropriate educational opportunities for all children, whatever their disabilities or learning needs (Griffin and Shevlin, 2007).

In 1998, the first comprehensive *Education Act* to regulate the system was enacted. This specifically set out to make provision in the common good for the education of every person in the state, including those with a disability or other special educational need. In 2000, the Task Force on Autism was set up and reported in 2001, addressing the educational provision and support of people with ASD, while the Task Force on Dyslexia also reported in 2001. The recommendations of these two reports resulted in a substantial expansion of educational services, especially for students with ASD. In 2004 the *Education for Persons with Special Educational Needs (EPSEN) Act* was passed. This established the National Council for Special Education (NCSE), which has an advisory, research and coordination role for special education. However, due to budgetary constraints, the full Act has not yet been commenced.

Thus, since the late 1990s government policy has favoured the inclusion of children with disabilities in mainstream schools and classes, while retaining a continuum of provision of special schools and classes to meet, in particular, the needs of children with more significant disabilities. In the 2013/14 school year, the NCSE enabled over 45,700 students with special educational needs to receive additional teaching in mainstream schools (NCSE, 2015). This represents 5.3% of the mainstream school population, both primary and post-primary (the mainstream population was 869,492 in that year – www.education.ie). While this is the proportion of children with special educational needs in mainstream schools as a whole, research

> " In 1998, the first comprehensive *Education Act* to regulate the system was enacted. This specifically set out to make provision in the common good for the education of every person in the state, including those with a disability or other special educational need. "

has shown that a small proportion of both primary and post-primary schools have much larger numbers with assessed disabilities/special educational needs and report that over 20% of their pupils fall into this category (O'Gorman and Drudy, 2011). As well as those receiving support in mainstream classes, in 2013/14 there were 737 special classes in mainstream schools with 4,997 places and an additional 7,500 pupils enrolled in special schools. By 2015/16 there were 11,820 special needs assistants (NCSE, 2015), compared to less than 300 in the late 1990s, and some 6,832 resource teachers, many of whom work alongside the mainstream teacher (NCSE, 2015). This represents a great improvement in the support of children with special educational needs, even through a period of economic difficulty.

A further welcome initiative in the field of disability/SEN was the introduction of Reasonable Accommodation in Certificate Examinations (RACE). RACE is targeted to candidates with permanent or long-term conditions, including visual and hearing difficulties, or specific learning difficulties. The stated aim is to remove, as far as possible, the impact of the disability on the candidate's performance and thus enable the candidate to demonstrate his or her level of attainment. It also aims to ensure that, whilst giving candidates every opportunity to demonstrate their level of attainment, the special arrangements will not give the candidate an unfair advantage over other candidates in the same examination (State Examinations Commission, 2016). However, a number of people have expressed dissatisfaction with the operation of the scheme, as evidenced by Dáil questions, and concern has been expressed that the recommendations of an expert advisory group have not been implemented (*Irish Times*, July 2, 2015).

The DES established the Special Education Support Service (SESS) in 2003, with the role of enhancing the learning and teaching of pupils with SEN by means of professional development for teachers. From 2017, the SESS will form part of the Inclusion Support Service within the NCSE, along with the National Behaviour Support Service (NBSS) and the Visiting Teacher Service for children who are deaf or hard of hearing and for children who are blind/visually impaired (VTHVI) – www.education.ie. In addition, there are now accredited postgraduate courses at Higher Diploma and Masters levels in special education for serving teachers in many of the universities. In its criteria for Initial Teacher Education (ITE), the Teaching Council has made inclusion, including special education, a mandatory element for all courses seeking professional accreditation. This is a very welcome initiative and formalises an element of the teacher education curriculum that was already well embedded in teacher education programmes. Research commissioned by the NCSE into the impact of teacher education for inclusion (as assessed by student teachers, NQTs and early stage professionals) should provide valuable insights into teacher professional formation in this area.

These developments represent significant progress for a group of pupils who until the end of the 1990s were very seriously marginalised in education. However, even these very vulnerable pupils have received cuts to their support services. As the Children Rights Alliance *Report Card* (2016) points out, the *Education for Persons with Special Educational Needs (EPSEN) Act 2004* is the key statute governing the education of children with special needs. However, in 2008, due to budgetary constraints the government deferred full implementation of this Act.

While acknowledging that very significant progress has been made by Irish policy-makers and schools in educational provision and support for students with disabilities and special educational needs, research has shown that there are still issues to be addressed. Research on Irish primary-age children shows that school experiences and attitudes towards school vary among children with SEN according to the type of need they have. At a descriptive level, the findings show that students with multiple disabilities - typically learning and physical disability or learning disability and emotional behavioural disorders (EBD) - are much more likely to dislike school compared to other students in the SEN group (such as those with physical, visual, hearing and speech difficulties) (McCoy and Banks, 2012).

A secondary analysis of wave one data from the GUI programme (Cosgrove et al., 2014) showed that children with SEN, particularly those identified with learning disabilities, face considerable barriers to engage fully in school life. They are considerably less likely to enjoy their time spent at school, a finding that holds when account is taken of their social and cultural background. A study of the experiences of children in all types of school settings shows that most pupils made academic progress, though often significantly below that achieved by their peer group. The two largest categories of special educational need identified in this study were social, emotional or behavioural difficulties (SEBD) and general learning difficulties (GLD). While there were, of course, considerable variations in background characteristics and, to a degree, by SEN categories, the analysis of the GUI data showed that children with special educational needs were disproportionately affected by a constellation of disadvantages. They were more likely to be from families with higher levels of socio-economic disadvantage than children without special educational needs; more likely to be in families under financial stress; more likely to have parents with poorer educational attainment than others; more likely to be from one-parent families; more likely to be attending DEIS schools (and thus in situations where there were higher levels of literacy and numeracy difficulties); and also more likely to be 'clustered' in classrooms – i.e. placed with other children with SEN (Cosgrove et al., 2014). Policy advice from the NCSE has been that the EPSEN Act (Government of Ireland, 2004) still represents the most effective blueprint for delivering resources to this cohort through its emphasis on individualised assessment processes, educational planning and monitoring of student outcomes (NCSE Working Group, 2014). Thus, pending the full implementation of EPSEN and due to concerns about possible inequities in the allocation of resources to schools, policy advice from this Working Group (2014) recommended a new and better model for the allocation of teaching resources. This is now to be extended from the pilot phase to all schools with 900 additional teaching posts, with effect from September 2017 (DES, 2017a).

A recent study of the experiences of students with SEN in post-primary schools has found that the majority of students have very positive experiences (Squires et al., 2016). However, some students experienced problems. A number of key lessons emerged from this study. Students should be at the centre of decisions made about them and actively involved in the process. School leaders need to consider how they can create a culture and climate in their schools that are supportive of all students, especially those who are vulnerable or have special educational needs. Friendship development and maintenance is harder for some students with SEN and particularly challenged at times of transition when existing friendships may change. When different teachers are involved in teaching an individual student or group of students, there needs to be good communication between the teaching team so that consistent approaches are used and opportunities for skill generalisation are developed. Schools should reflect on how they manage bullying in their schools and pay particular attention to students with special educational needs. Finally, school buildings need to be audited in terms of accessibility with the aim of improving access for different groups of students (Ibid., pp. 134-136).

It is likely that children with disabilities/SEN will have higher levels of unemployment. Since school engagement is crucial to helping people stay in education, the tendency for students with a disability to dislike school clearly needs to be addressed by teachers and schools. Therapeutic support services, such as speech and occupational therapy, psychological, physical and psychiatric supports, are also essential and primarily (apart from the National Education Psychology Service) provided by the HSE. Other research on the experiences and outcomes for students with SEN in Irish schools presents a mixed picture of the special education system in Ireland. It was evident from this research that the infrastructure to support special education provision has developed over recent years. It was also apparent, however, that serious systemic shortcomings exist. These include issues related to access to appropriate and timely assessments in order to avail of resources, the availability of therapeutic support, and failure to fully implement the EPSEN Act, with implications for the consistent development and application of individual education plans (Rose et al., 2015). Inadequacies in the provision of support services have been reported by many parents of children with disabilities. The barriers also include insufficient teacher knowledge and expertise, inconsistencies in development and implementation of IEPs and exclusionary clauses in school enrolment policies (ibid.). Research has also shown the greater likelihood of children with SEN being bullied at school (Cosgrove et al., 2014).

The likelihood of lower levels of employment among people with disabilities/special needs is borne out in a number of studies. For example, the CSO analysis of the 2011 census found that of people aged 15 and over, and who declared a disability, only 21% were at work. This compares to 50% for the overall population aged 15 and over who were at work (CSO, 2012). The National Disability Authority (NDA) has found that employment levels are higher among those with higher levels of education (Watson et al., 2015). Education greatly increases employment potential but also the independence levels of those not capable of unsupported employment and enhances their social inclusion and quality of life.

> " It is likely that children with disabilities/SEN will have higher levels of unemployment. Since school engagement is crucial to helping people stay in education, the tendency for students with a disability to dislike school clearly needs to be addressed by teachers and schools. "

Watson et al. (2015) suggest a broadening of the curriculum to include greater availability of programmes such as the Junior Cycle Schools Programme and Leaving Certificate Applied Programme. They also suggest the introduction of a Level 2 award under the proposed reform of the Junior Cycle, which should enhance the school experiences for young people with special needs for whom the traditional Junior Certificate is unsuitable. It is likely that, when implemented, the establishment of

Level 2 Priority Learning Units and the Level 1 Learning Programme envisaged in the implementation framework for the Junior Cycle (DES, 2015 b) will address these issues. Thus, in order to respect the rights of such individuals with disabilities and to fulfil the commitments consonant with international covenants and agreements, continuing support for pupils with disabilities (physical, sensory and learning), and for those with any kind of SEN must, remain a core part of the education agenda, as must professional development for teachers (O'Gorman, et al., 2009).

ETHNIC DIVERSITY

Many schools now cater for children from a variety of cultural backgrounds. In some schools there may be up to twenty nationalities and linguistic backgrounds, and children from a wide variety of religious backgrounds. By 2007, some 10% of primary school pupils were from immigrant or 'newcomer' families, of whom over three quarters were non-English speakers (Smyth et al., 2009, pp. 44-45). At second level, some 6% of pupils were from immigrant families, of whom 70% were non-English speakers. Again, some schools have a much higher proportion of their pupil populations comprising immigrant children. At primary and second level, there are some schools with over 20% of their pupils in this category (ibid.). There is evidence from other countries that allowing high concentrations of ethnic or racial minority children in some schools has a negative effect. For example, in the US, it has been found that school factors are very powerful and that black children are more likely to attend predominantly minority schools and that this leads to a black/white achievement gap (Condron, 2009). A study by the ESRI (Byrne et al., 2010) found little evidence of segregation in the Irish context but, in line with international studies, found that schools with a more socio-economically disadvantaged intake tend to have a higher proportion of immigrant students than other schools, and this was true for both urban primary and second-level schools. This finding, they argue, raises concern about whether 'choice' is available for immigrant families given that these schools tend to be undersubscribed relative to non-DEIS schools.

> " Many schools now cater for children from a variety of cultural backgrounds. In some schools there may be up to twenty nationalities and linguistic backgrounds, and children from a wide variety of religious backgrounds. "

Studies have shown the difficulties that some immigrant children face when attending school in Ireland and the need for more support for them in school contexts. The need for immigrant children to have language and intercultural support in school settings in Ireland is evident (Tyrrell et al., 2011). However, it is also evident that there are as many differences between immigrant children as there are similarities, suggesting that a 'one size fits all' approach to diversity in schools is not sufficient (Devine, 2011; Darmody et al., 2017). It is particularly important that schools and teachers are aware that, while there is evidence that the children of migrant families are frequently highly motivated, poor proficiency in English – which is the mother tongue to just a minority of migrant children – can seriously damage the achievements of migrant children (Darmody et al., 2017). This would suggest that there should be substantial investment in support for English as an additional language for migrant children.

Research in Ireland and other countries has shown that immigrant children reported lower life satisfaction than non-immigrant children (Unicef Office of Research, 2016). Research by Darmody and Smyth (2015) explored the views of Irish teenagers on immigrant peers. In general, they point out that what emerges from the interviews is complex, indicating that a number of factors influence their perspectives: the attitudes prevalent in broader society, their degree of contact with immigrant students and (most importantly from an educational point of view) the way that difference is handled within and outside the school. Unicef Office of Research (2016) refers to the finding that schools with a higher proportion of immigrant children also had higher levels of fighting and bullying, but that classmate support played an important role. When classmate support was high, regardless of the proportion of immigrant children in the school, levels of violent behaviour were lower. What is needed is a concerted effort to promote tolerance and to address anti-racism. A cross-national study, which includes Ireland, by Van Driel et al. (2016) provides useful research-based guidelines, advice and recommendations for schools. We would argue that, at its most basic, what is required is to make immigrant students feel welcome in whichever school or setting they happen to be.

Research shows that teachers' engagement with diversity and with ethnic minority students is often constrained by a lack of adequate statutory support and resources to schools and that curricular knowledge should be reconstituted from the point of view of those who are marginalized within society (e.g. immigrant groups) (Bryan and Bracken, 2011). In other words, the curriculum should reflect the families and cultures of minority groups, as well as those of the majority. In particular, teachers should be aware that the immigrant children who are likely to be in need of most support are those who themselves or their families have experienced trauma of one kind or another (Levels et al., 2008). Children in direct provision may be particularly at risk. The *Convention on the Rights of the Child* (CRC) states that states must ensure that education is offered to all children. Over one third of those in direct provision for asylum seekers are children. Research among people in direct provision for asylum seekers (Arnold, 2012) has identified a range of barriers for children in attempting to avail of their rights under the CRC. These include: difficulties in obtaining access to schools in some areas; difficulties in accessing transport to schools (sometimes centres are in remote locations); difficulties in full participation in education due to lack of space in direct provision, cost of books, and coming to school hungry. Arnold's Report to the Irish Refugee Council includes recommendations to address these and other issues arising from direct provision. While many of the recommendations would require implementation by other government departments, they are a clear case for the type of inter-departmental and inter-agency cooperation envisaged in the DES *Statement of Strategy*.

In addition to immigrant children, Travellers continue to suffer marginalisation, including discrimination in the Irish education system (Harmon et al., 2015). Although Travellers are recognised as an ethnic minority in Northern Ireland and the rest of the U.K. and although recognition of Traveller ethnicity has been urged by the Equality Authority, the Human Rights Commission and other expert groups, the government has not, as yet, provided that designation. The government has been asked to review the matter by the UN Human Rights Committee, by the Council of Europe Commissioner for Human Rights and the UN Committee on the Rights of the Child (www.paveepoint.ie). At the time of writing, it appears from newspaper reports that discussions at government level are underway. It is argued that a state recognition of Traveller (and Roma) ethnicity would lead to a better identification of problems such as racism and to better eventual outcomes.

A study by the Department of Education and Science (2005b) shows improvements in the Traveller participation and completion rates but continuing significant disadvantage in comparison to the population at large. The National Children's Rights Alliance awarded the government an E- in its annual *Report Card* (2016) in the context of its failure to recognise Travellers' ethnic minority status (in spite of the criticism by international bodies such as the UN Human Rights Committee) and in the context that, of the general Traveller population, 55% have left school by the age of 15 and some 18% of Travellers have no formal education, compared with less than 2% in the general population (ibid.). Currently, just 13% of Traveller children complete secondary education in comparison with 92% of the general population (Harmon et al., 2015; Watson et al., 2017). Only 1% of Travellers aged 25–64 years have a college degree compared to 30% of non-Travellers (Watson et al., 2017).

Travellers were disproportionately hit by cuts to public service provision since the recession. For example, from 2008-2013 Traveller-specific educational supports were cut by 86.6% (Pavee Point, 2015). From a cultural and inclusive education perspective, it should be noted that, while inclusive education is a mandatory element of all Initial Teacher Education programmes at primary and post primary level, it is not compulsory for teacher education programmes to include specific training on Traveller or Roma communities as part of their inclusive education programmes (ibid.).

Research on ethnicity and education in Ireland by Devine et al. (2002) has identified the current challenges facing schools who wish to be more ethnically inclusive. In order to be inclusive, ethnic diversity issues, anti-racism and inter-culturalism should be included in the school plan and should inform the practice of all staff, including ancillary staff. Appropriate administrative structures should be established, including translation facilities and translated texts, to enable accurate recording of information about children. Student and parental involvement and support are essential in areas such as discipline. Parents should be welcomed, involved on Boards of Management and good feedback from minority ethnic parents on the progress of their children should be encouraged (ibid.). These findings point to two requirements: additional support for marginalised children whose first language is not English or who are from the Traveller community, and to the need for professional development for teachers in best practice relating to diversity. However, it should be pointed out that the authors of the present *Towards a Better Future* report are aware of some outstanding examples of good practice in this area in primary and post-primary schools.

RELIGIOUS DIVERSITY

While Catholic and other Christian denominations still form the majority of the population, the 2011 Census showed that the non-Catholic population has increased significantly (Faas et al., 2016). The share of the Catholic Church in the population had declined to 84% in 2011. By far the two largest proportionate changes between 2006 and 2011 were in the 'Other' category (which would have included the increase in the Muslim population) and in the 'No religion' category. With a proportionate share of 84% of the population, a total of 91% of primary schools are Catholic (ibid.). Three other Christian denominations,

> " The multi-denominational sector has grown from the early 1990s when they had just 11 primary schools to 77 primary and four post-primary schools in 2016... still a modest share of the total number of schools. "

with 4% of the population together have 6% of the schools. Muslims, now the third largest denomination, have just two schools, while Jews have one school. The multi-denominational sector has grown from the early 1990s when they had just 11 primary schools to 77 primary and four post-primary schools in 2016 (www.educatetogether.ie), still a modest share of the total number of schools.

The fact that 96% of Irish primary schools have religious patrons, with 91% of these under the patronage of the Catholic Church is unique in the developed world (*Report of the Advisory Group on Patronage and Pluralism*, 2012). This has been raised four times with state representatives before the UN Human Rights Committee as part of the periodic reporting mechanism. This Committee has recommended that Irish schooling should be re-structured in order to protect freedom of religion and non-discrimination and that more non-denominational schools should exist throughout the country (Mawhinney, 2015). The *Report of the Advisory Group on the Forum on Patronage and Pluralism in the Primary Sector* was published in 2012 and updates indicate that little progress has been made to date, particularly in the area of divestment (www.education.ie).

The issue of religious freedom and the 'right to discriminate' in the matter of school admissions has become a matter of public concern as well as legal analysis (Daly and Hickey, 2011; Ó Foghlú, 2016). The *Education (Admissions to Schools) Bill*, published in 2015 did not proceed under the last government, but the 2016 version of this Bill is, at time of writing, before the Dáil (www.education.ie). However, it continues to permit discrimination in admissions on religious grounds:

> 'where, in the case of a school whose objective is to provide education in an environment which promotes certain religious values, where the school refuses to admit as a student a person who is not of that denomination and it is proved that the refusal is essential to maintain the ethos of the school'
> (S62, (c) (iv)).

This is currently a matter of intense debate. In January 2017, the Minister for Education formally opened a consultation process to explore four possible approaches to the admission of children of different denominations and none to primary schools in advance of legislation (DES, 2017b).

Barriers to 'reasonable accommodation' in educational provision for Islam (and other denominations and non-denominational groups) have been identified as three-fold: the established organization of education; population density; the integrated curriculum (Hogan, 2011). While many (especially faith groups) defend the present system, others have suggested educating *all* children in the state in non-denominational secular settings, leaving faith formation to the private domain of parents and communities (O'Toole, 2015). This is a debate that is certain to continue (Rougier and Honahan, 2015). Ireland is experiencing unprecedented change in relation to religious and other forms of diversity so there is a need for schools to value and support pupils from culturally and religiously diverse backgrounds. The need for leadership in order that schools and teachers can be supported to move away from any perception that they are only, or predominantly, 'Catholic, White and Gaelic' has also emerged from research (Parker-Jenkins and Masterson, 2013; Bryan, 2010).

As well as being the predominant form of organization at primary level, denominational education is also strong at second level. There is evidence that many denominationally-owned and controlled schools, however, admit pupils from other denominations and those with no religious affiliation (Smyth & Darmody, 2011). Given the extent of denominational control of the education system, and the likelihood that the churches will continue to be major players in the system, they have an enormously important role to play in the future of Irish society. Decisions that will be made by them in education will affect the shape of society for the future and will require fresh thinking and considerable generosity – not least in terms of how faith formation takes place. Schools are the one institution in which all citizens of the state and all immigrant children participate. Therefore, their potential for good or ill is enormous. Given their predominance in the ownership and management of schools, the churches must play a very significant role in promoting equality, inclusion and anti-racism. The challenges for the churches collectively, who own or manage so much of the education system, are that they must not only promote equality (and, indeed, the thorny question of admissions of children of other faiths and none) but must also face up to such roles as they play in the stratification of the school system and unequal outcomes at second level, in order to address inequality and disadvantage.

GENDER

In terms of educational inequality, gender is sometimes regarded as an unimportant differentiating variable. The reverse is actually the case. It is a variable, however, in which there have been important fluctuations in patterning over the past three decades. In Ireland and internationally, girls now generally outperform boys. In OECD countries, the average gender gap in reading performance is substantial. Boys are significantly more likely than girls to demonstrate a poor level of literacy performance. Boys tend to perform better on average in Mathematics than girls (OECD, 2010) whereas data on special educational needs show that boys outnumber girls by two to one (Dyson & Gallannaugh, 2008). From a position where girls achieved more poorly than boys in public examinations thirty years ago, girls now outperform boys in most areas (O'Connor, 2007). Pedagogical practices, which take account of pupils' different learning styles, are an essential tool in addressing male (and indeed female) underachievement (OFSTED, 2003).

The disadvantageous gender difference for boys is far from unique to Ireland. Unicef Office of Research (2016) points out that since the first PISA study in 2000, 15-year-old boys have consistently done worse than girls have in reading. The gaps in favour of girls are largest in reading: in 2012, girls outperformed boys in reading by a good margin (38 score points, or nearly one year of schooling) on average across OECD countries. In 37 of the 39 countries studied, boys were significantly more likely to be in the bottom decile of reading achievement than girls (ibid.).

There is one area where boys out-perform girls and this is at the higher end of the distribution in Mathematics. Doris, O'Neill and Sweetman (2013) examined this gender gap in Maths scores at age nine in primary schools. Examining the reasons for this gender gap, they argue, is important because of the under-representation of women in Science, Technology, Engineering and Mathematics (STEM) careers. While there was tentative evidence that boys performed better in single sex schools, there was no such evidence for girls. Thus, there was no evidence that the gender gap was smaller in single-sex than in coeducational schools – if anything it was larger. Other variables proved inconclusive in their effects.

The question of single-sex versus co-educational schooling arises in debate on policy from time to time. Back in the 1980s, the DES funded the first study on this topic, conducted by the ESRI. This was *Schooling and Sex Roles: Sex Differences in Subject Provision and Subject Choice in Irish Post-primary*

Schools (Hannan et al., 1983). At the time, the proportion of single-sex schools at post-primary level was 41%. This was the highest proportion at a European level (indeed Ireland still has the highest proportion of single sex post-primary schools at 33%). Debates in the UK, quickly taken up by the Irish media, developed into a moral panic that further development of the co-education sector (i.e. mainly the community and comprehensive sector) would disadvantage girls. The key findings by Hannan et al. pointed to the fact that, before any valid comparisons could be made, factors such as the social class intake of the schools had to be part of the control variables. The research, along with a review of international findings, pointed to the conclusion that it was less a question of whether schools were organised along single sex or coeducational lines than of examining what was done within these schools. The key issues were school policy and practices rather than whether the schools were single sex or co-educational. Thus, this research provided no grounds for the halting of the expansion of the co-educational sector.

A recent British birth cohort analysis of men and women born in 1958 showed that while the men and women in the study had different experiences of paid work and its remuneration at age 42, there was little evidence that having attended a single-sex secondary school had a direct impact on labour market success, or occupational segregation. The results suggested that the gendered nature of labour market (and other) institutions is the dominant feature of adult experience rather than any legacy of single-sex schooling. The authors point to the irony that, while the argument against single-sex schooling is that single-sex environments are 'unnatural' for young people, gender-segregated environments are seen as quite normal in adult life (Sullivan et al., 2011). A review of the international literature (Smyth, 2015) points to the fact that gender differences in educational processes and outcomes are constructed and reconstructed in both single-sex and coeducational settings. Indeed, the way in which schools 'manage' gender may ultimately be much more important than the gender mix of students in the class or school (ibid.).

> **"**
> What is sometimes forgotten is the impact of gender in the take-up of subjects.
> **"**

In the most recent DES strategy, there is a welcome focus on the Arts (DES, 2015a). The Arts foster creativity and entrepreneurship. They are essential in transmitting and creating cultural values, but are also vital to the economy. What is sometimes forgotten is the impact of gender in the take-up of subjects. Boys are still in the majority in the take-up of honours Mathematics and are substantially so in Physics and Engineering, whereas girls are significantly over-represented in the take-up of Art and Music at Leaving Certificate. At Senior Cycle in Ireland, outside a number of core subjects, boys' and girls' subject choices at Senior Cycle break down on very traditional lines (O'Connor, 2007). These choices have important labour market implications. Increasing the uptake of STEM subjects has been a priority for some years, fuelled by a general awareness of the importance of the take-up of STEM subjects for our economy. However, there is also a developing awareness of the importance of what are called the 'STEAM' subjects - i.e. the way in which combining the Arts with the teaching of Science, Technology, Engineering or Mathematics can foster greater creativity and innovation. The OECD has pointed out that, in Ireland, while 22% of men study Science, only 11% of women do, with an even smaller proportion of women studying Engineering, Manufacturing and Construction – 3%, compared to 22% of men (OECD, 2016b). Stereotypical choices have significant labour market implications for students and for social, cultural and economic development. There is substantial work to be done in schools of all types in fostering non-stereotypical subject choices among their pupils.

While female students out-perform boys in most subjects at Leaving Certificate level and predominate in Post Leaving Certificate (PLC) and other further education programmes (O'Connor, 2007), there is one area of education that is almost entirely male-dominated. This is the apprenticeship area. Apprenticeships are set to provide an increasingly important pathway for school leavers. Currently, apprenticeships operate primarily in a number of designated trades, including engineering, construction, motor, electrical, printing, and furniture, and men have typically accounted for 99.5% of graduates of such programmes (O'Connor, 2007). Submissions to the *Review of Apprenticeship Training in Ireland* (DES, 2014c), established by the Minister in 2013, considered that an improved gender balance would best be achieved by widening the scope of apprenticeships into new areas such as business administration, ICT, social care, hospitality, financial services etc. The widening of scope forms part of the strategic plan of Solas (Solas, 2014). Following the Review, the Apprenticeship Council was established. It commenced an invitation process for new apprenticeships in order to identify apprenticeships that could expand into new sectors of the economy, across a range of qualification levels and mapping out the sectors where new apprenticeships could make a real difference to both employers and employees (Apprenticeship Council, 2015). This would result in Ireland moving closer to the model that prevails in Germany, which includes both craft and service occupations, although there is evidence that there too such occupations are gender-typed (Smyth and Steinmetz, 2015). Addressing the gender inequality, which characterises this important avenue to employment, will need to be a strong focus both for government policy and for careers advice in schools.

Analyses of patterns in European countries, including Ireland, show the apparent advantages enjoyed at school by high-performing girls are not always 'cashed out' into later advantage in higher education and beyond (EU Commission, 2009). In Ireland, the OECD and the EU, at all levels of educational attainment and all age-groups women's earnings range from just 73-79% of those of men (OECD, 2016a, p.126). With regard to educational achievement, it must be borne in mind that gender intersects other differentiating variables and both boys and girls are often disadvantaged sufficiently by their family backgrounds to obscure the effects of gender differentiation (Gorard et al., 1999). For example, working-class girls are often both disadvantaged and not identified as such.

SEXUAL ORIENTATION

It is just over twenty years since homosexuality was decriminalised in Ireland. Since then successive Irish governments have introduced a range of legislation giving recognition and rights to people who are lesbian, gay, bi-sexual, transgender or intersex (LGBTI). The relevant legislation includes the *Equal Status Act 2000*, the *Civil Partnership and Certain Rights and Obligations of Cohabitants Act 2010*, the *Gender Recognition Act 2015*, the Marriage Referendum 2015, the *Marriage Act 2015* and the *Equality (Miscellaneous Provisions) Act 2015*. Thus, in the last two decades, Ireland has made significant advances in achieving equality for its LGBTI citizens. Ireland is now considered internationally as a forerunner in progress on equal civil rights of LGBTI people (Higgins et al., 2016).

There are, nonetheless, still problems to be addressed – especially among the school-going population. The advocacy agency GLEN (2016) has pointed out that it is highly likely that every school and classroom in Ireland has LGBT students. A recent survey of 8,000 young people found a sizeable minority did not identify as heterosexual – 8% identified as lesbian, gay or bisexual, while a further 3% were unsure of their sexual orientation. Applying the 8% figure to the current enrolment in second-level schools amounts to approximately 29,000 young people who identify as LGBT. Whether they are 'out' or not, this is a sizeable minority (ibid.).

A study on the mental health of the LGBTI population shows that 12 is the most common age for people to know they are LGBTI and that, in spite of the societal change, there has not been a significant reduction in anti-LGBTI bullying in schools (Higgins et al., 2016). Such bullying can have a devastating impact on LGBTI teenagers' mental health. This survey by Higgins et al. showed that, although the general levels of mental health in the LGBTI population were quite good, the youngest age group in the sample (14–18) had the highest level of mental health difficulties. Their rates of severe depression, anxiety and stress were four times higher than rates in a survey of general Irish adolescents (p. 25).

Bullying is a very serious issue and may affect any individual or category. The DES (2013b) defines bullying as

> 'unwanted negative behaviour, verbal, psychological or physical conducted by an individual or group against another person (or persons) and which is repeated over time. The following types of bullying behaviour are included in this non-exhaustive definition: (i) deliberate exclusion, malicious gossip and other forms of relational bullying; (ii) cyber-bullying; and (iii) identity-based bullying such as homophobic bullying, racist bullying, bullying based on a person's membership of the Traveller community and bullying of those with disabilities or special educational needs' (p. 8).

GLEN, in association with the DES, Tusla, school management bodies and teacher unions, has recently published a compendium of resources and guidelines for schools in order to assist them in addressing homophobic bullying and in supporting LGBTI students (GLEN, 2016).

Issues relating to employment of LGBTI teachers in religious-run schools have been a source of contention since the *Employment Equality Act 1998* and the *Equal Status Act 2000*. Under this previous law, the ethos of religious institutions was prioritised over workplace protection for employees. New amended sections of the *Equality (Miscellaneous Provisions) Act 2015* are aimed at protecting LGBTI employees in state-funded denominational schools and hospitals (*Irish Times* 03/12/2015).

There are also issues relating to curriculum. For example, the INTO LGBT group has developed resources for Social, Personal and Health Education such as '*Different Families, Same Love*' (www.into.ie). This is to encourage children to reflect positively on the variety and diversity of families in Ireland and to create a positive school climate.

CONCLUSION

What is needed in relation to the six areas relating to educational equality highlighted above is a serious commitment to equality by government and by the key educational interest groups – the churches, teacher unions, management bodies and parents' organisations. Even in times of austerity, such as those experienced over the recent past, educational policy should have been equality proofed. However, the values and goals expressed in the Department of Education and Skills' *Statement of Strategy 2015 – 2017*, if implemented, give grounds for optimism. An integrated public policy approach, involving the range of government departments, will have to be a core part of the new directions. So too will be a strategy of equality-proofing all budgetary policies and initiatives.

In order to facilitate educational equality, the government will have to radically reduce child poverty. This will, of course, require a cross-governmental multi-faceted approach, as pledged in *Better Outcomes, Better Futures* (DCYA, 2014) as well as in the DES *Statement of Strategy*. Clearly, social class inequalities will have to be addressed. While certain areas have high levels of social class disadvantage and require intensive resourcing, it must be borne in mind that disadvantaged children may be found in many non-designated schools. Support systems for Traveller and Roma pupils should be restored (including the Visiting Teacher service). There is a need to provide additional supports for pupils in direct provision and for other categories of immigrant children, especially for those who do not have English as a first language. It will also be essential to provide CPD on inter-culturalism, anti-racism and teaching English as an additional language for teachers, as well as requiring and supporting schools to incorporate ethnic diversity issues, anti-racism and inter-culturalism in all school plans. However, it would not be reasonable to expect schools to be the only challenge to racism and xenophobic tendencies of any kind. There needs to be a society-wide anti-racist programme, which would include legislation against hate crimes.

The government will need to continue to develop and increase investment in high quality and quality-assured early childhood education for children, especially for disadvantaged children and those with disabilities/special educational needs. Such increased investment should aim to ensure improved employment for staff and a minimum of not just Level 5 but, as quickly as possible, a Level 6 qualification for all staff and a Level 8 qualification for the leaders of early childhood education centres. Therapeutic supports for children with disabilities/SEN (especially speech and language and occupational therapies and psychological services) will need to be increased. Barriers to school completion for pupils with disabilities/SEN, such as bullying and/or disengagement from school, will need to be addressed. Bullying is still a major problem for many students but especially for pupils with SEN and for LGBTI pupils. The anti-bullying policy of the DES is a very welcome resource, as is the training available to primary and post-primary schools and teachers, provided by the Anti-Bullying Centre at Dublin City University.

In order to provide evidence- and research-based advice to the Minister, and to coordinate research and development in this vital area in a transparent and accountable manner, the Educational Disadvantage Committee should be re-established. This Committee was originally established by statute in the 1998 Education Act, was left dormant from 2005 and was finally abolished in 2012. To be effective, it would be necessary to ensure the Committee is comprised of representatives of the relevant government departments (e.g. Education & Skills, Health, Children & Youth Affairs, Social Protection, and Justice), the Human Rights and Equality Commission and people with expertise in the field of equality and education. Educational researchers, education partner representatives (e.g. teacher unions, management bodies), community group representatives and other relevant bodies should also be represented. Since improving the progress of learners at risk of educational disadvantage is a central goal of the DES *Action Plan 2016-2019* (DES, 2016j), this could be a valuable mechanism for evidence-based implementation of policy.

> " The government will need to continue to develop and increase investment in high quality and quality-assured early childhood education for children, especially for disadvantaged children and those with disabilities/special educational needs. "

The goals and vision in the Department's 2015 – 2017 strategy paper and those in the 2016-2019 *Action Plan* (DES, 2015a and DES, 2016j) provide a platform for development. While accepting that resources are always restricted, it is worth reminding ourselves that, as Ireland emerges from the shadow of the recent recession, the need for social, cultural and economic development is very clear. Education is central to this. Evidence from across the world shows that societies that are more equal provide better outcomes for their citizens. Education is a core mechanism for the advancement of equality (or its opposite). Equality is also closely linked to quality in modern educational systems. Educational outcomes are linked to health outcomes (OECD, 2015, p. 156) so there should not be a battle for resources between education and health. It is, as previously stated, essential that equality in education becomes a central focus. To deliver this, the resources must be provided. Increased investment in early years and other areas of education will involve substantial additional allocations to education, which can only be achieved through increased taxation (progressive, not regressive). This issue cannot be dodged and the public need to be prepared for this in a careful and measured way. In the end, it is about the kind of society we want for our children and ourselves.

To achieve the ambition of a more equal, peaceful and prosperous society, government and civil society will need to think long-term. We are now, post-Brexit, entering a most uncertain time. At this remove, it even seems likely that we will once again experience an economic slow-down and perhaps a further recession. We have seen the impact of austerity measures and cutbacks over the past eight years on the least well off. We have probably yet to experience the full social impact of these. If there is another economic downturn, Ireland, as a society will need, even more, to guard against measures that will create further inequality. On the contrary, as a society, Ireland needs to plan for the future with a set of twenty-year targets to reduce inequality. This work must begin now and with the youngest citizens. The work cannot be done by schools and the education system alone. For example, the elimination of consistent child poverty, and indeed homelessness, would do much to combat educational disadvantage but this can only be done through a multi-agency approach, and with government determination, through all departments of state.

There must be a national conversation and consensus on improving the conditions, opportunities and outcomes of all citizens through all facets of the social and economic structure. The social and cultural returns will be significant but so too will be the economic returns. There is, thus, a historic opportunity to make a radical difference to Irish society. In this way Ireland can not only make some progress on developing a more egalitarian system but it could advance the ambition of the signatories of the 1916 Proclamation that Ireland would guarantee the 'religious and civil liberty, equal rights and equal opportunities of all its citizens'.

CHAPTER EIGHT ● ● ● ● ● ● ● ● ● ● ● ● ● ● ●
The Changing Role of the Inspectorate

THE STAGE OF TRANSITION

The Education Act of 1998 was the first comprehensive Education Act in the history of the state. The Act was also a landmark in the development of the Inspectorate in that Section 13 of the Act gave statutory recognition to it, and gave a new definition to its role. It gave a more strategic and focussed role in contrast to the multi-tasked and diversified role that had hitherto prevailed. Its future role was to be an evaluative and advisory one – to evaluate and report on all aspects of the school system. Its statutory duty now required it to give advice on education issues to all key stakeholders and to provide policy advice to the Department and the Minister. The Inspectorate had also a legislative duty to consult with key stakeholders relevant to the promotion of quality education. Its remit could be summarised as system evaluation, system development and system support.

The changed role of the Inspectorate coincided with a major reform of the then Department of Education and Science (DES), following the Deloitte & Touche, 1999, and the Cromien, 2000, reports. The early years of the new century witnessed major changes in the structure and functions of the Department in an effort to declutter it from the vast range of diverse activities that were over-absorbing it, to the detriment of the strategic policy. A range of new agencies was set up to take over many responsibilities in areas such as psychological services, special education, ICT, state examinations, teacher education and registration. These developments assisted the Inspectorate to focus its professional work on evaluation and advice, as well as school- and system-improvement. To position itself for its changed role, the Inspectorate re-structured its organisational framework and introduced a range of new procedures and models of communication, which have had a major influence in the re-shaping of the school system in recent years. Leadership and staffing of the Inspectorate also underwent significant change, with a new recruiting policy shaped by its professional concerns (Coolahan, 2009, pp. 260-290). Among key internal structures were the Senior Management Group (SMG), the Evaluation Support and Research Unit (ESRU) and the Staff Development Unit (SDU). Improved inspector induction processes were introduced and more extensive forms of continuing professional development (CPD) were made available, reflective of the Chief Inspector's comment of the Inspectorate as 'a learning organisation'.

Among key early indicators of the changing pattern of work and communication of the Inspectorate in the early years of this century were the following: In 1999, the School Development Planning Unit was set up, which in subsequent years, would guide schools in implementing the school development planning policy. In 2002, the Inspectorate published its *Professional Code of Practice on Evaluating and Reporting,* making known to interested parties how it approached its work. In 2002, it also published *Fifty Reports: What Inspectors Say,* to inform on the viewpoints of the Inspectorate on

> " The changed role of the Inspectorate coincided with a major reform of the then Department of Education and Science (DES), following the Deloitte & Touche, 1999, and the Cromien, 2000, reports. "

practice evaluated. A publication to help schools in self-evaluation, *Looking at Our Schools,* was published in 2003.

The first new form of inspection, Whole-School Evaluation (WSE), took place in primary schools in 2003 and in post-primary schools in 2004. The first *Chief Inspector's Report,* for 2001-04, was published in 2005 (DES, 2005c). In 2006, a notable event took place with the first Inspectors' Reports on the evaluation of schools published on the DES website. The *Chief Inspector's Report* for 2008 is a good example of the changed culture of inspection that had been brought about in these years. It provides an overview of the range and scale of the various forms of inspection then operative and includes focussed comments on the strengths and weaknesses of aspects of the school system. It clearly emphasises the close engagement now operating by the Inspectorate with the work of teachers, school communities, and provision outside the mainstream system (DES, 2009). It provides incisive comment on what is working well in schools, what needs to be improved, and what needs to be done into the future. Overall, the *Report* is reflective of a significant shift in direction for much of the work of the Inspectorate in which evaluation and mentoring of educational quality, on the ground, is centre stage, extensive feedback is given to practitioners, policy advice is collated, and reflection occurs on emerging trends. It is also significant to note that, between 2002 and 2008, the

Inspectorate issued over sixty publications as well as a range of information leaflets and newsletters. This contrasts strongly with the previous paucity of published data and reflects an attitude of greater transparency, accountability, partnership and professionalism, to the benefit of schools and teachers, to policy makers and to the interested public.

THE CONTEMPORARY CONTEXT

Planning for the Future

As with the education system generally, the Inspectorate also suffered from the economic cutbacks of the recessionary era. A significant indicator of this was the decline in inspectoral staff from a total of 168 in 2008 to 118 in early 2016. The general inspectorate staff increased to 124 by the end of 2016. Furthermore, the appointment of a ten-person special inspectorate core for early childhood education has raised the overall personnel to 134. Despite the serious loss in numbers, what is very notable in the contemporary period is that the momentum for continuing reform and development has been sustained. The *Chief Inspectors' Report 2010-12*, published in 2013, acknowledges an era of 'change and challenge,' but committed the Inspectorate to address the concerns being posed.

Among significant educational policy changes for the school system, to which the Inspectorate contributed, were *The National Strategy for Literacy and Numeracy 2011-2020* (DES, 2011a), and the reform of the curriculum and assessment of the Junior Cycle in post-primary schools. Over recent years, the Inspectorate has issued a range of documents reflective of a very vibrant, reflective and mission-oriented agency. Among these, it developed *Strategic Plans for 2011-2013*, and for 2014–16. In the case of both plans, it also established an *Implementation Tracking process*. A new *Code of Practice for the Inspectorate was* published in 2015 (DES, 2015c). A *Guide to Early Years Education – Focused Inspection* (EYEI) was published in 2016. The Inspectorate has also been paying special attention to the induction and continuing professional development of inspectors as is evidenced in documents *The Induction and Initial Professional Development of Inspectors* and *Learning Strategy for the Inspectorate 2016-2020*.

Modes of Inspection

Among key changes in this mode of school inspection has been the use of a new form of Whole-School Evaluation, entitled *Whole-School Evaluation – Management, Leadership and Learning* (WSE – MLL), for schools. Following a trial period, Schools Self-Evaluation (SSE) became mandatory for schools in 2012. The focus for the first four years of this cycle has been very much on teaching and learning, as was indicated in the *SSE Guidelines issued* to schools, and was to be based on relevant assessment data. Schools embarking on SSE also benefit from advisory visits by the Inspectorate. By 2016, almost all schools have engaged in SSE processes. As well as the WSE, and SSE-oriented inspections, a wide range of inspection models is now in operation. Models include short, unannounced, one-day inspections, subject-focussed inspections, curriculum evaluations, programme evaluations and specialised inspections as, for instance, in disadvantaged schools or special needs provision. A key value of the range of models of inspection is that a particular inspection can be tailored more closely to needs. A major new development has been the introduction of 'follow through' inspections whereby, after a period of time, inspectors return to check on and discuss progress made by the school community in light of the earlier inspections and recommendations. Progress is recorded as 'very good', 'good', 'partial' or 'no progress'. Where schools are found to have serious weaknesses, a co-ordinated approach is adopted within the Department to effect remediation, with continued inspectoral involvement. A further innovative practice has been the issuing of confidential appraisal questionnaires to parents and students on their experiences and perceptions of the work of schools. Teachers' views on the running of schools are accessed through interviews or questionnaires. Post-inspection surveys of primary and post-primary teachers and principals, as well as of chairpersons of boards of management and parent associations on WSE evaluations in the most recent period – September 2015 to January 2016, are very positive, particularly from the primary personnel (Hislop, 2016).

Overall, one detects a comprehensive, professional approach to inspection in contemporary practice. An extensive process of consultation is engaged in before forms and processes of inspection are finalised. A good development from previous practice is greater advance preparation by inspectors in gathering data on the school's circumstances and context. This reduces the workload for school personnel in preparing documentation or data, but it also helps equip the Inspectorate to carry out its declared intention of bearing issues pertaining to the school's context very much in mind when evaluating practice. The fact that guidelines and criteria of inspection are available to school personnel in advance also facilitates communication and dialogue. The feedback from questionnaires is carefully noted and feeds into refining strategy and approaches. Following inspection, schools are given oral feedback and they are allowed to respond and proffer factual corrections before reports are finalised for publication. There is also provision for schools to submit appeals on evaluations.

The declared core approach of the Inspectorate is 'inspection for improvement.' The Inspectorate in Ireland does not favour league-table-type grading of schools, realising that this is a very blunt approach and ignores many relevant contextual issues in school appraisal. The Inspectorate aims to operate a co-professional approach with teachers, urging collaboration and collegiality, based on mutual respect of roles. This co-professional approach is a recognition of the quality of the teaching force, many of whose members possess post-graduate qualifications. This co-professional approach is also in alignment with the Teaching Council's rationale for teacher education in its policy on teacher education as a continuum. The sense of openness and transparency is aimed at fostering a positive approach by school communities, with the work of the Inspectorate being viewed as an aid to school improvement, and a sense of ownership cultivated in the process. A key objective in the moves by the Inspectorate on whole-school planning, SSE and WSE is to encourage greater collaborative and collegial work within school communities, breaking away from a more traditional model of teacher individualism and 'king/queen of the classroom syndrome.' The Inspectorate also regards its work emphases on teaching and learning to be in harmony with types of varied and active pedagogy and the varied forms of pupil learning and engagement which underpin the primary curriculum and the new Junior Cycle reforms.

The *Inspectorate's Strategic Plan for 2014-2016* indicates that the Inspectorate will use a programme of interlinked inspection models of different duration, intensity and purpose. The revised inspection planning process is aimed at ensuring some form of inspection in at least 25% of all schools in a school year. It is also aimed to have a published report on each post-primary school in each three-year period and a published report on each primary school within an eight-year cycle (DES, 2014a, p. 9).

A striking characteristic of the modern school Inspectorate is the continual process of reflection on the outcomes of consultation and experience to refine and upgrade its practice and guidelines to school communities. This trend is very evident in a range of documents being issued to school communities and to education partners for implementation from the school year 2016–17. Circulars have been issued to schools relating to the next phase of school self-evaluation, 2016-2022. These are accompanied by *School Self-Evaluation Guidelines 2016-2020* for both

> "
> The Inspectorate's Strategic Plan for 2014-2016 indicates that the Inspectorate will use a programme of interlinked inspection models of different duration, intensity and purpose.
> "

primary and secondary schools. These publications are complemented by new editions of *Looking at Our School, 2016,* setting out Quality Frameworks for primary and for post-primary schools. The Quality Frameworks focus on two key dimensions: teaching and learning; and leadership and management. It is planned that the Guidelines and the Quality Frameworks will assist schools in their self-development and will emphasise the complementarity of self-evaluation and external evaluation. They emphasise that the central focus of self-evaluation is on teaching and learning. The aim has been to simplify and streamline the Guidelines for clarity and ease of usage. International evidence would suggest that a system of school self-evaluation working in combination with forms of external monitoring/ evaluation lead to best outcomes. *Looking at Our School* is likely to be a key reference document for the school system for years to come.

In June 2016, the Department issued *Guides to Inspection for* both primary and post-primary schools (DES, 2016g; DES, 2016h). Each *Guide* includes summaries of each inspection model being used, using a consistent format, and setting out the rationale and procedures for each of the modes of inspection. The *Guides* also set out how the Quality Frameworks will be used to inform the work of the Inspectorate, in line with its *Code of Practice* (2015). To lessen the burden of work on schools, the number of documents typically requested in the course of an inspection has been reduced. The publication of this range of documents emphasises the importance being placed on consultation, clarification and communication in promoting a professional partnership between teaching and inspection. The Inspectorate is also preparing a Gaeltacht Education Policy at present, with a special focus on the issues involved in quality improvement for schooling in Gaeltacht areas.

Early Years Inspection

Following a period of extensive consultation, a new section was established within the Inspectorate, Early Years Education – Focussed Inspection (EYEI), in 2016. This is a corps of ten highly-specialised personnel. It evaluates the nature, range and appropriateness of the early years' experiences for children participating in the free pre-schools in ECCE programmes. Criteria of evaluation have been designed appropriate to this form of schooling. The EYEI model complements the monitoring and regulatory processes of other relevant agencies in respect of ECCE provision. A specific mode of operation has been designed to suit the early childhood educational settings. However, the numbers of involved inspectors in EYEI will need to be expanded if they are to cope with the number of settings. Published reports appear on the DES website and on those of the Department of Children and Youth Affairs and Pobal. These inspections are based on a quality framework that is informed by the principles of Aistear and Síolta. Quality outcomes are identified for four broad areas of ECCE (DES, 2016c):

- The quality of the context to support children's learning and development
- The quality of the process to support children's learning and development
- The quality of children's learning experiences and development
- The quality of management and leadership of learning.

The first formal inspections commenced in April 2016, with reports being published in June 2016. A challenge ahead will be aligning inspection in early years' settings with the inspection of infant classes in primary schools.

NEW APPROACHES TO TEACHER INDUCTION AND PROBATION

The Inspectorate has been seeking to bring about a significant change in a long-established practice – the probation of primary teachers. Working in association with the Teaching Council, this responsibility is being transferred to the teaching profession. This is part of a wider agenda of giving more authority to the profession for its own self-government and development. The Teaching Council has been operating a pilot scheme of teacher induction and probation, known as Droichead.

The National Induction Programme for Teachers (NIPT) is assisting the Council in the process. A formal review of the scheme was completed in 2016, which recorded 'high levels of satisfaction' with the scheme, but pointed up a range of issues to be addressed to ensure its effective implementation across all schools (ESRI, 2016, pp. 195-203). The new system is working more satisfactorily at post-primary level. At primary level, some difficulties have been encountered, particularly in small schools. Some principals are reticent about evaluating the work of newly-qualified teachers. The Inspectorate provides a range of workshops and information sessions to assist in the training of school staffs for this type of work. The Inspectorate plans to start phasing out its involvement in probation from September 2016, over a sequence of years up to 2019. However, it will continue to be available to offer advice to school personnel when particular difficulties are encountered in this area. At present, up to 2,200 inductees need to be probated per annum. Such a workload would make serious time-infringements on the Inspectorate's strategy for its inspection programme. However, attention also needs to be paid to the increased workload involved for school principals.

Interpreting National and International Tests

The Inspectorate keeps a close monitoring role on the outcome of national and international assessments of pupils' performance, particularly in Mathematics, Literacy and Science. It has close liaison with the Educational Research Centre, which among other things, has built up a very credible reputation in pupil testing and evaluation. The Inspectorate takes an active interest in international studies such as those of PISA, PIRLS and TIMSS. It interprets how Irish pupils compare with their international peers in these tests. Inspectors communicate relevant perspectives to the various school stakeholders and to policy-makers. These types of benchmarks are utilised to sustain qualitative performance, but are not fed into league table patterns. The approach taken is a critical perspective, which is also alert to possible methodological and contextual issues of the studies that might need to be borne in mind.

> " The Inspectorate plans to start phasing out its involvement in probation from September 2016, over a sequence of years up to 2019. "

In the past, the Irish education system has suffered from the lack of a comprehensive database of school pupils. The Inspectorate has been championing the provision of such a database, which has now been completed for the primary school sector, and it is understood that it is now in process for post-primary pupils. This database will provide a very wide range of information about pupils, including socio-economic background, and will be linked up with census data. It will allow for much more refined and discriminatory policy decision-making and in-build greater contextual refinements to the evaluation work of the Inspectorate. In November 2015, the Department established a Management Board on Quality, Evaluation and Assessment, chaired by the Chief

Inspector, to give an up-to-date, researched overview of this theme. The review will present initial findings by the end of 2016, with the work continuing into 2017 and 2018.

Induction and Continuing Professional Development

The Inspectorate has been very conscious of the need for staff, in view of its key evaluative and advisory roles in education, to pay focussed attention to the induction of new recruits to the corps and to provide high quality continuing professional development (CPD) for its established staff. The induction lasts for a period of six months, and experienced inspectors act as mentors for the inductees. In the course of the induction period, the inductees undertake a course of seven modules: introduction to school evaluation, models of school inspection, evaluating teaching and learning, evaluating leadership and management, data-gathering, communicating evidence, and inspections on professionals. Suggested readings and references are set out to accompany each module. A range of tasks is also set out for inductees during the induction period. The induction also includes work-shadowing opportunities to accompany and observe experienced inspectors in the course of their professional work (DES, *Induction of Inspectors*, n.d.).

The *Learning Strategy for the Inspectorate 2016-2020* sets out the following definition of CPD:

> **The means by which members of the Inspectorate learn, develop, update and improve their professional knowledge and skills and develop the personal capability and qualities required in their professional lives.**
>
> (DES, 2016d, p. 4)

To fulfil this aim, an annual plan for CPD is prepared. Current arrangements are based on six modes of delivery: centrally-delivered programmes; regionally-delivered programmes; blended learning programmes; specialised and self-managed programmes; remote learning courses; and collaborative learning programmes. Over the next few years (2016-2020), the priorities for CPD are focused on the following six areas: improving the quality of evaluation; improving the quality of teaching, learning and leadership; developing the skills of all inspectors, ensuring inspectors are up-to-date on curriculum developments; extending inspectors' participation on externally-accredited courses; and upskilling in ICT. An interesting development in recent times is the facilitation of inspectors to engage in post-graduate courses of the Institute of Education, London on inspection and regulation. It is also noteworthy that the Inspectorate maintains close contact with the Inspectorate in Northern Ireland, including periods of exchanging service and joint engagement on special projects. Collegial links are also well-established with Inspectorate in Scotland and Wales, and the Irish Inspectorate takes part in meetings of the Inspectorates of the UK and Ireland East-West arrangements. The international dimension is also emphasised by the Irish Inspectorate's active membership of the Standing International Conference of Inspectors (SICI). Irish inspectors have taken leadership roles in SICI and contribute papers to its international conferences. The Inspectorate maintains strong links with the European Agency for Special Needs and Inclusive Education. The Inspectorate also has links and periodic engagements with international policy agencies such as the OECD, the EU and the Council of Europe. Through these various linkages, the Inspectorate keeps itself abreast of international policy trends and perspectives on school inspection issues, in an era when such policy trends have been increasingly influential.

CHALLENGES AHEAD

It is clear that the Inspectorate has continued over recent years on the professional path shaped for it subsequent to its statutory establishment in the Education Act of 1998. It has been carrying out its mandate in a very focussed and developmental way. It has evolved major new forms of inspection, as well as extending the range of inspection models. It has been at pains to ensure good consultation and communication with all education stakeholders. It has established a tradition of publishing its school reports and its reports on special themes. The recently-introduced follow-through inspections provide a valuable stimulus for continuous improvement. The key focus on the evaluation and improvement of teaching, learning and school leadership and the eschewing of the league mode of accountability is noteworthy. The Inspectorate has adopted a more transparent approach than the older tradition of inspection. It also holds itself open to the formal appraisal of its mode of operation by the stakeholders. The policy of induction to the Inspectorate and continuing professional development of those in service is in line with best international practice. In summary, it can be argued that the Inspectorate is a strength of the contemporary Irish education system.

However, that is not to say that there are not problems on the horizon that need to be engaged with to ensure the harvesting into the future of the gains that have been made. One issue relates to the staffing of the traditional school Inspectorate, which experienced a decline of more than 20% from 2008 to 2016. It should also be noted that some inspectors are deployed to serve on agencies such as the NCCA, the Teaching Council and the Teacher Education Section of the Department. This reduction in staff occurred when, arguably, the

> " The key focus on the evaluation and improvement of teaching, learning and school leadership and the eschewing of the league mode of accountability is noteworthy. "

role of the Inspectorate was being extended. In circumstances where the work of the Inspectorate continues to expand while staff numbers are reduced, there is a danger of the role being qualitatively diluted and of staff being over-stretched. It is crucial that in the various forms of inspection, the inspectors have the time to establish evidence-based judgements on the quality of what they are evaluating. The inspectors need to be in a position to stand confidently behind the integrity of their reports, which are published for public scrutiny. To date, there is no evidence of a dilution in the quality of the Inspectorate's work. However, it would be prudent to ensure that the extensive range of its responsibilities is matched by the provision of requisite staff numbers, into the future, for the well-being of the system.

It is also the case that the overall range of change and reform sought from schools over recent years is very demanding. While this change agenda can be interpreted as progressive and representing good practice, it has coincided with a period of significant cutbacks in financial and personnel resources within the system. Significant elements of the reforms sought include new curricular and assessment reform; new forms of evaluation, particularly in the forms of whole-school assessment and school self-evaluation; new forms of partnership of school staff with higher education institutions particularly with regard to the induction and probation of newly-qualified teachers; the desirability of school staffs working more collegially and collaboratively, reducing the strong tradition of teachers operating as individuals; and the necessity for teachers to engage in CPD as a condition for continued registration. In accumulation, such policies, if successfully embedded, would amount to a virtual culture change for Irish schools, apart from contemporary consultation by the DES on advancing greater school autonomy in the Irish school system.

International research substantiates the fact that the successful achievement of significant educational reform is a time-consuming process, within which felicitous timing of initiatives, the availability of supportive resources, and qualitative leadership have significant impact. The embedding of stages of a reform before significant new layers are added on is desirable for success. Fundamentally, the cultivation of a sense of ownership of the reforms by key stakeholders can be an important harbinger of success. In reflecting on the admirable agenda for educational change that has been underway, one suggests that perhaps insufficient attention has been paid to prevailing conditions and circumstances in the schools by the Inspectorate, as a key professional agent in the change process. Their role puts them in a very good position to have a good awareness of the internal dynamics of the school system. It may well be that a *festina lente* approach, for a period, would best serve both the Inspectorate and the school system at this crucial era of change.

CHAPTER NINE ● ● ● ● ● ● ● ● ● ● ● ● ● ●
Initial Teacher Education and Induction

RECENT DEVELOPMENTS

In recent years, Initial Teacher Education (ITE) in Ireland has been undergoing its most fundamental change for four decades. A significant landmark, in this context, was the establishment of the Teaching Council, in 2006. The Council, comprised of various stakeholder interests, has a majority of teacher representatives. In 2007, the Teaching Council published a two-part bedrock document regarding the teaching profession. It was titled *Codes of Professional Conduct for Teachers* and contained a 'Code of Professional Practice' and a 'Code of Professional Conduct' (Teaching Council 2007). The aim was to enrich professional discourse and to encourage the universalisation of appropriate standards. The two codes were revised into one during 2011 and issued in 2012 as the *Code of Professional Conduct for Teachers* (Teaching Council, 2012).

In 2009, the Teaching Council drew up a *Draft Strategy for Review and Accreditation of Initial Teacher Education Courses* and between 2009 and 2011 conducted eight pilot course accreditations. The Council, as well as other agencies, had been urging the extension of the duration of the existing teacher education courses. In 2011, a dramatic decision was announced by the Department of Education and Skills (DES) that it was authorising the extension of ITE courses, undergraduate and postgraduate, by one year. This was to take effect for the concurrent courses from the academic year 2012/13 and for the consecutive courses from autumn 2014. This was a much awaited, landmark development for the teaching profession.

The Teaching Council set planning afoot in relation to the reconceptualisation of the new, extended duration courses. In August 2011, it published *Initial Teacher Education: Criteria and Guidelines for Programme Providers* and, in September, *Strategy for the Review and Professional Accreditation of Existing Programmes.* The higher education institutions also got to work in preparing and planning for the new programmes. In due course, the Council established accreditation review teams for all the institutions. Visits were made to each college and detailed discussions took place on the reconceptualised programmes based on the criteria and guidelines designed by the Council. As well as changes in course duration, significant reforms were introduced in areas such as course content, styles of teaching and engagement, school practice arrangements, relationships with schools, research training, staff-student ratio, and student resources. While demanding in terms of time, effort and resource, it is gratifying to record that all stakeholders worked hard to ensure that the new arrangements would lead to greatly enriched initial teacher education programmes. Under the reformed plan, the B.Ed. concurrent programme is a four-year honours degree course, while the new two-year consecutive course leads to a Professional Master of Education (PME). In the new course design for ITE, the Council stated:

> **The foundation studies, professional studies and the school placement should be carefully planned in the light of changing understandings of the nature of learning and the theory practice relationship, so that there is an appropriate balance between them and their inter-relationship is made explicit.**
>
> (Teaching Council, 2011b, p. 12)

Unlike the parlous position of Education as a subject in some other countries, as discussed in John Furlong's recent book, *Education – An Anatomy of the Discipline,* (Furlong, 2013, pp. 181-200), in Ireland the education foundation studies are still seen as providing an underpinning role. The Council's document states that the foundation studies should provide:

- research informed insights into student teachers' understanding of the practices of teaching, learning and assessment
- an illumination of the key dimensions of the professional context in which the thinking and actions of teachers are carried out
- the basis for a strong professional ethic in teaching
- the basis for reflective practice (Teaching Council, 2011b, p.13).

The focus on the teacher as reflective practitioner is supported by emphasis on small group teaching, tutorials and workshops, and the compilation of professional development portfolios. Student teachers are being oriented towards collaborative collegial engagement in the school as a learning community. Students receive research training and undertake a research project in their course work.

A very striking feature of the new courses is the much greater emphasis on partnership and collaboration between the HEIs and the schools, and the enhanced role beyond teaching practice for student teachers to experience the general life of the school. A much greater role is envisaged for the teaching professional in student teacher formation:

> Such models would see greater levels of responsibility devolved to the profession for the provision of structured support for its new members and a gradual increase in classroom responsibility for student teachers. Structured support would include mentoring, supervision and critical analysis of the experience as well as observation, and conversations with, experienced teachers.
>
> (Teaching Council, 2011b, p. 16)

School placements are to take place in a variety of settings and incorporate a variety of teaching situations and school contexts. While the new model of initial teacher education poses a challenge for principals and classroom teachers to take a more proactive role in the formation of new recruits to the profession, this is also a great opportunity for the profession's self-development. Practitioners in other established professions such as medicine and law engage in the formation of their future members.

Traditionally, in Ireland, the teaching career has enjoyed high social status and public trust. It has attracted a student clientele of very high academic achievement and personal commitment. The entrance to the traditional college courses has been very competitive. The *Report of the International Review Panel on the Structure of Initial Teacher Education Provision in Ireland* (DES, 2012b) stated,

> 'the academic standard of applicants (for teacher education) is among the highest, if not the highest, in the world,' and considered that it was incumbent that this 'rich resource should be highly valued … challenged and developed to its full potential'
>
> (International Review Panel, 2012, p. 12)

In recent years, a new private provider, Hibernia, has supplemented the traditional providers of teacher education courses. Initially, this agency engaged in teacher education for primary teachers but now also provides it for post-primary teaching. It employs a good deal of its provision online. Its courses are subject to accreditation by the Teaching Council, which requires staff to hold qualification grades higher than course participants. As a private institution, it is not restricted in student intake numbers by the state, as are the traditional institutions. It has also become a pattern that unsuccessful applicants for ITE courses in Ireland tend to go to other jurisdictions, particularly England, for their teacher education. There is some concern that the philosophy and qualitative approach to teacher education abroad may not be in harmony with that being pursued in Ireland. Concern is also being expressed that issues of over-supply of teachers may be diminishing appointment opportunities for graduates from the Irish institutions and may contribute to a dilution of teacher quality. In an over-supply situation, high quality candidates may be deflected from pursuing teaching as a career in favour of one with better career prospects.

As well as the reforms in the duration, content and mode of engagement of ITE courses, the framework for the national provision of teacher education has also come under scrutiny. A significant contextual factor in relation to the future of teacher education institutions is that, as part of government policy for collaboration, co-operation and integration of higher education institutions generally, major structural changes are planned for teacher education institutions. In her Background Paper, prepared for the International Review Panel on Teacher Education in Ireland, (2012), Professor Áine Hyland saw the restructuring 'as an opportunity to reconfigure the system of initial teacher education in Ireland to ensure the best possible learning experience for student-teachers that will compare favourably with the best in the world' (Hyland, 2012, p. 23). The Review Panel set out its vision for the future as follows:

> The Review Panel's vision for the structure of ITE provision in Ireland is that by 2030 Ireland will have a network of teacher education institutions based on a small number of internationally comparable institutes of teacher education. Each of these institutions will offer research-based teacher education in internationally inspiring environments, provided at Masters level initially or through continuing professional development. Each will also offer further professional development services on the continuum ranging from early childhood to in-service training of teacher and leaders.
> (DES, 2012b, p. 24)

The most significant development of this recommended process to date has been the incorporation of St. Patrick's College of Education, Church of Ireland College, Mater Dei Institute and the Education Department of DCU into a new Institute of Education within the framework of Dublin City University. This process was underway for four years, with the incorporation concluding in autumn 2016. The Froebel College of Education has already been incorporated within Maynooth University. St. Angela's College Sligo is incorporated within NUI Galway. Collaboration is being fostered between the Education Departments of UCD, TCD, National College of Art and Marino College of Education. In the mid-west region, links are being established between Mary Immaculate College of Education, University of Limerick, Limerick Technical Institute and St. Patrick's College Thurles. Time will tell how this planned restructuring of the teacher education institutions will evolve but there is much promise in the potential involved to enhance synergies of expertise, collaboration of effort, the promotion of educational research and improved quality of teacher education for all sectors (DES, 2012b, p. 25).

INDUCTION

The policy of what was known as a '3Is' approach to teacher education – initial, induction and in-service has long been sought in Ireland. This has now been achieved as a policy decision, and the Teaching Council is now promoting the policy on the continuum of teacher education. The Council sees the continuum as encompassing 'initial teacher education, induction, early continuing professional development and, indeed, later career support, with each stage merging seamlessly into the next and interconnecting in a dynamic way with each of the others' (Teaching Council, 2011, p. 8). It adopts a new set of '3Is' to underpin all stages of the continuum, namely innovation, integration and improvement.

The induction process is the second stage of the continuum. In August 2010, the Department of Education and Science announced that in the wake of the pilot induction programme, from 2012 a national teacher induction programme would become operative for all future teachers. Building on the pilot experience, a structured plan was devised involving the DES, the Teaching Council, the teacher education institutions and classroom teachers. Training was provided for 'mentor' teachers, and school leaders were expected to play an active role in promoting the scheme. The National Induction Programme for Teachers (NIPD) made, and continues to make, valuable contributions to teacher induction.

Following successful graduation, all beginning teachers now need to satisfactorily complete a programme of induction as a requirement for full registration by the Council. The Council also emphasises the role the profession should play in the induction process:

> Induction should be based on a whole-school approach which sees induction and mentoring as the professional responsibility of the whole community of teachers, supported by the ITE providers, school leadership and linked to the school's development plan.
> (Teaching Council, 2011a, p. 17)

Arising from a period of consultation with stakeholders, the Teaching Council, in May 2013, issued a policy termed *Droichead*, which set out a new model for the future induction and probation of newly-qualified teachers. The Council regards this policy as 'a way forward for induction and probation which positions school communities in a professional space where shared responsibility is the norm. In doing so, it supports the growth of collective professional confidence. A fundamental value underpinning the policies is professionally-led regulation' (Teaching Council, 2013, p. 3).

The ESRI has conducted a review of the pilot phase of Droichead (2016). The review provides a helpful summary of the key elements of Droichead, as follows:

> The Droichead pilot programme, which began in 2013, is designed to provide whole-school support for teacher induction in both primary and post-primary schools. The programme is innovative in a number of respects. It is led at school level by a Professional Support Team (PST) consisting of the principal, mentor(s) and other member(s), who have received training provided by the National Induction Programme for Teachers (NIPT) in relation to their roles and responsibilities. Newly-qualified Teachers (NQTs) in Droichead schools have support from a mentor and other members of the PST in the identification of their professional learning needs and in planning opportunities to address these needs. NQTs have the opportunity to observe and be observed by other teachers, and receive feedback on their teaching. NQTs also compile a learning portfolio which supports their learning and records their reflections on their learning. At the end of the process, the PST may make a recommendation to the Teaching Council that the Droichead condition be removed from a teacher's registration. In this process, emphasis is placed on the progress made by the teacher in terms of his or her professional learning and practice.
>
> (ESRI, 2016, p. viii)

As can be noted, the induction scheme allows very significant support and guidance to the beginning teachers, at what is often a challenging period for them as they find their feet in the profession. The Review rightly comments, 'Droichead represents a sea-change in relation to previous approaches to supporting newly-qualified teachers (NQTs) in its emphasis on whole-school support for the NQT and school ownership of the recommendation process' (ESRI, 2016, p. 195). The findings of the Review pointed 'to the high levels of satisfaction among principals, mentors, other PST members and the newly-qualified teachers with the Droichead pilot programme' (ESRI, 2016, p. 200). Droichead, of course, places extra demands on school personnel in a variety of ways. The Review indicated that there were significant problems in ensuring that Droichead would be adopted on a countrywide basis. Among concerns highlighted was the need to provide more time for the professionals involved, the centrality of the attitude of principals, the buy-in of staff at a period when, due to cutbacks etc., morale is low. It considered that building time for *Droichead* activities into the school day was likely to be crucial to the sustainability of the programme (ESRI, 2016, p. 201).

Induction is planned to incorporate the probation process. Up to the present, the probation process at primary level came under the role of the inspector. The number of teachers to be probated per annum has now reached the high level of 2,200. As part of the process of moves towards a largely self-governing teaching profession, the Inspectorate now plans to withdraw from probation by 2018-19, while continuing to give some assistance in emergencies. While many consider that the

Droichead induction process provides a more professionally satisfactory basis for decisions on probation, school personnel, particularly in small schools, do not relish taking on this responsibility.

At the Annual Conference of the INTO at Easter 2016, a motion was passed against continuing participating in the Droichead scheme. This may be linked to dissatisfaction with the salary and promotion cutbacks over recent years, and the fact that many principals feel they are already over-burdened with work. Interestingly, the IPPN *Leadership*[+] journal issue of June 2016 lists the views of principals who are familiar with the current Droichead process. In the advantages listed, there are many lauding the improved professional experience of NQT inductees. Problems are also raised with a list of recommendations to solve them. These include calls for more time / release days for staff involved, lifting the moratorium on posts of responsibility, further training for mentoring, probation, induction and quality control for consistency between schools (IPPN, June 2016, p. 15).

In an article in the same issue, Tomás Ó Ruairc, Director of the Teaching Council, sets out a range of changes that have been introduced in the light of the ESRI report. Various adjustments to the process have been made. Furthermore, three models of a Professional Support Team (PST) are now provided for in the policy. Additional release time has been secured for the Droichead process and a Shared Learning Bursary is made available for schools. The system at post-primary level is progressing without serious difficulties. It is intended that Droichead will continue to evolve over time. A policy review is planned for 2018. In the interim, further research is planned on the experience of teaching principals. The Director states that 'subject to the necessary resources and supporting actions, Droichead will be the enhanced route of induction for all NQTs from September 2018' (ibid, p. 17).

LOOKING TO THE FUTURE

From the above account of developments, it is quite clear that the last six years have witnessed a period of fundamental reform in the nature and content of initial teacher education. There have also been very significant developments in the planning and experimental developments for a new teacher induction and probation process. From a national perspective, these reforms can be seen to be built on earlier reports and recommendations seeking such reforms and now yielding results that should rebound greatly to the benefit of teaching as a profession. From an international perspective, the developments, and associated contextual factors such as the quality of candidates for teacher education, Ireland can be regarded as one of the most progressive countries in relation to initial teacher education and induction. Both national and authoritative international perspectives are at one in highlighting the many new challenges facing the teaching profession in contemporary and evolving society. It is heartening that Ireland has been taking progressive measures in equipping teachers and school communities to cope with these challenges.

Yet, aspects of the change agenda are still work in progress. The attitudinal change and sense of ownership by key stakeholders, particularly the teaching profession, need continued nurturing through good communication, affirmation of effort, and support. As part of this process, it is hoped that the various forms of cutbacks that the profession has experienced during the recessionary years may be alleviated. As well as changes in school personnel roles on new forms of teacher education, many other changes of operation are being sought from schools. The change agenda is heavy and somewhat intense. International research shows that the implementation of large-scale educational change needs to incorporate the requisite resources needed to operationalise it. It is to be hoped that greater political support for this aspect of the implementation process may be forthcoming in the years ahead.

In ensuring the quality of the future teaching force, critical attention needs to be paid to supply of teachers. In current circumstances, many teachers qualified under the reformed programmes are finding it difficult to ensure employment in Irish schools following graduation. Many are finding it difficult to secure satisfactory situations for their induction programmes. This, coupled with a scarcity of permanent teaching positions, is contributing to a sense of disillusion among highly-motivated young teachers who have participated whole-heartedly in the extended and reformed programmes. This situation can also have

> " The attitudinal change and sense of ownership by key stakeholders, particularly the teaching profession, need continued nurturing through good communication, affirmation of effort, and support. "

deleterious effects on those considering career paths on leaving school. The prospect of long duration, demanding and costly courses leading to qualifications but not job opportunities, is likely to have deterrent effects.

Ireland is now the home to a much more multi-ethnic and multi-cultural society than was formerly the case. Attention needs to be paid to the recruitment of teachers from the new ethnic groups. As part of this policy, financial supports need to be made available to enable suitable candidates from ethnic groups and from disadvantaged sectors to undertake long-duration, expensive courses. In this context the decision of the Minister for Education and Skills, Richard Bruton, on 19th September 2016, to 'increase access to teacher education for students from such target groups', as part of the Programme for Access to Higher Education (PATH), is to be welcomed. As he rightly remarked, 'teachers who have successfully accessed and progressed in higher education can have a really positive effect as role models' (DES, 2016).

Another contemporary issue causing concern is that the salaries available for newly-qualified teachers are significantly lower than those for their established colleagues are, and is a cause of serious dissatisfaction and is corrosive of esprit de corps within the profession. It is heartening that negotiations between the DES and some of the teacher unions have begun to address the amelioration of this salary discrepancy.

The lack of a satisfactory policy on teacher supply and demand has been an acknowledged weakness in Irish educational planning. A Technical Working Group (TWG) has been working on the issue and submitted its final *Report* in November 2015. It has made fourteen recommendations (TWG, 2015, pp. 37-42). Accepting the problems and complexities of the issue, its main recommendation was the establishment of a Standing Group on teacher supply, to be set up in June 2016, well-staffed and well-resourced, to continue the TWG's work on a continuous basis. This highlights the need for a much more focussed approach to teacher supply issues into the future than has been experienced in the past. It also points out the 'risk to the stability of planning if any one provider can recruit an unlimited number of student teachers in any given year' (TWG, 2015, p. 40).

The well-being of a teacher profession has many dimensions to it. The resource of a well-educated and committed teaching force for the continuing progress of a society is of central importance. Ireland has a valuable asset in its teaching force, but protecting its future quality requires vigilance and long-term planning. The major transition phase in teacher development that Irish society has been undergoing requires sustained public attention and support.

CHAPTER TEN •••••••••••••••••••
Professional
Development
in Teaching

REVIEW OF PATTERNS AND DEVELOPMENTS

For most of the twentieth century, the continuing professional development (CPD) of teachers was a neglected issue in Ireland. Once the teacher had received his/her qualifications, it was quite common that little was done by way of professional learning between then and retirement, other than some intermittent up-skilling prescribed by the Department of Education. Week-long summer courses for primary teachers were a long-standing feature in the yearly education calendar. Some of these were highly-regarded courses, but for the most part the provision was not part of any long-term strategy or vision.

In the last three decades of the century, there was considerable expansion in the provision of in-service courses for teachers. These were mainly linked to reforms in curricula, the first major reform being the introduction of the new primary school curriculum of 1971. A number of assumptions underlay the expansion. These assumptions were more implicit than part of a stated rationale. They were widely shared, however, among teachers and those organising and providing in-service courses. The assumptions included that in-service education:

- was intended primarily to serve the needs of the system, as distinct from the needs of schools as learning communities or of teachers as resourceful practitioners
- was largely something done to teachers by others – usually their superiors or employers
- because of its close link with national educational policy initiatives, was more a sporadic than a continuous undertaking
- was an 'add-on', as distinct from an integral part of the teacher's work and identity as a practitioner.

During the last decade of the 20th century, assumptions like these came under critical scrutiny, not least through the work of the National Education Convention (1993-94). The *Report on the National Education Convention,* 1994, placed in-service education in a life-long learning context (Ch.11) and called for the establishment of a Teaching Council. The 1995 White Paper, *Charting our Education Future,* drew heavily on the *Report on the National Education Convention* and prepared much of the ground for the 1998 Education Act. The White Paper dealt with in-career development of teachers in some detail (Ch.8). It identified different categories of need in professional development and envisaged a strategic framework under which 'the disparate elements of the present approach will be drawn together into a coherent strategy setting out priorities and associated budgetary allocations' (p.128).

The turn of the century saw the arrival of support services under DES provision, such as the School Development Planning Initiative (SDPI), Leadership Development for Schools (LDS), Second Level Support Service (SLSS) and Primary Curriculum Support Programme (PCSP). As these services set to work in the various regions of the country, teachers and school leaders became involved in new forms of CPD activity. Some notable progress was made by these services during the first decade of the new century. This fell short, however, of the kind of coherence anticipated in *Charting our Education Future.* Such coherence can scarcely be realised, moreover, until a well-designed national framework for professional development is in place and working well.

In this connection, the recently-issued *Action Plan for Education,* 2016, makes the following point in its remarks on professional development:

> A key theme of the ongoing reform of teacher professional development will be to develop the collegial responsibility of the teacher, not only as an expert teacher, but also as a participant in the collegial work of the school – in improving standards, in developing innovations, and in assessing, monitoring and improving students' learning. (DES, 2016j, p.31)

The *Action Plan* states further that 'Continuous professional development will be transformed with the creation of a centre of excellence to support in-school improvement, peer-learning and peer-exchange' (p.32). These are worthy policy aspirations. Yet something more concrete and specific is called for in an Action Plan. For instance, reference is made in the Action Plan to the finalising of the Teaching Council's *National Framework for Teacher CPD* as an 'ongoing' action (p.36), but there is no mention of the Council's key policy document on professional development, *Cosán,* or on any of its contents. As will be seen from the following pages, concrete action is called for under a range of specific headings if a framework for professional development is to be adequate to its task and if professional development itself is to make clear and meaningful advances.

The Teaching Council's *Strategic Plan for 2015-17* included the establishment of a national framework for professional development as one of its four main goals. In March 2016, the Council launched *Cosán: Framework for Teachers' Learning*. The Foreword to the *Cosán* document states:

> *Cosán* recognises that teachers are already committed to their professional learning. It acknowledges the many ways in which teachers have told us that they learn. It thus provides a clear and accessible framework for that ongoing professional learning to be recognised, in the context of teachers' status as registered professionals. It also provides a clear context for new conversations to happen about teaching and learning, between teachers, parents, students, and all stakeholders.
> (Foreword)

An important statement of the values underlying professional development for teachers is contained in *Cosán*. Among the values that are elucidated are: teachers as autonomous professionals; flexibility as a feature of the framework; facilitation of teachers in identifying and pursuing relevant professional learning opportunities; allowing for innovative approaches to quality assurance; opportunities to acknowledge and recognise teachers' learning; and facilitating teachers in prioritising learning that benefits themselves and their pupils.

In addition to the affirmation of educational values like these, the *Cosán* document recognises that teachers' learning is not merely an up-skilling or functional matter; that it is a formative process involving a number of intermingling dimensions. These dimensions it identifies as: formal and informal, professional and personal, collaborative and individual, school-based and external. The document also stresses the importance of critical reflection in teachers' professional learning and gives attention in short, numbered sections to each of the following: planning for learning and reflecting on its impact; standards to guide learning and reflection; and quality assurance processes. The final chapter envisages a development phase from 2016 to 2019, to be followed by an implementation phase commencing in 2020.

LOOKING AHEAD

The *Cosán* document provides a valuable context – in fact the key regulatory context – in which to consider the development of CPD policy and practice for teachers in Ireland. Its rationale marks a welcome contrast to the kinds of assumptions underlying more traditional approaches to 'in-service', such as the four identified in the opening paragraphs above. Despite its extended title, however, *Cosán* is less a framework than a first outline of the elements of an envisaged framework. It is important to recognise this; otherwise, some key matters that *Cosán* does not mention, or touches on only lightly, might be seen as structural gaps in the framework. In making provision for a three-year developmental phase, *Cosán* allows for opportunities to concentrate minds on strategic matters. To the fore in such matters must be a careful thinking-through of the range of features necessary to make the framework a practicable and a fruitful one when it comes to implementation. What follows here is an attempt to engage constructively in such thinking-through. In this attempt, a number of headings are considered in turn.

(a) A professional development spectrum

At one end of such a spectrum might lie the minimum requirements for the amount of professional development teachers might be required to undertake over a given period to renew their registration. At the other end of the spectrum might lie the kinds of requirements that enable teachers to accomplish advanced levels of professional standing. While the former requirements would be obligatory for all registered teachers, the latter would be optional – viz. identifying professional development routes that teachers might elect to follow in pursuing such advanced standing. The kinds of courses needed to cater to this spectrum range from short courses provided under the auspices of PDST or other national support agencies, to locally-organised courses that are submitted for accreditation through the Education Centres, to university-linked courses in the Education Centres, to Post-graduate Diplomas or M.Ed. degrees or indeed professional doctorates in the universities themselves. Designing a flexible career enhancement structure, a readily-understandable credit-weighting system and a credible system of equivalences for such a spectrum is a necessary task to carry out in moving toward a fully-fledged framework for professional learning.

> " Designing a flexible career enhancement structure, a readily-understandable credit-weighting system and a credible system of equivalences for such a spectrum is a necessary task to carry out in moving toward a fully-fledged framework for professional learning. "

(b) Accreditation of professional development

The references under the previous heading to minimum requirements for renewal of registration, and to more advanced levels of professional accomplishment, point to an important conclusion: an accreditation system is an inescapable element of a framework for professional learning. In keeping with the values underlying *Cosán*, such an accreditation system would need to be a flexible one, recognising the kinds of autonomy and the degrees of autonomy that are inherent to teaching as a practice. It would also need to be an easily understood and transparent one. Developments in recent decades in the accreditation of prior learning (APL) and in the modularisation of study courses make the design of an accreditation system a much less daunting task than it would previously have been. It is now a common practice to recognise modules at different levels (i.e. quality) and to allocate a different number of credits to modules of different duration (i.e. quantity). The pages of *Cosán* have little to say on this matter, but the matter itself is a cornerstone for the entire framework and a priority task for attention during the 2016-19 development phase envisaged in *Cosán*.

Provision of accredited modules could take place through a range of routes, perhaps sometimes through joint providers. Providers could include higher education institutions, Education Centres, ETBs, professional associations like IPPN and NAPD, subject associations and so on. In the accrediting of such modules, it is important that close attention be given to things like the focus and relevance of each module. For instance, each module should be able to show its promise for enhancing the kinds of capacities needed to lead high-quality teaching and learning initiative in the classroom, or in the school more widely.

(c) Time provision for professional development

There are recurring references in *Cosán* to facilitating teachers in pursuing professional development, to collaboration between teachers, and to providing new opportunities for teachers to engage in professional development. These references do not broach the issue of allocated time for professional development. Yet, making available the opportunities envisaged in *Cosán* unavoidably raises the question of time, and in more ways than one. For instance, is professional development to be regarded as an 'add-on' to the teacher's existing working week? Could some portion of 'Croke Park hours' (or a duly-negotiated replacement for them) be earmarked for professional development activities? How much time per week or per month would be needed to satisfy minimum requirements of professional development? How do other countries deal with the provision of time for professional development for teachers? In relation to the first question, unless professional development is seen as integral to the teacher's professional identity and capability, devoting time to it is likely to be regarded as an optional 'add-on'. Secondly, 'Croke Park hours' are a good example of such an 'add-on', though in this case not an optional one. Although deftly used by many schools, the fact remains that the 'Croke Park hours' are widely resented by teachers as an imposition, associated very directly with government austerity measures. International experience shows that time for professional development is best provided for as part of a negotiated settlement on which teachers have freely voted. As already mentioned in other chapters of this review, the post-McCrone settlement in Scotland is instructive in this regard, though not necessarily a model to copy. In Ireland's case, it has been difficult to find time for any of the non-classroom responsibilities of teaching within the packed weekly schedules of schools. The reference in Circular 0024/2016 (DES, 2016a) to making some non-teaching time available to post-primary teachers (p.16), albeit not explicitly for professional development purposes, might be a propitious straw in the wind. The provision in the circular for four-and-a-half days for subject-specific CPD (p.18) is a significant measure, but there are two important caveats that need to be made in relation to it. Firstly, this measure is designed more to serve the needs of the system than the needs of the teacher, or indeed of the school. Of course, benefits may accrue to the latter two from well-designed CPD initiatives whose main function is to support national curricular reforms; but not if conceived in 'delivery' formats that fail to engage teachers and school leavers in sustained, constructive ways. Secondly, the four-and-a-half days in question mean a loss of teaching time. Even if cover is provided, what students are receiving is something other than, and normally less than, what their entitlement should be. This underlines the necessity for a more strategic provision, as suggested below.

The provision of time for professional development would be more appropriately viewed as one element in a larger package of measures addressing a range of issues that have caused disquiet in recent years, or even for decades (curriculum, assessment, different pay scales for the same work, removal of promotion posts etc.) Chapter 11 of this review provides some illuminating comparative data on how time in school is spent in the different jurisdictions covered by OECD surveys. For instance, a study of that data (Ch. 11, Fig.3) shows that the quantity of teaching time in lower secondary school in Ireland is higher than the OECD average. The point is also made in that chapter that the proportion of statutory working time spent in teaching in Ireland is by far the highest of the OECD countries.

To conclude, the larger question of a package of measures that properly reflects the changed nature of teaching in the 21st century needs to be properly acknowledged and tackled. Unless this happens, professional development for Ireland's teachers is likely to be attenuated, as distinct from progressive, in the years ahead. Nor is it likely to receive the central importance it receives in practices like nursing, pharmacy or medicine.

(d) The role of Education Centres

The Education Centres have a central role to play in a national framework for professional development for teachers. They are referred to in *Cosán* mainly as workshop locations for gathering feedback in consultations with teachers (pp.5, 12), though there is a reference to them as 'learning hubs' in the Appendix to the draft of the *Cosán* document published in May 2015 (p.23). The strategic and active role of the Education Centres needs to be fully acknowledged and promoted. This includes not only their role as venues for providing courses under the auspices of PDST or any of the national support services. Equally significant is their leadership and developmental role, for instance, in designing and providing participatory seminars or programmes that cultivate professional learning communities among teachers. The Education Centres are key players in planning and implementing the modular, credit-bearing system mentioned under headings (a) and (b) above.

(e) The role of Professional Associations

Professional associations like IPPN and NAPD are primarily seen as support and advocacy bodies for their own members. Of course, they are that, but their members are themselves the leaders of professional practice in the schools. The wealth of insight and expertise accumulated by members as practitioners of educational leadership is an invaluable resource for professional development of school leaders. Some of that expertise is currently being drawn upon in the provision of leadership development courses. To make the most of it at national level, however, it needs to be 'taken on the road' more widely, as suggested in Chapter 6 above, and in myriad ways. Such ways could include, for instance, feeding regularly into the professional development work of the newly-established Centre for School Leadership; contributing key ideas to the development of the Teaching Council's framework for professional learning; and influencing the relevant policy making arms of the DES.

> " Professional associations like IPPN and NAPD are primarily seen as support and advocacy bodies for their own members. Of course, they are that, but their members are themselves the leaders of professional practice in the schools. "

Other professional associations, such as the subject teaching associations at secondary level, have similarly important roles to play in advancing the provision of professional development for teachers. This is also true of the teacher unions, not only where the contribution of ideas that are both promising and practicable are concerned. One of the teacher unions for instance – INTO – has had extensive experience in organising professional development courses for its members.

(f) Quality assurance

Allowing for innovative approaches to quality assurance for professional learning is one of the educational values highlighted in *Cosán*. Section 9 of the document calls attention to the Teaching Council's statutory responsibilities in evaluating teacher education programmes – in this case continuing professional learning courses. It also cites Thomas Guskey's research, which has continually highlighted the necessity to make evaluation a more meaningful exercise than surveying participants' levels of enjoyment or satisfaction with a particular course. Guskey stresses the point that the evaluation of professional learning courses for teachers needs to focus centrally on the resulting difference the course makes in the quality of learning experienced by pupils and students (Guskey, 2000). To this key criterion can be added a second one: the difference the course makes to the professional *capacity* of the teacher: i.e. enhanced professional insights, capabilities and practices. This notion of enhanced professional capacity stresses qualities like originality and initiative, which are inherent to good teaching. It contrasts strongly with any conception of professional development that sees it mainly as 'upskilling' of a workforce.

These two criteria could profitably be taken into account in what *Cosán* has to say at the end of section 9 on 'Conceptual Framework' and on 'Design and Evaluation'. The design and piloting of an accreditation system, as envisaged for instance in paragraphs (a) and (b) above, are pivotal to achieving a quality assurance provision that is equal to *Cosán's* own vision. In this connection, it is necessary to point out that what *Cosán* identifies as 'standards' (Section 8) are more properly described as aspirations, or aims-in-view, viz. a commitment to 'quality teaching and learning' and to 'continued professional growth' (p. 32). Standards, if they are to do the work expected of them, need to embody criteria for assessment of the levels of capability achieved, not merely the identification of desirable professional qualities. The Teaching Council itself already acknowledges this in another area of its work: namely, the standards specified in its *Codes of Professional Conduct.* These provide the necessary criteria for the operation of the Council's fitness to practise responsibilities.

(g) Availing of relevant research insights
It is now widely accepted that the promotion of good professional practice in education is a research-informed activity, no less than it is in other, widely different practices – e.g. engineering, medicine, librarianship, accountancy, and nursing. Where the practice of education is concerned, case studies and action research studies have in recent decades added very substantially to what has been traditionally provided by empirical research. *Cosán* cites many research sources from other countries (mostly the UK and the USA). Strangely, however, it cites no Irish research. Its only references to Irish sources are to the Teaching Council's own policy documents. There is a considerable body of Irish research in recent years – including action research studies, case studies and R & D initiatives – that are relevant to the building of a framework for professional development (e.g. Hyland, 2000; Hogan et al, 2008; Conway et.al, 2009; Sullivan et al, 2016). Such studies not only illustrate how something that might work well in another jurisdiction might work less well, or well but differently, within an Irish schooling context; they can also highlight some difficulties and some possibilities that are peculiar to the Irish context. It is to be hoped that the Teaching Council will pay more systematic attention to relevant Irish research and to good research from European jurisdictions with broadly comparable populations and GDP per capita – e.g. Scotland, Denmark, and Finland. This could yield richer fruits than might otherwise be harvested in the three-year development period during which the national framework for professional learning for teachers takes shape.

(h) Leadership and Professional Development
Throughout these chapters, there has been a recurring emphasis on educational leadership, highlighting the distinctions between it and other important concerns such as educational management, educational administration and educational governance. Perhaps it is worth stressing once more that the key goal of educational leadership is that of promoting, monitoring and sustaining high quality educational experiences in classrooms and other formal learning environments. The leadership of capacity development initiatives for teachers needs continually to keep this goal to the fore.

The Teaching Council is now the main statutory agency with responsibility for regulation of the teaching profession, including the professional learning of teachers, from its initial phase right through to advanced professional development. Previously, such statutory responsibilities lay in a less specific way with the DES. The opening paragraphs of this chapter mention the CPD initiatives taken under

DES auspices in the wake of the 1998 Education Act – e.g. SDPI, PCSP, SLSS, and LDS. DES initiatives since the arrival of the Teaching Council in the CPD arena have sought to streamline the Department's CPD work. These include the establishment of the Professional Development Service for Teachers (PDST), the Project Maths support programme, and Junior Cycle for Teachers (JCT). Particularly significant is the recent setting up of the Centre for School Leadership (CSL), the consequence of joint efforts by IPPN and NAPD with the DES. This succession of initiatives marks a welcome advance on the changes inaugurated in the late 1990s, where national policy on the development of the teaching profession largely lacked a leadership perspective. In the recently-issued *Action Plan for Education,* there are a few references that link professional development with educational leadership, including the following:

> In the coming years, new innovative programmes to support the professional development of school leaders will commence. This will provide for professional coaching services and the introduction of a post-graduate qualification for aspiring school leaders.
>
> (DES, 2016j, p.31)

The coaching service is designed to support those who are already school principals (pp.35, 36) and the post-graduate programme to support aspirants. Both are welcome developments, although the reference to new innovative courses commencing fails to credit the dramatic rise that has already taken place in the numbers pursuing post-graduate courses for aspiring educational leadership within the last decade.

In any case, to build profitably on the succession of initiatives mentioned above, it is crucial that the experience gained by the different agencies is regularly shared so that there is a continuing exchange of perspectives, including constructive criticisms, between the agencies. Such exchange is also conducive to the emergence of new leadership ideas. This, in short, is an essential form of professional development for the agencies themselves. In its absence, it is only to be expected that the effects of corporate insulation will come to prevail, including unawareness of new cognate expertise that could yield valuable insights and synergies. In addition to the support agencies and statutory bodies like the NCCA and DES (including TES and the Inspectorate), other bodies need to be active participants in this exchange. These include the Teaching Council, the educational research community, the Education Centres and not least, IPPN and NAPD. The State Examination Commission is another key agency to include here. As suggested in the remarks on partnership at the close of Chapter 6, a sustained commitment to such exchange builds a tradition with its own singular benefits. Prominent among these is a regular renewal of the springs from which flow promising and practical ideas for realising the real potential of professional development itself, and for leading this potential to fresh woods and pastures new.

CHAPTER ELEVEN • • • • • • • • • • • • • • •

The Financing and Resourcing of Education at Primary and Post-Primary Levels: What Can We Learn from the OECD's *Education at a Glance?*

INTRODUCTION

The Organisation for Economic Co-operation and Development (OECD) has its roots in the establishment of the Organisation for European Economic Cooperation (OEEC) in 1948 to run the Marshall Plan for the re-construction of post-war Europe. In 1961, with the addition of the U.S., Canada and 18 other countries to its membership and a new OECD Convention, the OECD officially came into being. There are now 35 member countries in Europe, North and South America and Asia, of which 22 are members of the European Union. Ireland joined in 1961. The stated mission of the OECD is to promote policies that will improve the economic and social well-being of people around the world.

(www.oecd.org)

The OECD Directorate for Education and Skills develops and analyses quantitative, internationally comparable indicators and it publishes these annually in a volume entitled *Education at a Glance*. Together with OECD country policy reviews, the stated purpose of these indicators is to assist governments in building more effective and equitable education systems. The most recent editions of this report at the time of writing were 2015 and 2016. As with so many compendiums of official statistics, there is a time lag in the availability and analysis of data. Most of the figures in the 2015 *Education at a Glance* refer to the years 2012 or 2013 and the figures in the 2016 edition refer mainly to the year 2013/14. In this chapter, we draw upon these two volumes to provide a picture of the financing and resourcing of selected aspects of education in Ireland, in comparison with OECD and EU averages, and with selected other countries. All references to *Education at a Glance 2015* and *2016* will be indicated by page numbers.

SOME DEFINITIONS

Some key terms must be understood when reading the comparative information provided by the OECD on financing and resourcing. The indicators on costs, salaries and expenditure are normally expressed in US dollars (USD). To provide more accurate comparisons, the data for each country are also converted using Purchasing Power Parities (PPPs). When expressing costs/expenditure etc. they are calculated for each country in relation to its Gross Domestic Product (GDP). All definitions can be reviewed on the OECD website www.oecd.org.

Purchasing Power Parities
These are the rates of currency conversion that equalize the purchasing power of different currencies by eliminating the differences in price levels between countries. In their simplest form, PPPs are simply price relatives that show the ratio of the prices in national currencies of the same goods or services in different countries. PPPs are also calculated for product groups and for each of the various levels of aggregation up to and including GDP. Expenditure and costs are expressed in USD throughout the *Education at a Glance* volumes. We will use the $ to indicate USD where relevant.

Gross Domestic Product
The OECD state that Gross Domestic Product or income (GDP) is the aggregate used most frequently to represent the economic size of countries and, on a per capita basis, the economic well-being of residents. Calculating PPPs is the first step in the process of converting the level of GDP and its major aggregates, expressed in national currencies, into a common currency to enable these comparisons to be made.

Reading from an Irish perspective there are a couple of things to consider. A country's progress can be measured in a number of ways. The most commonly-used measures are the rate of national economic growth (or income) as measured by Gross National Product (GNP) or Gross Domestic

Product (GDP). GDP, which includes the income generated by multi-national firms (some repatriated to parent countries), is used extensively in the European Union and by the OECD. GNP is a somewhat better measure as it relates to the income accruing to the country, as opposed to GDP, which in many cases, and especially in Ireland, masks significant repatriation of profits. However, both measures are subject to serious criticism and should be regarded as inadequate indicators of progress due, inter alia, to their failure to take account of the distribution of income and the prevalence of poverty. Due to recent controversies about the use of GDP as it is affected by the activities of the large Irish multi-national sector, the use of statistics based on GDP has raised queries about the value of GDP as an indicator of economic growth in Ireland - notoriously described as 'leprechaun economics'. Nevertheless, because of the use of GDP by most countries, and specifically by the OECD, and because the figures in *Education at a Glance* are converted to common currencies using PPPs, reference will be made to it throughout this chapter, bearing in mind these cautionary comments.

> " Due to recent controversies about the use of GDP as it is affected by the activities of the large Irish multi-national sector, the use of statistics based on GDP has raised queries about the value of GDP as an indicator of economic growth in Ireland "

Core Educational Services

Expenditure on core educational services includes all expenditure that is directly related to instruction and education. This should cover all expenditure on teachers, school buildings, teaching materials, books, tuition outside schools and administration of schools.

Intended Instruction Time/Instructional Hours

Intended instruction time refers to the number of hours per year for which students receive instruction in both the compulsory and non-compulsory parts of the curriculum. For countries with no formal policy on instruction time, the number of hours was estimated from survey data. Hours lost when schools are closed for festivities and celebrations, such as national holidays, are excluded. Intended instruction time does not include non-compulsory time outside the school day. It does not include homework, individual tutoring or private study taken before or after school.

Teaching Time/Teaching Hours

Teaching time is defined as the net contact hours of teaching. It is calculated based on the annual number of weeks of instruction multiplied by the minimum/maximum number of periods, which a teacher is scheduled to spend teaching a class or a group, multiplied by the length of a period in minutes and divided by 60. Periods of time formally allowed for breaks between lessons or groups of lessons, and days when schools are closed for public holidays and festivities, are excluded. In primary education, however, short breaks that teachers spend with the class are typically included.

Post-Primary/Secondary Institutions

The OECD uses the term 'secondary' institutions to refer to what are mainly called 'post-primary' institutions in Ireland. They sometimes divide the data into lower and upper secondary education and occasionally combine these data with figures for non-tertiary post-secondary institutions. When looking at the figures for Ireland, it makes most sense to draw on those for combined lower and upper secondary. In this chapter, we make use of the OECD's practice of referring to post-primary institutions as secondary ones.

Tertiary Education

As this report focuses on the school system up to the end of post-primary (i.e. upper secondary education), for the most part we do not explore changes in the financing of third-level education. We acknowledge that the cuts to state resources have been proportionately greater at third level than in the rest of the educational system. However, some of the figures in *Education at a Glance* include primary through tertiary education and these are included below, where appropriate.

THE AMOUNT SPENT PER STUDENT

In 2012, on average OECD countries spent $10,220 per student from primary through tertiary education: $8,247 per primary student, $9,518 per secondary student, and $15,028 per tertiary student. These are, of course, average figures and mask substantial differences between countries. The relevant figures for Ireland in the year 2012 were $8,681 per primary student, $11,298 per secondary (i.e. post-primary) student, and $14,922 per tertiary student (including R&D activities). This put Ireland's per-student spending above average for primary and secondary, but below average for tertiary education. In 2012, Ireland's expenditure per student for primary ranked 13th out of the 34 countries for which data were available. Its per student expenditure for primary was less than that of, for example, Luxembourg, Switzerland, Norway, the U.S., Denmark, and the U.K. It was greater than, for example, Finland, France, Germany, Japan, Australia and the Slovak Republic, among others.

In 2012, Ireland's per-student expenditure ranked eighth for all secondary (upper and lower secondary combined). Its per-student expenditure was less than that of, for example, Luxembourg, Switzerland, Norway, Austria, the US and Belgium. It was greater than, for example, France, Germany, Japan, New Zealand, Sweden and the UK, among others (OECD, 2015, pp. 208 & 219).

The figures for the year 2013 are presented in Table 1 and Figure 1:

Table 1: Annual expenditure on educational institutions per student (2013)
(In equivalent US$ converted using purchasing power parities for GDP)

	Primary	Secondary	Tertiary (Including Research and Development)	Primary to Tertiary
Ireland	8,002	10,804	13,663	10,065
OECD average	8,477	9,811	15,772	10,493
Ranking (OECD)	19th of 34	14th of 33	19th of 34	18th of 34

Source: Table B1:1, *Education at a Glance 2016a*, p. 192; DES Statistics Section, 2016, p. 10

Figure 1: Annual expenditure by educational institutions per student,
by types of service (2013) (In equivalent USD converted using PPPs,
based on full-time equivalents, for primary through tertiary education)

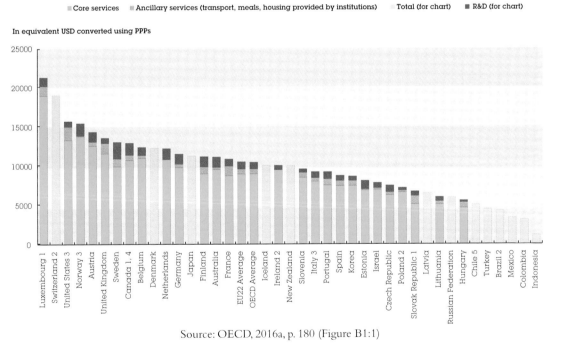

Source: OECD, 2016a, p. 180 (Figure B1:1)

Comparison of the 2012 figures with the 2013 figures presented in Table 1 shows that spending per school pupil and third-level student deteriorated significantly between the years 2012 and 2013 as the effects of budget cuts (due primarily to the financial emergency) were felt throughout the system. Ireland's rank on expenditure per student at primary level fell from 13th to 19th and for secondary students from 8th to 14th. Tables B1:1 in *Education at a Glance*, both years, show a reduction in expenditure per student, primary to tertiary, of 6.3% (2015, p. 219; 2016, p, 192). Ireland's overall expenditure in 2013 ranked below several of the countries where it was ahead the previous year, e.g. France and Australia and the overall OECD average. In 2013, Germany, Japan, Sweden and the UK were ahead of Ireland's ranking on this variable. Ireland, however, remained ahead of Estonia, Latvia, Poland, Portugal, Spain, Turkey and, perhaps more surprisingly, slightly above New Zealand. In 2013, it fell below the OECD average (OECD, 2016a, p. 192). However, as Table 1 illustrates, expenditure per student in secondary education remained above the OECD average. As Figure 1 shows, Ireland's per-student expenditure in 2013 was almost exactly in the middle of all the countries for which information was presented, but was slightly below the OECD average. While the decrease in Irish expenditure was 6.3% between 2012 and 2013, it was 7% compared to 2008 levels, while the average across the OECD increased by 8% over the 2008-2013 period (OECD, 2016b).

On average, across OECD countries, expenditure on core education services represents 84% of total expenditure per student from primary through tertiary education, and exceeds 90% in Ireland, Luxembourg, Mexico and Poland. It should be noted that, in common with a number of other countries, Ireland's expenditure per student increased from 2000 to 2010 but, due to the economic crisis, it decreased 2011-2012 (OECD, 2015, p. 222). Between 2012 and 2013, as we have seen above, it decreased even further (OECD 2016). In OECD countries, expenditure per student by educational institutions averages 22% of per capita GDP at the primary level and 25% at the secondary level. The relationship between per capita GDP and expenditure per student by educational institutions is difficult to interpret. However, there is a clear positive relationship between the two at both the primary and secondary levels of education – in other words, poorer countries tend to spend less per student than richer ones. Although the relationship is generally positive at these levels, there are variations, even among countries with similar levels of per capita GDP, and especially those in which per capita GDP exceeds $30,000. Ireland and Austria, for example, have similar levels of per-capita GDP but spend very different proportions of it on primary and secondary education. In Ireland, the proportions are 19% at the primary level and 25% at the secondary level (below or at the OECD averages of 22% and 25%, respectively), while in Austria, the proportions are 21% and 31%, respectively, and are among the largest at the secondary level (OECD, 2015, p.213).

Expenditure per student by educational institutions is largely influenced by teachers' salaries, pension systems, instructional and teaching hours, the cost of teaching materials and facilities, the programmes provided (e.g. general or vocational) and the number of students enrolled in the educational system (OECD 2015, p.209). Countries have different priorities for allocating their resources. For example, among the ten OECD countries with the largest expenditure per student by educational institutions at the lower secondary level, Denmark, Ireland, Luxembourg, Switzerland and the United States have among the highest teachers' salaries after 15 years of experience at the lower secondary level. Austria, Finland, Luxembourg and Norway have some of the lowest student-teacher ratios at that level.

THE PROPORTION OF NATIONAL INCOME SPENT ON EDUCATION

Since the beginning of the economic crisis in 2008 and up to 2012, GDP decreased, in real terms, in 20 countries with available data. Public expenditure on educational institutions started to fall between 2010 and 2012 – later than decreases in GDP – as a result of the necessary time gap to adjust public budgets. Over the period 2010-12, public expenditure on educational institutions decreased in 11 countries, including Ireland (OECD, 2015, p. 231). The average expenditure on educational institutions as a percentage of GDP at primary and secondary levels in 2012 was 3.7% in OECD countries and 3.6% in 21 EU countries for which data were available. At 4.1%, Ireland's expenditure was above the average. It ranked 9th, less than countries such as New Zealand, Denmark, Norway, Iceland and the UK but more than countries such as Australia, Austria, Mexico and Finland (OECD, 2015, p. 233). *Education at a Glance 2016* shows that the most recent figure on expenditure on educational institutions, primary to tertiary, is the same as the OECD average at 5.2% of GDP but that Ireland spends proportionately more on primary education (2% of GDP compared to the OECD average of 1.5%) and less on tertiary education (1.2% of GDP compared to the OECD average of 1.6%) (OECD, 2016a).

Changes in the proportion of national income spent on education, as measured by GDP, between 2008 and 2013 are provided in *Education at a Glance 2016* and are presented in Figure 2 below.

Figure 2: Change in public expenditure on educational institutions in percentage of GDP (2013)

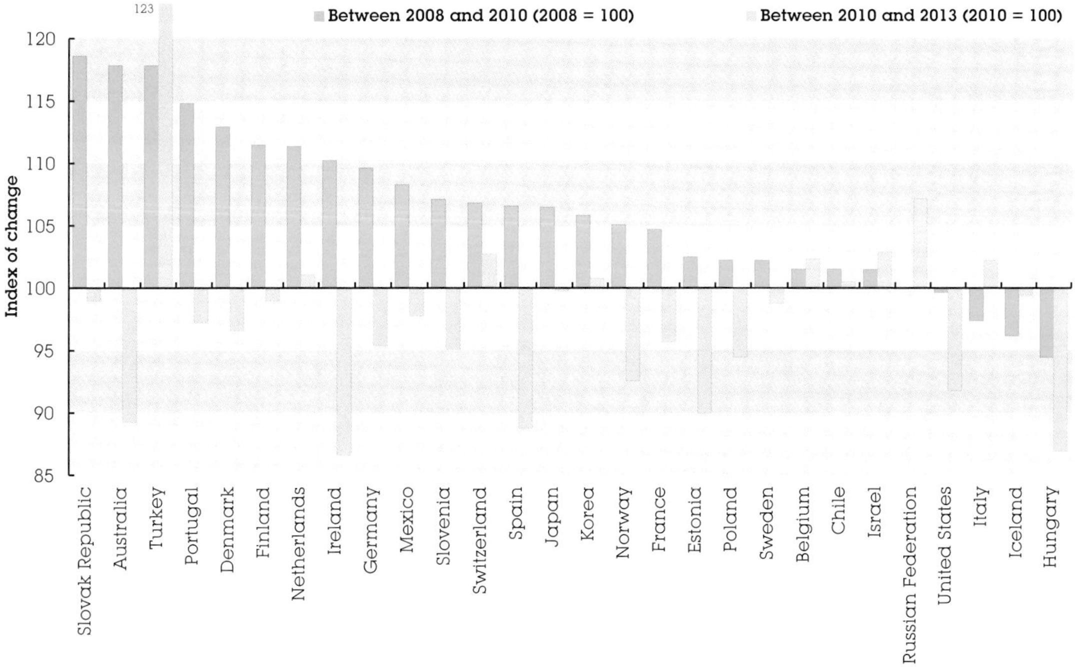

Index of change between 2008 and 2010 and between 2010 and 2013 in public expenditure on educational institutions as a percentage of GDP, for primary to tertiary education (2013 constant prices) Source: OECD, 2016a, p.203

The figures for the years 2010 – 2013 provided in *Education at a Glance 2016* present a clear picture of the reduction in funding arising from the financial crisis. The proportionate change was greater in Ireland than in all other listed countries except Hungary. However, there is a need for a certain level of caution in interpreting this chart as some of the countries which proportionately increased their public expenditure during this period, such as Turkey, or which decreased very slightly, such as Portugal, had lower expenditure per student in 2013, primary to tertiary, than Ireland (respectively, Turkey $4,482; Portugal $9,218; Ireland $10,065). The 2013 expenditure per student figure for the other country which had the same proportionate decrease in spending 2010-2013 (i.e. Hungary) was $5,591, in other words just over half of the Irish expenditure per student in that year.

THE RESOURCES AND SERVICES ON WHICH EDUCATION FUNDING IS SPENT

Across OECD countries, on average, the largest share of expenditure on education is devoted to current expenditure, given the labour intensive nature of instruction. Current expenditure is expenditure on goods and services consumed within the current year, which needs to be made recurrently to sustain the production of educational services. Minor expenditure on items of equipment, below a certain cost threshold, is also reported as current spending. Current expenditure includes final consumption expenditure, property income paid, subsidies and

> " The figures for the years 2010 - 2013 provided in *Education at a Glance 2016* present a clear picture of the reduction in funding arising from the financial crisis. "

other current transfers, e.g., social security, social assistance, pensions and other welfare benefits (www.oecd.org). In Ireland's case, the proportions for current expenditure at primary and secondary levels are greater than the OECD averages of 92.5 and 93.2% respectively. In Ireland, current expenditure as a percentage of the total was 94.6 for primary and 95.6 for secondary institutions in 2012 (OECD, 2015, p. 287).

FACTORS THAT INFLUENCE THE LEVEL OF EXPENDITURE ON EDUCATION

Factors that influence expenditure on education are the instruction time of students, the teaching time of teachers, teachers' salaries and estimated class size. Consequently, a given level of the salary cost of teachers per student may result from different combinations of these four factors. Teachers' salaries are most often the primary factor influencing the difference from the average salary cost of teachers per student at each level of education; estimated class size is the second factor (OECD, 2015, pp. 290-291). The OECD data indicate that, between 2010 and 2013 at primary level in Ireland, teachers' salaries went down and class sizes went up. Secondary level teachers' salaries went down but class size went down by a small amount, also resulting in a smaller decrease in salary cost of teachers per student than that at primary (OECD, 2015, p.295, see Fig 3).

Figure 3: Change in the salary cost of teachers per student, teachers' salaries and estimated class size, primary and lower secondary education (2010, 2013)

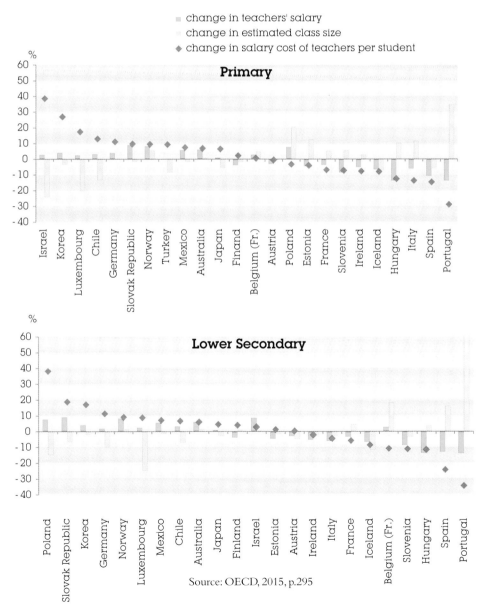

Source: OECD, 2015, p.295

In 2013, the average salary cost of teachers per student in OECD countries was $2,677 at primary and $3,350 at lower secondary level. Ireland's costs were higher than the OECD average at $3,426 at primary and $4,063 at lower secondary level. The pattern was the same in Ireland at upper secondary level although a number of countries had higher costs at upper secondary. While Ireland's teacher salary costs per student were higher than the OECD average, they were by no means the highest, with eight countries having higher costs at primary and 11 having higher costs at lower secondary level (OECD, 2015, p.299).

As the OECD points out, teachers' salaries represent the largest single cost in formal education and have a direct impact on the attractiveness of the teaching profession. They influence decisions to enrol in teacher education, to become a teacher after graduation (as graduates' career choices are associated with relative earnings in teaching and non-teaching occupations, and their likely growth over time), to return to the teaching profession after a career interruption, and/or to remain a teacher (as, in general, the higher the salaries, the fewer the people who choose to leave the profession).

> " As the OECD points out, teachers' salaries represent the largest single cost in formal education and have a direct impact on the attractiveness of the teaching profession. "

Burgeoning national debt, spurred by governments' responses to the financial crisis of late 2008, have put pressure on policy-makers to reduce government expenditure – particularly on public payrolls. Since compensation and working conditions are important for attracting, developing and retaining skilled and high-quality teachers, *Education at a Glance* advises that policy-makers should carefully consider teachers' salaries as they try to ensure both quality teaching and sustainable education budgets (OECD, 2015, p.426).

The OECD figures show that the financial and economic crisis that hit the world economy in late 2008 significantly affected the salaries for civil servants and public sector workers in general. On average across OECD countries with available data, teachers' salaries decreased, for the first time since 2000, by about 5% at all levels of education between 2009 and 2013. In England, Estonia, Greece, Hungary, Ireland, Italy, Portugal, Scotland and Spain, teachers' salaries were significantly affected by the crisis (see Figure 4 below for a picture of the OECD as a whole.

Figure 4: Change in teachers' salaries in OECD countries (2005-13)

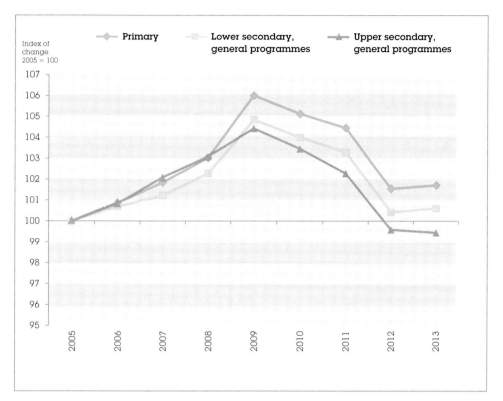

OECD average index of change, among countries with data for all reference years, for teachers with 15 years of experience and minimum qualifications (2005 = 100, constant prices). Source: OECD, 2015, p.434

In Ireland, as most Irish readers will know, teachers' salaries were reduced as of 1 January 2010 as part of a public service-wide reduction in pay. In addition, teachers who entered the profession after 1 January 2011 are paid according to a new salary scale that is lower than the salary scale that applied to those previously recruited. (OECD, 2015, pp. 426, 434-5). At the time of writing, agreement has been reached between the DES and two of the teacher unions about the restoration of some pay allowances for new recruits (www.education.ie). In spite of the reductions which occurred from 2010, the data on teachers' salaries, expressed in USDs converted using PPPs for private consumption, show that Irish teachers' salaries in 2013 at different points in their careers at both primary and secondary levels were higher than the OECD or EU averages (although a number of countries were higher – e.g. Canada, Germany and Luxembourg) (OECD, 2015, pp. 440-1). However, again, caution is required when interpreting the figures, as they do not show the structure of the teaching career, e.g. the number of part-time or temporary teachers in the system in Ireland or any other country.

STUDENT TEACHER RATIO AND CLASS SIZE

The OECD describes the relationship between class size and student teacher ratio as follows:

> 'the student–teacher ratio is calculated by dividing the number of full-time equivalent students by the number of full-time equivalent teachers at a given level of education and type of institution. Class size, on the other hand, takes into account a number of different elements: the ratio of students to teaching staff, the number of classes or students for which a teacher is responsible, the amount of instruction time compared to the length of teachers' working days, the proportion of time teachers spend teaching, how students are grouped within classes, and team-teaching arrangements'.
>
> (OECD, 2015, p.421)

As regards class size, the only figure presented for Ireland in 2013 and in 2014 was for primary level. Average class size, at 25, for Irish primary schools was higher than that of the OECD average of 21 or the EU average of 20. This was the fifth highest figure, with Chile, Israel, Japan and the UK being higher (OECD, 2015, p. 423; 2016a, p. 401).

In the years 2013 and 2014, Ireland also had higher ratios of students to teaching staff than the OECD and EU ratios at both primary and secondary levels. Ireland's ratios were 16 for primary and 14 for secondary, while the OECD's were 15 at primary, 13 at secondary overall, and the EU's were 14 at primary and 11 (2013) and 12 (2014) at secondary (OECD, 2015, p.424; 2016a, p. 403).

THE TIME TEACHERS SPEND TEACHING

The amount of time teachers spend teaching also affects the financial resources countries need to allocate to education. Irish teachers will be very conscious of occasional perceptions in the media and among the public that they teach fewer hours than is the case in other countries. Comparisons provided by *Education at a Glance 2015* and *2016* illustrate that this is not so. The number of teaching hours per year by Irish teachers in primary schools is higher than in secondary schools and is higher than the OECD average (OECD, 2015, p. 452). Teaching hours in Ireland are significantly longer than the OECD average, at 915 hours per year at primary level (compared to the OECD average of 776 hours) and 735 hours at upper secondary level (compared to the OECD average of 644 hours) (OECD, 2016a). The number of teaching hours per year by Irish teachers in lower secondary education is above the OECD average and rose slightly due to agreements during the economic crisis (see Figure 5 below – those for upper secondary were not provided in this figure).

Figure 5: Number of teaching hours per year in general lower secondary education, in 2000, 2005 and 2013

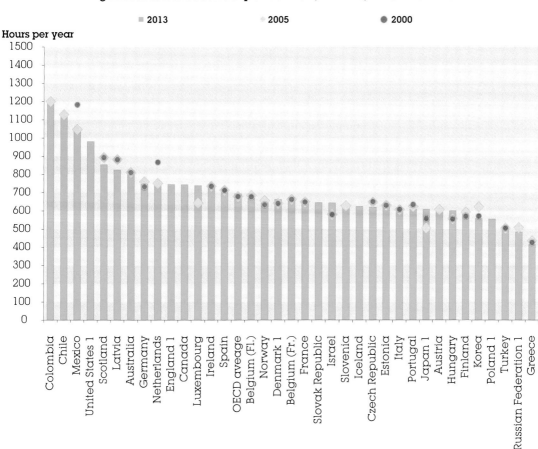

Source: OECD, 2015, p. 450

Obviously, the amount of time teachers spend teaching affects the financial resources countries need to allocate to education. The OECD points out that most countries regulate the number of working hours per year that teachers are formally required to work, including teaching and non-teaching activities (2015, p.451). It is also noted that, although teaching time is a substantial component of teachers' workloads, assessing students, preparing lessons, correcting students' work, in-service training and staff meetings may also be taken into account when analysing the demands placed on teachers in different countries. The amount of time available for these non-teaching activities varies across countries, and a large proportion of statutory working time spent teaching may indicate that less time is devoted to activities such as assessing students and preparing lessons (2015, p. 454). As regards the percentage of statutory working time spent teaching in Ireland, at more than 90% it is by far the highest in the OECD (2015, p. 455). However, the arrangements for the implementation of the framework for Junior Cycle will allow 22 hours of professional time for each full-time teacher each year, as well as an additional two hours to be allocated by school management to a teacher on a rotational basis for the coordination of subject learning and assessment reviews (DES, 2016a). These allocations are intended to be implemented in the 2016/17 school year in schools in which the members of the teacher unions have supported by ballot the recommendations of an agreement between the DES and the two second-level teacher unions.

CONCLUSIONS

The comparative figures and analysis provided by the OECD's *Education at a Glance* show that, by comparison with OECD and EU averages, Ireland's resourcing and financing of education – in spite of the recent time of austerity – is not by any means at the lowest level among OECD and EU countries. However, the data also show that there have been serious cutbacks and that Ireland's financing of education is in the mid-range, generally below that of more economically-developed countries. Even within the parameters of existing resources, it is also important to remember (and the OECD points this out in a number of places) that different policy choices can be made.

Due to the economic crisis, Ireland has been through a period of substantial cuts to public services and education did not escape. While the cuts are too numerous to list in full, successive budgets in Ireland have seen the following: pay-cuts for teachers (along with all public servants), substantial cuts to education budgets from 2011 to 2014, including substantial reductions in the allocations to higher education institutions, reductions in rates of student support grants and grants to programmes for marginalised youth and disadvantaged adults, 'rationalisation' of teacher support services and 'efficiencies' in school transport (i.e. cutbacks) (Department of Finance, various years). There was an overall reduction in teacher allocations and school guidance services. Perhaps most seriously from the perspective of educational participation and achievement, there were serious cuts in Social Welfare, including Child Benefit. Analysis of austerity budgets suggests that they are economically regressive and that they will copper-fasten educational inequalities (e.g. Social Justice Ireland, 2012). As already indicated, there was a cut that removed the allowances attaching to masters and doctoral qualifications for new entrants to the profession, in addition to substantial cuts in the money for continuing professional development (CPD). The allowances, while not large, did provide an

> " The comparative figures and analysis provided by the OECD's Education at a Glance show that, by comparison with OECD and EU averages, Ireland's resourcing and financing of education – in spite of the recent time of austerity – is not by any means at the lowest level among OECD and EU countries. "

incentive to teachers undertaking certified CPD – important when one considers the lower proportion of Irish teachers taking advanced qualifications in comparison to their international colleagues – and indeed, the substantially lower number of days of all kinds of CPD taken by Irish teachers (OECD, 2009).

At the time of writing, there are on-going discussions between the DES and other stakeholders on the issue of pay arrangements for newly-qualified teachers. These discussions are taking place within the context of the acceptance by two of the teacher unions (the INTO and the TUI) of the Lansdowne Road Agreement (DES, 2016e). The matter of CPD in relation to the implementation of the new Junior Certificate programme has been outlined in a circular letter from the Department (DES, 2016a). As the economic indicators improve, there has been a series of allocations by the Department of Finance to educational services. There is now an opportunity for the restoration of many of the cuts that were implemented, especially those that affected the most marginalized pupils.

Education at a Glance each year provides a snapshot of indicators for each participating country. These are necessarily time-bound. The value is that they provide a mechanism for policy-makers, educators and citizens to evaluate the progress, or otherwise, in their education systems, in comparative perspective.

CHAPTER TWELVE ● ● ● ● ● ● ● ● ● ● ● ● ●
Conclusion

Irish schooling faces significant challenges into the future. Ireland's is not a perfect system, no more than any other schooling system in the world. While perfection is not achievable, it is incumbent on every society to apply its best efforts to ensuring that the school system is as good as possible so that that this and future generations are assisted at achieving their potentials. The eleven chapters of this review paint a very creditable picture of how Irish schooling policy and provision has been evolving and of the manner in which this is being achieved. The various stakeholders and educational partners in this small island state have focussed constructively in establishing the present structure. Each of the headings reviewed in the chapters indicates that Ireland's educational system is on the cusp of major attempts at reform. Building on accumulated achievements, it is poised for qualitative breakthroughs on a range of fronts.

As detailed in the foregoing chapters, the agenda for necessary advances and improvements in our schooling system is clear. The crucial contemporary question is that of achieving it as the country emerges from a painful recession and as the key economic indicators improve. An underlying, dynamic pulse of Ireland's educational system is the interest in, and concern for educational improvement by parents, teachers and policy-makers. The achievement of major educational reform, in a sustainable way, has been shown to be a demanding challenge in all societies. A number of pre-requisites is needed to help promote success. These include the quality of prevailing policies and how they have been arrived at. Good communication on the proposed advantages of the proposed changes is integral to the process. A sense of engagement and ownership needs to be cultivated among key practitioners. Appropriate training and capacity development may be required for implementers of reform. The timing of reforms and the gradation span for change needs to be well planned. The administrative structures need to be such that this can be seen to facilitate implementation. Integral to the whole question of sustainable improvements is the judicious planning of policy initiatives, and the budgeting for the necessary resources, to make the right things happen, in the right ways and at the right times.

It is rare to get all such pre-requisites to full satisfaction. This review nevertheless indicates that many of them are on track in Ireland. The weakest of the pre-requisites relates to the governance and administrative structure and the inadequate resources available for a strategic development programme in education. With regard to governance and administrative structures, it has been a striking feature of the school system that there is no intermediate tier of administration between the Department of Education and Skills and the individual school, albeit the ETBI fulfils some such role for about 35% of post-primary schools (254/735). Over the last forty years, a number of attempts were made to establish such a middle tier, without success. The lack of such a tier places a heavy burden on the administration of individual schools. Many of the changes envisaged in current plans for the conduct of schools emphasise school planning, school self-evaluation and school communities working in collaborative, collegial ways. In line with international trends, significant emphasis is being placed, in Ireland, on the quality of educational leadership. Within that, the emphasis is being particularly placed on the leadership of the core functions of the school – teaching and learning. However, Ireland has inherited an older model of school leadership, whereby the principal and deputy principal (if one exists) carry forward a multiplicity of duties that seriously impede close engagement with the leadership of teaching and learning. The duties involve relationships with parents, pupils, staff, procurement, maintenance of premises, relationships with the DES, examination agencies etc., and a great deal of bureaucratic activity. As referenced repeatedly in the

> "
> In line with international trends, significant emphasis is being placed, in Ireland, on the quality of educational leadership. Within that, the emphasis is being particularly placed on the leadership of the core functions of the school – teaching and learning.
> "

preceding chapters, this exerts a huge clogging influence on the work of real educational leadership. Many school leaders experience great stress in coping with this very varied and burdensome workload. Indeed, there is evidence that the post of principal is not now attractive to many high-quality teachers, who see it as an unwelcome distraction from their core educational interests. However it is achieved, remedy is needed in this area and in the characterisation of responsibility posts in schools, if the aspired-for quality of educational leadership is to be realised.

Another legacy issue from the past is the question of what a teacher's contract entails. Irish teachers have a very good record in devoting voluntary time to school cultural events and sports. However, increasingly, the teacher's contract is being interpreted as his/her allocated teaching hours in the school. This tends to fragment teachers' sense of professional identity, leading to internal tensions and incoherences. An unfortunate, but by no means an infrequent, consequence is that principals seeking to involve staff in school activities such as school planning, collaborative subject teaching, school self-evaluation activities etc. can be faced with significant obstacles in co-operation. The so-called "Croke Park hours" were an attempt to establish the time for such planning activities, but they have been fraught with controversy, linked to industrial relations problems and to resentments of an imposed reign of austerity. Since at least the early 1990s, this issue has been regarded as a problem in the way of much-needed advances in Ireland's schooling, but it remains to be satisfactorily resolved, if these delayed advances are to be made.

The other major requisite which is missing is adequate budgetary resourcing to enable and to nurture these advances. While the promotion of education is a sectoral issue, in the sense that it is the immediate responsibility of the Department of Education and Skills, it is also a government issue in that it impinges on a very wide range of society's concerns. In common with other public services, education suffered during the recession. However, over the past twenty years or so, education has lost out vis-à-vis the other main spending Departments where its share of the overall national budget is concerned. In a recent newspaper article, John Walshe pointed out that in 1950, spending on health, education and social welfare accounted for only a third of government spending. Today, these three departments account for almost 80% of government spending. However, in relative terms, health and social welfare have benefited significantly more than education has from this increase. Since the year 2000, all three increased their share for reasons such as demographics, rising costs etc. Nevertheless, while social welfare has increased from 26.7% to 38% of the overall national budget and health has increased from 19.6% to 26%, education has only increased from 13.9% to 17% over this period (Walshe, 2016).

The findings and suggested policy paths arising from this review of our schooling indicate the unsustainability of this situation. The references to a New Deal in the preceding chapters are not rhetorical or tendentious. The state has in recent years endorsed a reform agenda for schooling with many commendable features, including advances in the induction procedures for newly-qualified teachers, self-evaluation by practitioners, and a more learner-focused curriculum at post-primary Junior Cycle. However, for all its merits, it is an agenda that has not ignited the wide-scale enthusiasm of Ireland's teachers. More inclusive and more imaginative policy approaches are called for. A new vision is needed to redress structural shortcomings of some decades and inequities that have become more overt in a time of recession. Without such a vision, including the serious long-term commitment to increased educational expenditure needed to realise it, the chances of successful implementation of any agenda for improvement are seriously in jeopardy.

To assist in the articulation and pursuit of such a vision, we have summarised below some key issues needing attention and action. For ease of reference, the issues are grouped under the headings of the eleven foregoing chapters. The remarks under each of the eleven headings are necessarily concise. They are not intended as a list of recommendations. Rather, they are designed to invite constructive, practical forms of engagement with ideas arising from a fuller reading of the chapters themselves.

1. TEACHING AND LEARNING

The more dominant conceptions of teaching and learning in the public arena – often even among teachers themselves – fail to do justice to the daily realities of educational practice. In particular, they have an inadequate understanding of learning. Any adequate understanding of teaching needs to overcome uncritical notions of transmission, and associated one-sided notions like 'delivering the curriculum' or 'covering the course'. The prevalence of many variants of the transmission idea in the everyday workings of policy and practice places too much emphasis on so-called transfer of knowledge and skills. It places too little on the enduring attitudes *to* learning and practices *of* learning that take shape, beneficially or otherwise, in educational experience as it unfolds. Preoccupation with transmission, and with the examining of its results, hinders a professional requirement of first importance among practitioners of teaching. That is: the systematic perceptiveness called for in devising and promoting a high quality of educational experience among students. This perceptiveness is crucial in evaluating or validly assessing anything important in education, including the short-term and lasting consequences of the learning experiences that take place in our schools and colleges. Where it is embodied in the work of practitioners, such perceptiveness ensures a continuing focus on the monitoring and enhancement of students' capabilities and genuine accomplishments. It also highlights the inadequacies of the omnipresent notion of 'delivering' a curriculum and of measuring the 'outcomes' of such delivery. These points are centrally relevant to the cultivation of a strong capacity for self-evaluation among teachers and schools.

2. EARLY CHILDHOOD EDUCATION

In this chapter it was suggested that the percentage of GDP allocated to Early Childhood Education should be increased to 0.8%. More attention and support needs to be given to the education and training of staff for this area. Support needs to be sustained for the implementation of Aistear. The synchronisation of Aistear with the infant years in the primary school curriculum needs to be achieved. There should be a cap on the size of reception classes in primary schools. Continuing efforts are needed for the incorporation of children with disabilities in free pre-school provision.

3. CURRICULUM

Chapter 3 outlined the history of curriculum policy in primary and second-level schools in Ireland and focused on current curriculum reform. It summarised the recent revision of the Primary Language Curriculum and the upcoming revision of Primary Maths. It traced the many efforts over the past forty years to reform Junior Cycle curriculum and welcomed the new Junior Cycle Framework, which was agreed between the teacher union leaders and the Minister in May 2015. The new framework and the associated assessment changes herald a new and welcome era where the professionalism of teachers will be recognised and given scope, and the learning environment will be more engaging for students.

The strengths and weaknesses of a learning outcomes approach to curriculum design, as currently adopted by the NCCA, were explored. The potential of this approach for teaching and learning are recognised, but undue or slavish adherence to specifying curriculum solely in terms of topics and learning outcomes must be avoided, especially when the Leaving Certificate syllabi are being revised. Information about the depth of treatment of subjects, teacher guidelines and details of examination requirements will have to be provided to bring the Leaving Certificate curriculum into line with international good practice. This is also needed to ensure that the Leaving Certificate will continue to be of the high standard expected by society and the higher education sector.

4. ASSESSMENT – PRIMARY AND JUNIOR CYCLE

Assessment is an integral component of the curriculum process: it should serve the curriculum, not dominate it. It is multi-faceted and ideally employs a combination of modes and techniques so as to match intended programme/subject outcomes. Conducting assessment should not be seen as an end in itself. The findings should form the basis for improving teaching and learning practices. The involvement of teachers in the assessment of their own pupils up to certificate levels is widely acknowledged and is recommended. Assessment findings should be shared widely with interested stakeholders and couched in a language that is accessible to each audience.

While the proposals on assessment at Junior Certificate level currently being implemented represent a significant, if modest, breakthrough in extending the range of assessments, the terminal examination still remains the dominant mode of assessment, with a minor allocation for coursework. An increased allocation of school-based, teacher-led assessment would enhance the system and benefit the students. Hopefully, this will eventually lead to the full implementation of the DES 2015 reform proposals. In this context, a system of external monitoring is regarded as essential in the interests of maintaining standards across the system and ensuring the credibility of the system.

> " Conducting assessment should not be seen as an end in itself. The findings should form the basis for improving teaching and learning practices. "

Teachers need the support of ongoing professional development in all aspects of assessment relevant to their involvement in implementing a system of school-based assessment, while research into all aspects of any new system of assessment is deemed essential so that standards of implementation can be monitored on an ongoing basis.

5. TRANSITION FROM SECOND LEVEL TO HIGHER EDUCATION

This chapter focused on the transition of students from second to third-level education. It outlined the process used by higher education institutions to select school leavers, and the central role played by the Leaving Certificate in this process. It traced the history of the Central Applications Office and the development of the Points system. It outlined upcoming changes to the Leaving Certificate grading system as well as associated changes in the Points system. It suggested alternatives to the Leaving Certificates a mechanism for selection and explored approaches in other jurisdictions. It concluded that there is no perfect system of selection nor is there a 'one size fits all' solution. As long as demand exceeds supply, either in an aggregate sense or for individual courses, some system of selection has to be put in place and there will be winners and losers. However, every system of selection should be regularly reviewed and if necessary reformed, if and when the evidence points to a more successful selection system.

> " As long as demand exceeds supply, either in an aggregate sense or for individual courses, some system of selection has to be put in place and there will be winners and losers. "

6. EDUCATIONAL LEADERSHIP AND GOVERNANCE

Where the conduct of educational practice is concerned, it is important to distinguish from the start between the different kinds of responsibilities that belong to management, to administration, to governance and to leadership. The last of these has a particular importance as we look ahead. Its central purpose is identifying and promoting initiatives that yield a higher quality of educational experience for pupils and students.

Educational leadership within schools involves not only the principal and deputy principal, but also the teaching staff and, where appropriate, the students. The exercise of such leadership needs dedicated time, however, for planning and consulting, for implementing and monitoring, for evaluating and amending. Such dedicated time has been far too scarce in Ireland's schools and tackling this problem requires a restructuring of time-in-school.

Educational leadership is also important beyond the gates of the school. The constructive voice of school leaders needs to be heard more influentially in policy-making quarters, not least on the kinds of initiatives that have enhanced educational experiences in Irish schools. The new Centre for School Leadership is a welcome development in this context. It needs a strong research dimension, allied to the freedom to initiate and promote enhanced professional practice and to speak fearlessly for and with school leaders.

7. THE SCHOOL SYSTEM: EQUALITY, INCLUSION AND RIGHTS

Equality, inclusion and human rights are core concepts in education. While progress has been made in these areas, research on the school system shows there are still significant inequalities arising from disadvantage linked to six sources: social class/socio-economic background; disability/SEN; ethnic diversity; religious diversity; gender; and sexual orientation. None of these issues can be addressed by the education system alone. For example, child poverty is a significant factor in poor educational outcomes. A substantial reduction in poverty requires action by Government and by all departments of state. What is needed in relation to these six areas is a serious commitment to equality, not only by government but also by the key educational interest groups – the churches, teacher unions, management bodies and parents' organizations. All educational policy should be equality-proofed. The values and goals expressed in the Department of Education and Skills' *Statement of Strategy 2015 – 2017* and *Action Plan for Education 2016 - 2019*, if continuously reviewed and developed as planned, and if implemented, give grounds for optimism. Indeed, as the DES itself points out in its 2016- 2019 *Action Plan*, all public bodies are required to consider human rights and equality issues and, therefore, these issues are a driving force in the Department's work. An integrated public policy approach, involving the range of government departments, will have to be a core part of the new directions. So too will be a strategy of equality-proofing all budgetary policies and initiatives. The approach of equality-proofing all school plans and initiatives will have to be adopted at school and management body levels if there is to be significant progress. The approach to policy should be research- and evidence-based and subject to on-going review. Increased investment in high-quality and quality-assured education from pre-school to higher education should be the target, especially for the most marginalized groups.

8. THE CHANGING ROLE OF THE INSPECTORATE

The staffing of the Inspectorate should be increased to enable it to implement satisfactorily its extensive work agenda. As key agents in promoting reforms in teaching and learning and in the dynamics of school life, the Inspectorate needs to use discretion and prudence in nurturing the pace of change to ensure its embeddedness. The Inspectorate should act in close liaison with the Teaching Council in relation to the implementation of the Council's teacher induction and continuing professional development policies.

9. INITIAL TEACHER EDUCATION AND INDUCTION

Policies aimed at greater collaboration between teacher education institutions need to be supported, financially and otherwise. Greater support needs to be provided for school personnel to engage fully with the teacher induction policy so that it becomes a normal part of professional engagement. Issues of teacher supply, particularly as it affects newly-qualified teachers, need greater attention. The recruitment of potential teachers from immigrant ethnic groups should be promoted.

10. FINANCING AND RESOURCING:

The comparative figures and analysis provided by the OECD's *Education at a Glance* illustrate that, by comparison with OECD and EU averages, Ireland's resourcing and financing of education – in spite of the recent time of austerity – is not by any means at the lowest level among OECD and EU countries. However, the data also show that there have been serious cutbacks and that Ireland's financing of education is in the mid-range, generally below that of more economically-developed countries. Even within the parameters of existing resources, it is important to remember (and the OECD points this out in a number of places) that different policy choices can be made. Increased investment in education will be essential as the economy recovers if the government and the DES are to achieve the targets set out in the DES *Action Plan 2016 – 2019* and other targets that may be considered necessary as policy develops, particularly in relation to marginalised pupils.

11. PROFESSIONAL DEVELOPMENT IN TEACHING

Traditionally, the professional development of teachers was not a priority area for educational policy in Ireland. Within the last two decades, that has changed considerably. The real significance of professional development is missed, however, if it is viewed as being mainly about skills and up-skilling. Professional development is essentially about the betterment of teachers' capacities to build vibrant and inclusive learning environments. Of course, this involves skills, but skills can remain mere competences unless they become purposefully at home in each teacher's cultivation of his/her professional capabilities.

The Teaching Council's *Cosán* publication (March 2016) marks a welcome step in devising a framework for professional development for Ireland's teachers. Important work remains to be done over the next few years in building that framework, not least in putting together a flexible system for accrediting valuable professional development activities undertaken by teachers. In this work, educational leaders, Education Centres, teachers' representatives and the educational research community have a central part to play.

Bibliography • • • • • • • • • • • • • • • • • • •

- Aho, E., Pitkanen, K., Sahlberg P. (2006) *Policy Development and Reform Principles of Basic and Secondary Education in Finland since 1968.* Washington DC: The World Bank Apprenticeship Council (2015) 'Report on New Apprenticeship Programme Proposals' https://www.education.ie/en/Publications/Policy-Reports/Apprenticeship-Council-Report-on-New-Apprenticeship-Programme-Proposals.pdf

- Arnold, S. (2012) *Poverty and Exclusion: The case of Children in State Accommodation for Asylum Seekers.* Dublin: Irish Refugee Council

- Baird, J-A, Hopfenbeck, T.N., Elwood, J., Caro, D., Ahmed, A. (2014) *Predictability in the Irish Leaving Certificate.* Oxford: Oxford University Centre for Educational Assessment and Queen's University, Belfast

- Baker, J., Lynch, K., Cantillon, S., Walsh, J. (2006) 'Equality: Putting the theory into action' *Res Publica*, Vol. 12, Issue 4

- Baker, J. K. Lynch, S. Cantillon and J. Walsh (2009) *Equality: From Theory to Action. 2nd Edition*, London: Palgrave Macmillan

- Boyd, W. & King, E.J. (1999) *The History of Western Education.* 12th edition, Lanham, MD: Rowman & Littlefield

- Bowen, J. (2003) *A History of Western Education: Volume Two: Civilisation of Europe – Sixth to Sixteenth Century*; Volume Three: The Modern West–Europe and the New World. London: Routledge

- Bryan, A. & Bracken, M. (2011) ' "They Think the Book is Right and I am Wrong": Intercultural Education and the Positioning of Ethnic Minority Students in the Formal and Informal Curriculum', in Darmody, M., Tyrrell, N., Song, S. (eds.) *The Changing Faces of Ireland: Exploring the Lives of Immigrant and Ethnic Minority Children.* Rotterdam/Boston/Taipei: Sense Publishers

- Bryan, A. (2010) 'Corporate Multiculturalism, Diversity Management, and Positive Interculturalism in Irish Schools and Society', Irish Educational Studies, Vol. 29, Issue 3

- Buckley, H. & McGarry, K. (2011) 'Child Protection in Primary Schools: a Contradiction in Terms or a Potential Opportunity?' *Irish Educational Studies*, Vol. 30, Issue 1

- Byrne, D., McCoy, S., Watson, D. (2008) *School Leavers Survey Report 2007*, Dublin: Economic and Social Research Institute

- Byrne, D. McGinnity, F., Smyth, E., Darmody, M. (2010) 'Immigration and School Composition in Ireland', *Irish Educational Studies*, Vol. 29, Issue 3

- Carr, W. (2006) 'Education Without Theory?', British Journal of Educational Studies Vol. 54, Issue 2

- CEB (Curriculum and Examinations Board) (1984) I*ssues and Structures in Education.* Dublin: CEB.

- CEB (1986a) *Senior Cycle: Development and Direction.* Consultative Document, Dublin: The Curriculum and Examinations Board

- CEB (1986b) *In Our Schools.* Dublin: The Curriculum and Examinations Board

- Central Board of Secondary Education, India, (2015) *Senior School Curriculum 2015-16.* http://cbseacademic.in/web_material/Curriculum/SrSecondary/2015%E2%80%9316_Senior%20School%20Curriculum%20Volume%201.pdf

- Cheng, Cheong, Yin (1996) *School Effectiveness and School-based Management: A Mechanism for Development.* London: Falmer Press

- Children's Rights Alliance (2010) *The United Nations Convention on the Rights of the Child.* http://www.childrensrights.ie/sites/default/files/submissions_reports/files/UNCRCEnglish_0.pdf

- Children's Rights Alliance (2016) *Report Card 2016.* Dublin: Children's Rights Alliance

- Clandinin, D. & Connelly, F. (1992) 'Teacher as Curriculum Maker' in Jackson, P. (ed.), *Handbook of Research on Curriculum.* New York: Macmillan

- Clerkin, A., Perkins, R., Cunningham, R. (2016) *TIMSS 2015 in Ireland: Mathematics and Science in Primary and Post-Primary Schools.* Dublin: Educational Research Centre

- Condron, D. (2009) 'Social Class, School and Non-School Environments, and Black/White Inequalities in Children's Learning', *American Sociological Review*, Vol. 74, Issue 5

- Conference of Religious of Ireland (1997) *Religious Congregations in Irish Education: A role for the future?* Dublin. Conference of Religious of Ireland

- Constant, C. & Connolly, T. (2014) 'An Exploration of formative assessment practices on children's academic efficacy' *Irish Teachers' Journal*, Vol. 2, Issue 1

- Conway, P. F., (2002) 'Learning in communities of practice: Rethinking teaching and learning in disadvantaged contexts'. *Irish Educational Studies*, Vol. 21, Issue 3

- Conway, P. F., Murphy, R., Rath, A., Hall, K. (2009) *Learning to Teach and its Implications for the Continuum of Teacher Education: A Nine Country Cross-national Study.* Maynooth: The Teaching Council

- Coolahan, B. (2014) *The Reform of Junior Cycle Education as an issue in Irish Education 1970-2014*, Dublin: Parkmore Press

- Coolahan, J. (1979) *University Entrance Requirements and their Effect on Second Level Curricula*, Dublin: Irish Federation of University Teachers

- Coolahan, J. (1981) *Irish Education: History and Structure*, Dublin: Institute of Public Administration

- Coolahan, J. & O'Donovan, P. (2009) *A History of Ireland's School Inspectorate.* Dublin: Four Courts Press

- Coolahan, J., Hussey, C., Kilfeather, F. (2012) *The Forum on Patronage and Pluralism in the Primary Sector: Report of the Forum's Advisory Group.* https://www.education.ie/en/Press-Events/Events/Patronage-and-Pluralism-in-the-Primary-Sector/The-Forum-on-Patronage-and-Pluralism-in-the-Primary-Sector-Report-of-the-Forums-Advisory-Group.pdf

- Coolahan, J. (2016) *Newsletter on the Arts in Education Charter.* Summer 2016 http://artsineducation.ie/en/home/

- Commission on the Points System (1999) *Final Report and Recommendations.* Dublin: Department of Education and Science

- Cosgrove, J., Shiel, G., Archer. P., Perkins, R. (2010) 'Comparisons of Performance in Ireland PISA 2000 to PISA 2009' Dublin: Educational Research Centre www.erc.ie/documents/p09erc_technical_report.pdf

- Cosgrove, J. (2015) 'Changes in achievement in PISA from 2000 to 2009 in Ireland: Beyond the test scores' *Irish Journal of Education*, Vol .40

- Cosgrove, J., McKeown, C., Travers, J., Lysaght, Z., Ní Bhroin, O., Archer, P. (2014) *Educational Experiences and Outcomes for Children with Special Educational Needs: A Secondary Analysis of Data from the Growing Up in Ireland Study.* NCSE Research Report No 17

- Council of the European Union (1990) 'Resolution of the Council and the Ministers for Education meeting within the Council of 31 May 1990 concerning integration of children and young people with disabilities into ordinary systems of education' http://eurlex.europa.eu/search.html?qid=1468428381117&wh OJ=NO_OJ%3D162,YEAR_OJ%3D1990&type=advanced&lang=en&SUBDOM_INIT=ALL_ALL&DB_COLL_OJ=oj-c

- Coyne, B., Devitt, N., Lyons, S. & McCoy, S. (2016) 'Perceived Benefits and Barriers to the Use of High-Speed Broadband in Ireland's Second-level Schools' *Irish Educational Studies*, Vol.34, Issue 4

- CSO (2012) (Central Statistics Office / An Phríomh-Oifig Staidrimh) 'Census 2011 Profile 8 Our Bill of Health – Health, Disability and Careers in Ireland' http://www.cso.ie/en/census/census2011reports/census2011 profile8ourbillofhealth–healthdisabilityandcarersinireland/

- CSO (2015) 'Survey on Income and Living Conditions (SILC) 2013 Results' http://www.cso.ie/en/releasesandpublications/er/silc/survey onincomeandlivingconditions2013/

- CSO (2016) 'Annual Population Change' http://www.cso.ie/px/pxeirestat/statire/SelectVarVal/Define. asp?Maintable=PEA15&PLanguage=0 And: 'Persons in Full-time Education, by Level', http://www.cso.ie/en/releasesandpublications/ep/p-syi/statisticalyearbookofireland2015/society/education/

- Cullinan, J., Flannery, D., Walsh, S. & McCoy, S. (2013) 'Distance Effects, Social Class and the Decision to Participate in Higher Education in Ireland' *The Economic and Social Review*, Vol.44, Issue 1

- Daly, E. & Hickey, T. (2011) 'Religious Freedom and the Right to Discriminate in the School Admissions Context: a Neo-republican Critique' *Legal Studies*, Vol. 31, Issue 4

- Darmody, M. & Smyth, E. (2015) ' "When You Actually Talk to Them …" – Recognising and Respecting Cultural and Religious Diversity in Irish Schools', in Honohan, I. & Rougier, N. (eds.) *Tolerance and Diversity in Ireland, North and South*. Manchester: Manchester University Press

- Darmody, M. McGinnity, F. and Kingston, G. (2016) 'The Experiences of Migrant Children in Ireland', in Williams, J., Nixon, E., Smyth, E., Watson, D. (eds.) *Cherishing All the Children Equally? Ireland 100 years on from the Easter Rising*. Dublin: Oaktree Press/ESRI

- Department of Children and Youth Affairs (2011) *Children First: National Guidance for the Protection and Welfare of Children*. http://www.dcya.gov.ie/documents/Publications/ ChildrenFirst.pdf

- Department of Children and Youth Affairs (2014) *Better Outcomes Brighter Futures: The National Policy Framework for Children and Young People 2014-2020* http://www.dcya.gov.ie/documents/cypp_framework/Better OutcomesBetterFutureReport.pdf

- Department of Education (1934) *Revised Programme of Primary Instruction*. Dublin: The Stationery Office

- Department of Education (1948) *Revised Programme for Infants*. Dublin: The Stationery Office

- Department of Education (1954) *Report of the Council of Education on the Curriculum of the Primary School*. Dublin: The Stationery Office

- Department of Education (1962) *Report of the Council of Education on the Curriculum in the Secondary School*. Dublin: The Stationery Office

- Department of Education (1965a) *Investment in Education: Report of the Survey Team Appointed by the Minister for Education in October 1962*. Dublin: The Stationery Office

- Department of Education (1965b) *Rules for National Schools*. Dublin: The Stationery Office

- Department of Education (1971) *Primary School Curriculum: Teachers' Handbook*. Dublin: The Stationery Office

- Department of Education (1975): *Final Report of the Committee on the form and function of the Intermediate Certificate Examination*. (The ICE Report) Dublin: The Stationery Office

- Department of Education (1990) *Report of the Review Body on the Primary Curriculum*. Dublin: The Stationery Office

- Department of Education (1999) *Primary School Curriculum* (Box set of volumes containing syllabus and Teacher Guidelines for the different subjects) Dublin: The Stationery Office *Teachers' Handbook*. Dublin: The Stationery Office

- DES (Dept. of Education and Science; became Dept. of Education and Skills in 2010) 'Annual Statistical Reports' http://www.education.ie/en/Publications/Statistics/Statistica l-Reports/Other-Statistical-Reports.html ; also 'Annual Statistical Reports International' http://www.education.ie/en/Publications/Statistics/ International-Statistical-Reports/International-Statistical-Reports.html

- DES (2000) *The Junior Certificate: Issues for Discussion*. Dublin: Department of Education and Science

- DES (2004) *Rules and Programmes for Secondary Schools 2004/05*. Dublin: Government Publications

- DES (2005a) *Literacy and numeracy in disadvantaged schools: challenges for teachers and learners: an evaluation by the Inspectorate of the Department of Education and Science* https://www.education.ie/en/Publications/Inspection-Reports-Publications/Evaluation-Reports-Guidelines/insp_literacy_numeracy_05_pdf.pdf

- DES (2005b) *Survey of Traveller Education Provision*. Dublin: The Stationery Office

- DES (2005c) *Chief Inspector's Report 2001-2004*. Dublin: Department of Education and Skills

- DES (2009) *Chief Inspector's Report, 2008*. Dublin: Department of Education and Skills

- DES (2010) *Incidental Inspection Findings 2010: A Report on the Teaching and Learning of English and Mathematics in Primary Schools*. Dublin: Department of Education and Skills – Evaluation Support and Research Unit

- DES (2011a) *Literacy and numeracy for learning and life: The National Strategy to Improve Literacy and Numeracy among Children and Young People 2011-20*. Dublin: Department of Education and Skills

- DES (2011b) *Child Protection Procedures for Primary and Post-Primary Schools*. https://www.education.ie/en/Circulars-and-Forms/Active-Circulars/cl0065_2011.pdf

- DES (2012a) *OECD Review on Evaluation and Assessment Framework for Improving School Outcomes: Country Background Report for Ireland, March 2012*. Dublin: Department of Education and Skills

- DES (2012b) *Report of the International Review Panel on the Structure of Initial Teacher Education Provision in Ireland*. Dublin: HEA

- DES (2012c) *A Framework for the Junior Cycle* Dublin: Department of Education and Skills.

- DES (2013a) *Chief Inspector's Report 2010-2012: Promoting the Quality of Learning*. Dublin: Department of Education and Skills

DES (2013b) 'Anti-bullying Procedures for Primary and Post-Primary Schools' https://www.education.ie/en/Publications/Policy-Reports/Anti-Bullying-Procedures-for-Primary-and-Post-Primary-Schools.pdf

DES (2014a) *Inspectorate's Strategic Plan 2014-16*. Dublin: Department of Education and Skills

DES (2014b) *Projections of Demand for Full Time Third Level Education 2014-2018*. Dublin: Department of Education and Skills

DES (2014c) 'Review of Apprenticeship Training in Ireland' http://www.education.ie/en/Publications/Policy-Reports/Review-of-Apprenticeship-Training-in-Ireland.pdf

DES (2015a) *Statement of Strategy 2015 – 2017*, https://www.education.ie/en/Publications/Corporate-Reports/Strategy-Statement/Department-of-Education-and-Skills-Statement-of-Strategy-2015-2017.pdf

DES (2015b) *Framework for Junior Cycle 2015*. Dublin: Department of Education and Science https://www.education.ie/en/Publications/.../Framework-for-Junior-Cycle-2015.pdf

DES (2015c) *Code of Practice for the Inspectorate*. Dublin: Department of Education and Skills. https://www.education.ie/en/Publications/Inspection-Reports-Publications/Evaluation-Reports-Guidelines/Professional-Code-of-Practice-on-Evaluation-and-Reporting-for-the-Inspectorate.pdf

DES (no date) *The Induction and Initial Professional Development of School Inspectors*. Dublin: Department of Education and Skills

DES (2016a) 'Arrangements for the Implementation of the Framework for Junior Cycle with Particular Reference to School Years 2015/16 and 2016/17' *Circular Letter 0024/2016* https://www.education.ie/en/Circulars-and-Forms/Active-Circulars/cl0024_2016.pdf

DES (2016b) *Education (Admissions to Schools) Bill 2016*

DES (2016c) *A Guide to Early-Years Education-focused Inspection (EYEI)*. Dublin: Department of Education and Skills

DES (2016d) *Learning Strategy for the Inspectorate*. Dublin: Department of Education and Skills

DES (2016e) 'FAQs on the Lansdowne Road Agreement/Post-Primary Teachers, 12 August 2016' http://www.education.ie/en/Education-Staff/Information/Public-Service-Stability-Agreement-Haddington-Road/FAQs-on-the-Lansdowne-Road-Agreement-Post-Primary-Teachers.pdf

DES (2016f) *Review of National and International Reports on Literacy and Numeracy*. Dublin: Department of Education and Skills

DES (2016g) *A Guide to Inspection in Primary Schools. Dublin: Department of Education and Skills* https://www.education.ie/en/Publications/Inspection-Reports-Publications/Evaluation-Reports-Guidelines/A-Guide-to-Inspection-in-Primary-Schools.pdf

DES (2016h) *A Guide to Inspection in Post-Primary Schools*. Dublin: Department of Education and Skills https://www.education.ie/en/Publications/Inspection-Reports-Publications/Evaluation-Reports-Guidelines/A-Guide-to-Inspection-in-Post-Primary-Schools.pdf

DES (2016j) *Action Plan for Education 2016-19: Department of Education and Skills Strategy Statement*. Dublin: Department of Education and Skills

DES Statistics Section (2016) *Education at a Glance 2016: OECD Indicators: A Country Profile for Ireland*. Dublin: Department of Education and Skills

DES (2017a) http://www.education.ie/en/Press-Events/Press-Releases/2017-Press-Releases/PR2017-01-18.html

DES (2017b) http://www.education.ie/en/Press-Events/Speeches/2017-Speeches/SP2017-16-01.html

Dept. of Education and Skills, State Examinations Commission, Irish Universities Association, Institutes of Technology Ireland, Higher Education Authority, Quality and Qualifications Ireland, National Council for Curriculum and Assessment (2013) *Supporting a Better Transition from Second Level to Higher Education: Key Directions and Next Steps*. Dublin: March 2013

Dept. of Education and Skills, State Examinations Commission, Irish Universities Association, Institutes of Technology Ireland, Higher Education Authority, Quality and Qualifications Ireland, National Council for Curriculum and Assessment (2015) *Supporting a Better Transition from Second Level to Higher Education: Implementation and Next Steps*. Dublin: April 2015

Department of Finance (2010, 2011, 2012) 'Summary of Budget Measures Policy Changes' http://www.budget.gov.ie/Budgets/2017/2017.aspx

Department of Finance (2013, 2014, 2015) 'Budget Leaflet' http://www.budget.gov.ie/Budgets/2017/2017.aspx

Devine, D. (2011) 'Securing Migrant Children's Educational Wellbeing: Perspectives on Policy and Practice in Irish Schools', in Darmody, M., Tyrrell, N., Song, S. (eds.) *The Changing Faces of Ireland: Exploring the Lives of Immigrant and Ethnic Minority Children*. Rotterdam/Boston/Taipei: Sense Publishers

Devine, D., Kenny, M., McNeela, E. (2002) *Ethnicity and Schooling: a Study of Ethnic Diversity in Selected Irish Primary and Post-Primary Schools*. Dublin: Report presented to the Department of Education and Science

Dewey, J. (1938/1995) *Experience and Education*. New York: Macmillan

Doris, A., O'Neill, D., Sweetman, O. (2013) 'Gender, Single-sex Schooling and Maths Achievement' *Economics of Education Review*, Vol. 35, August 2013

Drudy, S. & Kinsella, W. (2009) 'Developing an Inclusive System in a Rapidly Changing European Society' *International Journal of Inclusive Education*, Vol. 13, Issue 6

Drudy, P. & Punch, M. (2005) *Out of Reach: Inequalities in the Irish Housing System*. Dublin: Tasc at New Island

Duignan, P. (2011) *Educational Leadership: Together creating ethically inspired learning environments*. Cambridge: Cambridge University Press

DuFour, R. & Marzano, R. J. (2011) *Leaders of Learning: How District, School and Classroom Leaders Improve Student Achievement*. Bloomington IN: Solution Tree Press

Dunne, J. (2005) 'What's the Good of Education?', in Carr, W., ed. *The Routledge Falmer Reader in Philosophy of Education*. Abingdon & New York: Routledge

Dyson, A. & Gallannaugh, F. (2008) 'Disproportionality in Special Needs Education in England' *The Journal of Special Education*, Vol. 42, Issue 1

Educational Disadvantage Committee (2005) *Moving Beyond Educational Disadvantage: Report of the Educational Disadvantage Committee*. Dublin: Educational Disadvantage Committee

Eivers, E. & Clerkin, A, (2012) 'PIRLS and TIMSS: Reading, Mathematics and Science Outcomes for Ireland'. Dublin: Educational Research Centre. www.erc.ie/2012/12/31/publications-2012/

ESRI (Economic and Social Research Institute) (2016) *Review of the Droichead Teacher Induction Pilot Programme.* Dublin: The Economic and Social Research Institute

European Agency for Development in Special Needs Education (2012) *Profile of Inclusive Teachers.* Odense, Denmark: European Agency for Development in Special Needs Education

European Commission (2013) *Key Data on Teachers and School Leaders in Europe: Eurydice Report 2013 edition* http://eacea.ec.europa.eu/education/eurydice/documents/key_data_series/151EN.pdf

Faas, D., Darmody, M., Sokolowska ,B. (2016) 'Religious Diversity in Primary Schools: Reflections from the Republic of Ireland' *British Journal of Religious Education,*Vol. 38, Issue1

Fullan, M. (2003) *The Moral Imperative of School Leadership.* Thousand Oaks CA: Corwin Press and Ontario Principals' Council

Furlong, J. (2013) *Education – An Anatomy of the Discipline.* London: Routledge

Geoghegan, P. (2014) 'Professor Patrick Geoghegan defends admissions experiment' *The Irish Times,* 17th October 2014.

Geoghegan, P. (2016) 'In Identifying Ways to Determine Potential in the Leaving Cert, Debate and Scrutiny are Welcome' *University Times* (Trinity College Dublin), 27th January, 2016

Gleeson, J. (2010) *Curriculum in Context: Partnership, Power and Praxis in Ireland.* New York: Peter Lang

GLEN (2016) *Being LGBT in School: A Resource for Post-Primary Schools to Prevent Homophobic and Transphobic Bullying and Support LGBT Students.* Dublin: GLEN Gay and Lesbian Equality Network

Gorard, S., Rees, G., Salisbury, J. (1999) 'Reappraising the Apparent Underachievement of Boys at School' *Gender and Education,*Vol. 11, Issue 4

Government of Ireland (1992) *Education for a Changing World: Green Paper on Education.* Dublin: The Stationery Office

Government of Ireland (1995) *Charting our Education Future: White Paper on Education.* Dublin: The Stationery Office

Government of Ireland (1998) *Education Act 1998*

Governmeent of Ireland (1999) *Ready to Learn: White Paper on Early Childhood Education.* Dublin: The Stationery Office

Government of Ireland (2000) *Equal Status Act 2000*

Government of Ireland (2004) *Education for Persons with Special Educational Needs* (EPSEN) Act 2004

Government of Ireland (2010) *The Civil Partnership and Certain Rights and Obligations of Cohabitants Act 2010*

Government of Ireland (2012) *Education Amendment Act 2012*

Government of Ireland (2015) *Gender Recognition Act 2015*

Government of Ireland (2015) *Equality (Miscellaneous Provisions) Act 2015*

Government of Ireland (2015) *Gender Recognition Act 2015*

Griffin, S. & Shevlin, M. (2007) *Responding to Special Educational Needs: An Irish Perspective.* Dublin: Gill and Macmillan

Guskey, T.R. (2000) *Evaluating Professional Development.* Thousand Oaks CA: Corwin Press

Hammond, J., Halbert, J., O'Shea, M. (2011) 'Three Steps to a Better Way' *Le Chéile,* Issue No. 5 Dublin: National Association of Principals and Deputy Principals

Hannan, D., Smyth, E., McCullagh, J., O'Leary, R., McMahon, D. (1996) *Coeducation and Gender Equality: Exam Performance, Stress and Personal Development.* Dublin: Oak Tree Press in association with The Economic and Social Research Institute

Hannan, D., Breen, R., Murray, B., Hardiman, N., Watson D. (1983) *Schooling and Sex Roles: Sex Differences in Subject Provision and Subject Choice in Irish Post-primary Schools.* Dublin: Economic and Social Research Institute

Hargreaves, A. (1989) *Curriculum and Assessment Reform.* Toronto: Ontario Institute for Studies in Education

Hargreaves, A. & Fink, D. (2006) *Sustainable Leadership.* San Francisco: Jossey-Bass

Harmon, H., Pohjolainen, L., Curran, S., Mallon, M. (2015) *Irish Traveller and Roma Children Shadow Report: A Response to Ireland's Consolidated Third and Fourth Report to the UN Committee on the Rights of the Child.* Dublin: Pavee Point and Roma Centre

Harris, A. & Jones, M.S. (2016) *Leading Futures: Global Perspectives on Educational Leadership.* Thousand Oaks CA: Sage

Heywood, J., McGuinness, S., Murphy, D (1980) *Final Report of the Public Examinations Evaluation Project.* Dublin: School of Education, University of Dublin

Heywood, J. (2012) 'So Near Yet So Far: A Comparison of the 2011 Proposals of the National Council for Curriculum and Assessment (NCCA) for the Reform of the Junior Certificate Examination with the 1975 Proposals of the Committee on the Form s and Function of the Intermediate Certificate Examination (ICE)' *European Studies in Educational Management ,*Vol 1, Issue 2

HGSCE (2015) (Harvard Graduate School of Education) *Turning the Tide: Inspiring Concern for Others and the Common Good Through College Admissions; The Making Caring Common Project.* Cambridge MA: Harvard Graduate School of Education

Higgins, A., Doyle, L., Downes, C., Murphy, R., Sharek, D., DeVries, J., Begley, T., McCann, E., Sheerin, F., Smyth, S. (2016) *The LGBT Ireland Report: National Study of the Mental Health and Wellbeing of Lesbian, Gay, Bisexual, Transgender and Intersex People in Ireland.* Dublin: GLEN and BelongTo

HEA (Higher Education Authority) (2011) *National Strategy for Higher Education to 2030.* Dublin: Higher Education Authority

HEA (2014) *A Study of Progression in Irish Higher Education Institutions,* Dublin: HEA

HEA (2016) 'Information on HEAR and DARE schemes' http://www.accesscollege.ie

Higher Education Authority and National Council for Curriculum and Assessment (2011) *From Transaction to Transition: Outcomes of the conference on the transition from second to third-level education in Ireland.* Dublin: Higher Education Authority

Hislop, H. (2016) 'Ensuring and Assuring Quality in Education,' Dublin: Department of Education and Skills

Hogan, C. (2011) 'Accommodating Islam in the Denominational Irish Education System: Religious Freedom and Education in the Republic of Ireland' *Journal of Muslim Minority Affairs,*Vol. 31, Issue 4

Hogan, P. (2003) 'Teaching and Learning as a Way of Life' *Journal of Philosophy of Education,*Vol. 37, Issue 2

Hogan, P., Brosnan, A., deRóiste, B., MacAlister, A., Malone, A., Quirke-Bolt, N., Smith, G. (2008) *Learning Anew: Final Report of the Research and Development Project 'Teaching and Learning for the 21st Century' 2003-07.* Maynooth: Education Department, National University of Ireland Maynooth

- Hogan, P. (2010) *The New Significance of Learning : Imagination's Heartwork*. London & New York: Routledge
- Hopkins, D. (2008) *Every School a Great School: Realizing the potential of system leadership*. Maidenhead & New York: Open University Press
- Hord, S. & Sommers, W.A. (2007) *Leading Professional Learning Communities: Voices From Research and Practice*. Thousand Oaks CA: Corwin Press and National Association of Secondary School Principals
- Hyland, Á. (1998) *Innovations in Assessment in Irish Education*. Cork: Education Department, University College Cork
- Hyland, Á. (1999) 'The Curriculum of Vocational Education 1930-1966' in Logan, J. *Teachers' Union: The TUI and its Forerunners in Irish Education 1899-1994*. Dublin: Teachers' Union of Ireland
- Hyland, Á. (2000) *Multiple Intelligences, Curriculum and Assessment: Final Report of the Project*. Cork: University College Cork
- Hyland, Á. et al. (2005) *Final Report on the Bridging the Gap Project*. Cork: University College Cork
- Hyland, Á., Kennedy, D. & Ryan, N. (2007) 'Writing and Using Learning Outcomes in Your Institution' in *Implementing Bologna in Your Institution*. Brussels: European Universities Association
- Hyland, Á. & McCarthy, M. (2009) 'Multiple intelligences in Ireland', in Che, J-Q., Moran, S, Gardner, H. (eds.) *Multiple Intelligences Around the World*. San Francisco: Jossey-Bass
- Hyland, Á. (2011) *Entry to Higher Education in Ireland in the 21st Century: Discussion Paper for the NCCA/HEA Seminar 21st Sep. 2011*. Dublin: HEA and NCCA
- Hyland, Á. (2012) *A Review of the Structure of Initial Teacher Education Provision in Ireland*. Dublin: Higher Education Authority
- Hyland, Á. (2013) *Entry Requirements and Matriculation for Admission into Higher Education*, paper delivered at conference organised by DES, SEC, IUA, IoTI, HEA, QQI, and NCCA, NUI Maynooth June 2013
- Hyland, Á. (2014a) *The Design of Leaving Certificate science syllabi in Ireland: an international comparison*. Dublin: Irish Science Teachers' Association. http://www.ista.ie/news/hyland-report-0
- Hyland, Á. (2014b) '100 Years of Junior Cycle Curriculum 1914-2014' *Le Chéile* Issue No. 8, Dublin: National Association of Principals and Deputy Principals
- INTO (Irish National Teachers' Organisation) (1997) *Teaching & Learning: Issues in Assessment*. Dublin: Irish National Teachers' Organisation
- INTO (2001) *Literacy in the Primary School*. Dublin: Irish National Teachers' Organisation
- INTO (2005) *The Primary School Curriculum: INTO Survey 2005 & Proceedings of the Consultative Conference on Education*. Dublin: Irish National Teachers' Organisation
- INTO (2008) *Assessment in the Primary School: Discussion Document and Proceedings of the Consultative Conference on Education*. Dublin: Irish National Teachers' Organisation
- INTO (2011) *Literacy in a Changing World: Discussion Document and Proceedings of the Consultative Conference on Education*. Dublin: Irish National Teachers' Organisation
- INTO (2013) *Numeracy in the Primary School: A Discussion Paper INTO Education Conference*. Dublin: Irish National Teachers' Organisation
- IPPN (Irish Primary Principals' Network) (2016). *Leadership+* Vol. 7, June Issue, 2016
- IUA (Irish Universities' Association) (2012), *Reform of Selection and Entry to University in the Context of National Educational Policy: Communication from the IUA Council to Minister for Education and Skills, Ruairi Quinn*. Dublin: Irish Universities Association
- IUA (2014) *Progress Report of the Task Force on Reform of University Selection and Entry (TGRUSE)*. Dublin: Irish Universities Association
- Irish Universities' Association and Institutes of Technology Ireland (2015) *New Leaving Certificate Grading Scale and Revised Common Points Scale*. Dublin: Irish Universities Association and Institutes of Technology Ireland
- Jeffers, G. (2007) *Attitudes to Transition Year*. Maynooth: Education Department
- Kavanagh, L, Shiel, G, Gilleece, L, Kinity, J (2015). *The 2014 National Assessments of English Reading and Mathematics, Vol. 11: Context Report*. Dublin: Educational Research Centre
- Kellaghan, T. & Millar, D. (2003) *Grading in the Leaving Certificate Examination: A Discussion Paper*. Dublin: Educational Research Centre
- Kennedy, D. (2006) *Writing and Using Learning Outcomes: A Practical Guide*. Cork: Education Department, University College Cork
- Klenowski, V. (2016) 'Restoring Teacher Judgement: the key to quality assessment.' Address to the Maynooth Education Forum: 'Dismantling "The Murder Machine"? – Interrogating Cultures of Assessment'. National University of Ireland Maynooth, June 2016
- Lawlor, A. (2014) 'Transitions Toward Transformation: Exploring Continuing Professional Development for Teachers in Ireland' Unpublished PhD Thesis, Education Department, National University of Ireland Maynooth
- Lave, J. & Wenger, E. (1991) *Situated Learning: Legitimate Peripheral Participation*. Cambridge: Cambridge University Press.
- Levels, M., Dronkers, J., Kraaykamp, G. (2008) 'Immigrant Children's Educational Achievement in Western Countries: Origin, Destination, and Community Effects on Mathematical Performance' *American Sociological Review*, Vol. 73, Issue 5
- Lieberman, A. & Miller, L. (2004) *Teacher Leadership*, San Francisco: Jossey-Bass
- Lieberman, A. & Rosenholtz, S. (1987) 'The road to school improvement: Barriers and Bridges', in Goodlad, J.I. (ed.) *The Ecology of School Renewal*. Chicago: University of Chicago Press
- Looney, A. (2014) 'Curriculum politics and practice: from implementation to agency' *Irish Teachers' Journal*, Vol. 2, Issue 1
- Lynch, K. & Lodge, A. (2002) *Equality and power in schools: redistribution, recognition and representation*. London and New York: RoutledgeFalmer
- Lynch, K. & Moran A. (2006) 'Markets, Schools and the Convertibility of Economic Capital: the Complex Dynamics of Class Choice' *British Journal of Sociology of Education*, Vol. 27, Issue 2
- Lysaght, Z. & O'Leary, M. (2013) 'An instrument to audit teachers' use of assessment for learning' *Irish Educational Studies*, Vol. 32, Issue 2
- Mac Aogáin, E. (2005) 'The Points System and Grading of the Leaving Certificate Examination' *Irish Journal of Education*, Vol. 36. Dublin: Educational Research Centre
- MacBeath, J. (1999) *Schools Must Speak for Themselves*. London: Routledge
- MacBeath, J. (2012) *Learning in and Out of School*. London & New York: Routledge

- Madaus, G. & Macnamara, J. (1970) *Public Examinations: A Study of the Irish Leaving Certificate.* Dublin: Educational Research Centre
- Madaus, G., Airasian, P., Kellaghan, T (1980) *School Effectiveness: A Reassessment of The Evidence.* New York: McGraw-Hill Book Company
- Madaus, G. & Greaney, V. (1985) 'The Irish Experience in Competency Testing: Implications for American Education' *American Journal of Education,* Vol. 93, Issue 2
- Mawhinney, A. (2015) 'International Human Rights Law: Its Potential and Limitations in Effecting Change to the Place of Religion in the Irish Education System', *Journal of Intercultural Studies,* Vol. 36, no. 3
- McCoy, S. & Banks, J. (2012) 'Simply Academic? Why Children with Special Educational Needs Don't Like School' *European Journal of Special Needs Education,* Vol., 27, Issue 1
- McCoy, S., Quail, A., Smyth, E. (2012) *Growing up in Ireland: National Longitudinal Study of Children, Report 3: Influences on 9-Year-Olds' Learning: Home, School and Community.* Dublin: Government Publications
- McCoy, S., Smyth, E., Watson, D., Darmody, M. (2014) *Leaving School in Ireland: A Longitudinal Study of Post-School Transitions.* Dublin: ESRI, Research Series, No. 36
- Moon, J. (undated) 'Linking Levels, Learning Outcomes and Assessment Criteria' (Exeter University) http://www.ehea.info/uploads/seminars/040701-02linking_levels_plus_ass_crit-moon.pdf
- Murphy, D.E. (1974) 'Problems associated with the implementation of a new national system of educational assessment in Ireland'. Unpublished M.Ed. Dissertation, University of Dublin
- Murray, N. (2007) 'Leaving Cert reform to introduce project work' in *Irish Examiner,* 19th November 2007 http://www.irishexaminer.com/ireland/education/leaving-cert-reform-to-introduce-project-work-48281.html
- NCCA (National Council for Curriculum and Assessment) (1993) *A Programme for Reform: Curriculum and Assessment Policy Towards the New Century.* Dublin: The National Council for Curriculum and Assessment
- NCCA (1999) *The Junior Cycle Review: Progress Report: Issues and Options for Development.* Dublin: The National Council for Curriculum and Assessment
- NCCA (2003a) *Towards a Framework for Early Learning.* Dublin: The National Council for Curriculum and Assessment
- NCCA (2003b) *Developing Senior Cycle: Issues and Options.* Dublin: The National Council for Curriculum and Assessment
- NCCA (2004) *Proposals for the Future of Senior Cycle Education in Ireland: Overview.* Dublin: The National Council for Curriculum and Assessment
- NCCA (2005) *Primary Curriculum Review.* Dublin: The National Council for Curriculum and Assessment
- NCCA (2007) *Assessment in the Primary School Curriculum: Guidelines for Schools.* Dublin: The National Council for Curriculum and Assessment
- NCCA (2009) *Leading and Supporting Change in Schools – Discussion Paper.* Dublin: The National Council for Curriculum and Assessment
- NCCA (2010) *Innovation and Identity: Ideas for a new junior cycle,* Dublin: The National Council for Curriculum and Assessment
- NCCA (2011) *Towards a Framework for Junior Cycle: Innovation and Identity,* Dublin: The National Council for Curriculum and Assessment
- National Council for Curriculum and Assessment, Supporting a Better Transition from Second to Higher Education; Directions for Change Conference in National University of Ireland Maynooth, 24th June 2013
- NCCA (2015a) *Aistear Síolta Practical Guide.* Dublin: The National Council for Curriculum and Assessment
- NCCA (2015b) *Focus on Learning: Ongoing Assessment Booklets.* Dublin: The National Council for Curriculum and Assessment
- NCCA (2016) *Proposals for structure and time allocation in a redeveloped primary curriculum: For consultation.* Dublin: The National Council for Curriculum and Assessment
- NCSE(National Council for Special Education) (2015) Annual Report 2014, http://ncse.ie/wp-content/uploads/2015/06/NCSE-Annual-Report-2014.FINALWEBVERSION15.04.15.pdf
- NCSE Working Group on a Proposed New Model for Allocating Teaching Resources for Students with Special Educational Needs (2014) *Delivery for Students with Special Educational Needs: A better and more equitable way.* Trim: NCSE
- NESF (National Economic and Social Forum) (2005) *Early Childhood Care and Education.* Dublin: The National Economic and Social Forum
- National Programme Conference (1922) *National Programme of Primary Instruction,* Dublin: The Educational Company of Ireland
- National Programme Conference (1926) *Report and Programme Presented by the National Programme Conference to the Minister for Education,* Dublin: Stationery Office
- Nussbaum, M.C. & Sen, A. (1993) (eds.) *The Quality of Life.* Oxford: Clarendon Press
- Oakeshott, M. (1981) 'The Voice of Poetry in the Conversation of Mankind', in *Rationalism in Politics and Other Essays.* London: Methuen & Company
- O'Connor, M. (2007) *Sé Sí - Gender in Irish Education.* http://www.education.ie/en/Publications/Statistics/Se-Si-Gender-in-Irish-Education-Introduction-to-Chapter-9.pdf
- O'Gorman, E. & Drudy, S. (2011) *Professional Development for Teachers Working in the Area of Special Education/Inclusion in Mainstream Schools.* http://ncse.ie/wp-content/uploads/2014/10/Professional_Development_of_Teachers.pdf
- Ó Foghlú, S. (2016) Speech by Seán Ó Foghlú, Secretary General, Department of Education and Skills at the 2016 Catholic Primary School Managers Association AGM http://www.education.ie/en/Press-Events/Speeches/2016-Speeches/SP2016-02-26.html
- O'Gorman, E., Drudy, S., Winter, E., Smith R., Barry, M. (2009) *Professional Development for Post-Primary Special Educational Needs (SEN) Teachers in Northern Ireland and the Republic of Ireland.* Armagh: Centre for Cross-Border Studies
- O'Toole, B. (2015) '1831–2014: An Opportunity to Get it Right this Time? Some Thoughts on the Current Debate on Patronage and Religious Education in Irish Primary Schools' *Irish Educational Studies,* Vol. 34, Issue 1
- OECD (Organisation for Economic Co-operation and Development) (2001) *Reviews of National Policies for Education: Ireland.* Paris: OECD
- OECD (2004a) *Thematic Review of Early Childhood Education and Core Policy in Ireland.* Paris: OECD Publishing

- OECD (2004b) *Learning for Tomorrow's World: First Results from PISA 2003*. Paris: OECD Publishing
- OECD (2008) *Improving School Leadership Volume 2: Case Studies on System Leadership*. (eds.) Pont, B., Nusche, D., Hopkins, D. Paris: OECD Publishing
- OECD (2009) *Creating effective teaching and learning environments: First results from TALIS*. Paris: OECD Publishing. https://www.oecd.org/edu/school/43023606.pdf
- OECD (2010) *Education at a Glance 2010: OECD Indicators*. Paris: OECD Publishing
- OECD (2015) *Education at a Glance 2015: OECD Indicators*. Paris: OECD Publishing. http://dx.doi.org/10.1787/eag-2015-en
- OECD (2016a) *Education at a Glance 2016: OECD Indicators*. Paris: OECD Publishing http://dx.doi.org/10.187/eag-2016-en
- OECD (2016b) 'Ireland', in *Education at a Glance: OECD Indicators*. Paris: OECD Publishing DOI: http://dx.doi.org/10.1787/eag-2016-62 en
- OFSTED (Office for Standards in Education, England & Wales) (2003) 'Boys' Achievement in Secondary Schools', OFSTED Publication Centre, HMI 1659
- Palmer, N., Bexley, E., James, R. (2011) *Selection and Participation in Higher Education: University Selection in Support of Student Success and Diversity of Participation - Report prepared for Group of Eight*. University of Melbourne: Centre for the Study of Higher Education
- Parker-Jenkins, M. & Masterson, M. (2013) 'No longer "Catholic, White and Gaelic": Schools in Ireland Coming to Terms with Cultural Diversity' *Irish Educational Studies*, Vo. 32, Issue 4
- Pascal, C. & Bertram, T. (2013) 'The Impact of Early Education as a Strategy in Countering Socio-Economic Disadvantage', Centre for Research in Early Childhood (CREC) www.ofsted.gov.uk/accessandachievement
- Pavee Point (2015) 'Irish Traveller and Roma Children: An Update to Pavee Point Traveller and Roma Centre's Shadow Report in Response to Ireland's Consolidated Third and Fourth Report to the UN Committee on the Rights of the Child', http://www.paveepoint.ie/wp-content/uploads/2015/04/Update_-Shadow-Report-on-Traveller-and-Roma-Children-UNCRC-Latest.pdf
- Piketty, T. (2014) *Capital in the Twenty-First Century*. Cambridge, MA: The Belknap Press of Harvard University Press
- Randles, E. (1975) *Post-Primary Education in Ireland 1957-1970*. Dublin: Veritas Publications
- Rose, R., Shevlin, M., Winter, E., O'Raw, P. (2015) *Project IRIS – Inclusive Research in Irish Schools*. Trim: National Council for Special Education, Research Report, No. 20
- Rougier, N. & Honohan, I. (2015) 'Religion and Education in Ireland: Growing Diversity – or Losing Faith in the System?' *Comparative Education*, Vol. 51, Issue 1
- RTÉ News website (26th May 2016) 'Survey finds patchy broadband in rural areas' http://www.rte.ie/news/2016/0525/790991-survey-finds-patchy-broadband-in-rural-areas/
- Rutter, M., Maugham, B., Ouston, J., Mortimore, P. (1980) *Fifteen Thousand Hours: Secondary Schools and Their Effects on Children*. London: Open Books
- Sahlberg, P. (2011) *Finnish Lessons: What can the world learn from educational change in Finland?* New York: Teachers College Press
- Scottish Government/Rialghtas na h-Alba (2001) 'A Teaching Profession for the 21st Century –Agreement reached following recommendations made in the McCrone Report' www.gov.scot/Resource/Doc/158413/0042924.pdf
- Scottish Government/Rialghtas na h-Alba (2016) 'Scotland's International GDP Per Capita Ranking' www.gov.scot/Resource/0049/00495208.pdf
- Sergiovanni, T. J. (1996) *Moral Leadership: Getting to the Heart of School Improvement*. San Francisco: Jossey-Bass
- Sheehan, J. (1992) *Education, Training and the Culliton Report*. Dublin: School of Economics, University College Dublin
- Shiel, G., Kellaghan, T., Moran, G. (2010) *Standardised Testing in Lower Secondary Education*. Dublin: Educational Research Centre
- Shiel, G., Kavanagh, L., Millar, D. (2014) *The 2014 National Assessments of English Reading and Mathematics* Volume 1: Performance Report, Dublin: Education Research Centre
- Shiel, G., Kelleher, C., McKeown, C., Denner, S. (2016) *Future Ready: The Performance of 15-year-olds in Ireland on Science, Reading Literacy and Mathematics*. Dublin: Educational Research Centre.
- Smith, G. (2012) 'The Western Seaboard Science Project: An Innovative Model of Professional Development to Enhance the Teaching and Learning of Primary Science'. Unpublished PhD thesis, National University of Ireland Maynooth
- Smyth, E. (1999) *Do Schools Differ?* Dublin: Oaktree Press
- Smyth, E., McCoy, S., Darmody, M. (2004) *Moving Up: The Experiences of First Year Students in Post-Primary Schools*. Dublin: The Liffey Press in association with the Economic and Social Research Institute
- Smyth, E., Byrne, D., Hannan, C. (2004) *The Transition Year Programme: an assessment*. Dublin: The Liffey Press in association with The Economic and Social Research Institute
- Smyth, E., Dunne, A., McCoy, S., Darmody, M. (2006) *Pathways Through the Junior Cycle: The Experiences of Second Year Students*. Dublin: The Liffey Press in association with The Economic and Social Research Institute
- Smyth, E. & Hannan, C. (2007) 'School Processes and the Transition to Higher Education' *Oxford Review of Education*, Vol. 33, Issue 2
- Smyth, E. & Steinmetz, S. (2015), 'Vocational Training and Gender Segregation Across Europe', in Imdorf, C., Hegna, K., Reisel, I (eds.) *Gender Segregation in Vocational Education* (Comparative Social Research, Volume 31) Emerald Group Publishing
- Smyth, E., Dunne, A., McCoy, S., Darmody, M. (2007) *Gearing Up for the Exam: The Experience of Junior Certificate Students*, Dublin: The Liffey Press in association with The Economic and Social Research Institute
- Smyth, E. and S. McCoy (2009) *Investing in Education: Combating Educational Disadvantage*. Dublin: The Economic and Social Research Institute, Research Series, No. 6
- Smyth, E., Darmody, M., McGinnity, F., Byrne, D. (2009) *Adapting to Diversity: Irish Schools and Newcomer Students*. Dublin: The Economic and Social Research Institute, Research Series, No. 8
- Smyth, E. (2015) 'What Does the Research Tell Us about Single-Sex Education?', in de Waal, A. (ed.) *The Ins and Outs of Selective Secondary Schools*, London: Civitas
- Smyth, E. & Darmody, M. (2011) 'Religious Diversity and Schooling in Ireland', in Darmody, M., Tyrrell, N., Song, S. (eds.) *The Changing Faces of Ireland: Exploring the Lives of Immigrant and Ethnic Minority Children*, Rotterdam/Boston/Taipei: Sense Publishers

■ Smyth, E. (ed.) (2011) *Transitions Into and Out of Higher Education*. Special Issue of *Irish Educational Studies*, Vol. 30, Issue 2

■ Smyth, E. & Calvert, E. (2011) *Choices and Challenges: Moving from Junior Cycle to Senior Cycle Education*. Dublin: The Liffey Press in association with the Economic and Social Research Institute

■ Smyth, E., McCoy, S., Kingston, G. (2015) *Learning from the Evaluation of DEIS*. Dublin: The Economic and Social Research Institute, Research Series, No. 39

■ Smyth, E., Iannelli, C., Klein, M. (2016) 'Higher Education Selection: implications for social inequality' *ESRI Research Bulletin*, January 2016

■ Social Justice Ireland (2012) 'Budget 2012: Analysis and critique' http://www.socialjustice.ie/sites/default/files/file/Budget/2012/2011-12-07 per cent20- per cent20Budget per cent202012 per cent20Analysis per cent20and per cent20Critique.pdf

■ Solas (2014): Further Education and Training Strategy 2014 – 2019. http://www.solas.ie/SolasPdfLibrary/FETStrategy2014-2019.pdf

■ Special Education Review Committee (1993) *Report of the Special Education Review Committee*. Dublin: The Stationery Office

■ Spillane, J. P. (2015) 'Leadership and learning: Conceptualizing relations between school administrative practice and instructional practice' in *Societies*, Vol. 5, No. 2

■ Squires, G. Kalambouka, A. Bragg, J. (2016) *A Study of the Experiences of Post Primary Students with Special Educational Needs*. Trim: NCSE

■ Starratt, R. J. (2011) *Refocusing School Leadership: Foregrounding Human Development Throughout the Work of the School*. New York and Abingdon: Routledge

■ State Examinations Commission (2016) 'Reasonable Accommodations' https://www.examinations.ie/?l=en&mc=ca&sc=ra

■ Sullivan, A., Joshi, H., Leonard , D. (2011) 'Single-sex Schooling and Labour Market Outcomes' *Oxford Review of Education*, Vol. 37, Issue 3

■ Sullivan, B., Glenn, M., Roche, M., McDonagh, C. (2016) *Introduction to Critical Action Research for Teachers*. London & New York: Routledge

■ Task Force on Autism (2001) *Educational Provision and Support for Persons with Autistic Spectrum Disorders: the Report of the Task Force on Autism*. http://www.sess.ie/sites/default/files/Autism%20Task%20Force%20Report.pdf

■ Task Force on Dyslexia (2001) *Report of the Task Force on Dyslexia*. http://www.sess.ie/sites/default/files/Dyslexia_Task_Force_Report_0.pdf

■ Teachers' Union of Ireland, Association of Secondary Teachers in Ireland, Department of Education and Skills (2015) *Junior Cycle Reform: Joint Statement on Principles and Implementation*. https://www.education.ie/en/Publications/Education-Reports/Junior-Cycle-Reform-Joint-Statement-on-Principles

■ The Teaching Council /An Comhairle Mhúinteoireachta (2007) *Codes of Professional Conduct for Teachers*. Maynooth: The Teaching Council

■ The Teaching Council /An Comhairle Mhúinteoireachta (2011a) *Policy on the Continuum of Teacher Education*. Maynooth: The Teaching Council

■ The Teaching Council / An Comhairle Mhúinteoireachta (2011b) *Initial Teacher Education: Criteria and Guidelines for Programme Providers*. Maynooth: The Teaching Council

■ The Teaching Council /An Comhairle Mhúinteoireachta (2012) *Code of Professional Conduct for Teachers*. Maynooth: The Teaching Council

■ The Teaching Council /An Comhairle Mhúinteoireachta (2013) *Droichead: Policy on a New Model of Induction and Probation*. Maynooth: The Teaching Council

■ The Teaching Council / An Comhairle Mhúinteoireachta (2016) *Cosán: Framework for Teachers' Learning*. Maynooth: Teaching Council / An Comhairle Mhúinteoireachta http://www.teachingcouncil.ie/en/Teacher-Education/Continuing-Professional-Development/

■ Technical Working Group (2015) *Striking the Balance: Teacher Supply in Ireland*. Dublin: Dept. of Education and Skills

■ Trant, A. (2008) *Curriculum Matters in Ireland*, Dublin: Blackhall Publishing.

■ Tyrrell, N., M. Darmody and S. Song (2011) 'Introduction', in Darmody, M., N. Tyrrell and S. Song (eds.) *The Changing Faces of Ireland: Exploring the Lives of Immigrant and Ethnic Minority Children*, Rotterdam/Boston/Taipei: Sense Publishers

■ UNESCO (1996) 'Links between Early Childhood Development and Education and Primary Education – Monograph No.6' Paris: UNESCO http://unesdoc.unesco.org/images/0010/001055/105505E.pdf

■ UNESCO (2016) 'The Right to Education' Paris: UNESCO http://www.unesco.org/new/en/education/themes/leading-the-international-agenda/right-to-education/

■ UNICEF (2016) 'Fairness for Children: A League Table of Inequality in Child Well-being in Rich Countries', *Innocenti Report Card 13*, Florence: UNICEF Office of Research – Innocenti

■ University of California (2016) *'Comprehensive Review' Selection Criteria (2016)* – on http://admission.universityofcalifornia.edu/counselors/freshman/comprehensive-review/

■ Van Driel, B., Darmody, M., Kerzil, J. (2016) 'Education policies and practices to foster tolerance, respect for diversity and civic responsibility in children and young people in the EU' NESET II report. Luxembourg: Publications Office of the European Union

■ Walsh, T. (2016) '100 years of primary curriculum development and implementation in *Ireland: a tale of a swinging pendulum*' in Irish Educational Studies Vol. 35, Issue 1

■ Walshe, J. (2016) 'We shouldn't rob Peter to pay for Paul's basic education – if we fail to invest we will never see long-term benefits' *Irish Independent*, 10th September 2016. http://www.independent.ie/opinion/comment/we-shouldnt-rob-peter-to-pay-for-pauls-basic-education-if-we-fail-to-invest-we-will-never-see-longterm-benefits-35037585.html

■ Watson, D., Banks, J., Lyons, S. (2015) *Educational and Employment Experiences of People with a Disability in Ireland: An Analysis of the National Disability Survey*. Dublin: The Economic and Social Research Institute, Research Series, No. 41

■ Watson, D., Kenny, O. and McGinnity, F. (2017) *A Social Portrait of Travellers in Ireland*. Dublin: ESRI.

■ Wilkinson, R. & Pickett, K. (2009) *The Spirit Level: Why More Equal Societies Almost Always Do Better*. London: Allen Lane

■ Williams, K. (2007) *Education and the Voice of Michael Oakeshott*. Exeter: Imprint Academic

■ Wordsworth, W. (1994) 'Louisa' in *The Collected Poetry of William Wordsworth*. Ware, Herts: Wordsworth Editions Ltd.